THE WAY OF MYTH: STORIES' SUBTLE WISDOM

Other Books by Dennis Patrick Slattery

The Idiot: Dostoevsky's Fantastic Prince. A Phenomenological Approach (1984)

William Faulkner and Modern Critical Theory. Ed. Dennis Patrick Slattery (1987)

The Wounded Body: Remembering the Markings of Flesh (2000)

Depth Psychology: Meditations in the Field. Co-edited with Lionel Corbett (2000)

Psychology at the Threshold: Selected Papers from the Proceedings of the International Conference at University of California, Santa Barbara, 2000. Coedited with Lionel Corbett (2003)

Grace in the Desert: Awakening to the Gifts of Monastic Life (2004)

Harvesting Darkness: Essays on Literature, Myth, Film and Culture (2006)

A Limbo of Shards: Essays on Memory, Myth and Metaphor (2006)

Varieties of Mythic Experience: Essays on Religion, Psyche and Culture. Co-edited with Glen Slater (2008)

Reimagining Education: Essays on Reviving the Soul of Learning. Co-edited with Jennifer Leigh Selig (2009/2019)

Day-to-Day Dante: Exploring Personal Myth Through The Divine Comedy. (2011)

Re-Ensouling Education: Essays on the Importance of the Humanities in Schooling the Soul. Co-edited with Jennifer Leigh Selig and Stephen Aizenstat (2012/2019)

Riting Myth, Mythic Writing: Plotting Your Personal Story (2012)

Creases in Culture: Essays Towards a Poetics of Depth (2014)

Our Daily Breach: Exploring Personal Myth Through Herman Melville's Moby-Dick (2015)

Bridge Work: Essays on Mythology, Literature and Psychology (2015)

A Pilgrimage Beyond Belief: Spiritual Journeys through Christian and Buddhist Monasteries of the American West (2017)

Deep Creativity: Seven Ways to Spark Your Creative Spirit. Co-authored with Deborah Anne Quibell and Jennifer Leigh Selig (2019)

Correspondence: 1927-1987 Joseph Campbell. Co-edited with Evans Lansing Smith (2019)

From War to Wonder: Recovering One's Personal Myth Through Homer's Odyssey (2019)

An Obscure Order: Reflections on Cultural Mythologies (2020)

Poetry

Casting the Shadows: Selected Poems (2001)
Just Below the Water Line: Selected Poems (2004)
Twisted Sky: Selected Poems (2007)
The Beauty Between Words: Selected Poetry of Dennis Patrick Slattery and Chris Paris (2010)
Feathered Ladder: Selected Poems of Dennis Patrick Slattery and Brian Landis. (2014)
Road, Frame, Window: A Poetics of Seeing. Selected Poems of Timothy Donohue, Donald Carlson and Dennis Patrick Slattery (2015)
Leaves from the World Tree: Selected Poems of Craig Deininger and Dennis Patrick Slattery (2018)

Novel

Simon's Crossing. A Novel. Co-authored with Charles Asher (2010)

Unpublished Titles

Sticky Blood: Redeeming the Violent and Violated Body in Fyodor Dostoevsky's Crime and Punishment (1982)
From Your First Mile to Your First Marathon Without Injury. Co-authored with Jerry Poole (1984)

THE WAY OF MYTH: STORIES' SUBTLE WISDOM

DENNIS PATRICK SLATTERY

Mandorla Books
WWW.MANDORLABOOKS.COM

ISBN: 978-1-950186-32-7

Cover photograph: "The Book Looks At You"
by Timothy Donohue
Cover background photograph © Can Stock Photo / phloem
Back cover photograph © Can Stock Photo / anna_stasia
Cover design: Jennifer Leigh Selig

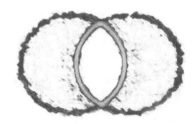

MANDORLA BOOKS
WWW.MANDORLABOOKS.COM

Dedication

To my family: Marty, Bob, Bill and Mary Beth; our sons Matt and Steve; our three granddaughters Kris, Eleanor and Siena; Francesca, Jennifer, Char, Debbie, and Phil.

To Pacifica Graduate Institute—faculty, staff and students—for gifting me with a home and an imaginal field to play in for almost three decades.

To my good friend Toni D'Anca, who wrote to me one day and suggested I write a book during the Covid-19 pandemic.

To my good friend, former student and creative genius, Jennifer Leigh Selig. What a wonder to work with you on so many writing projects and for your care in publishing several of my books. So much gratitude for your creative soul.

Most especially to Sandy, my spouse, friend, confidante, and constant support for over five decades.

What you come to remember becomes yourself. Learning will be to cultivate the awareness of that governing order.
~W. S. Merwin, "Learning a Dead Language,"
Migration: New and Selected Poems, 41.

Ideas spring from something greater than the personal human being. Man does not make his ideas: we could say that man's ideas make him.
~C. G. Jung. *Freud and Psychoanalysis,* par. 769.

The bones are the framework. I am excavating deeper and deeper for the lost parts of myself. I mourn them deeply. Where have they gone?
~Maureen Murdock, *The Heroine's Journey,*
Tenth Anniversary Edition, 97.

Poetic composition is a metaphorical weaving, the result of which is a 'richly patterned' fabric.
~John Scheid and Jasper Svenbro,
The Craft of Zeus: Myths of Weaving and Fabric, 120.

We could perhaps say, then, that a myth, whatever its origins, first begins to be known through the mythopoeic imagination, which is like the prophetic imagination in being the property of individual persons, even though the reality that it reveals is for a whole people.
~Louise Cowan, "Myth in the Modern World" in *Texas Myths,* 12.

Sometimes a person needs a story more than food to stay alive.
~Barry Lopez (qtd. in Phil Cousineau, *The Oldest Story in the World,* 32.

TABLE OF CONTENTS

I

Mining the Myths Anew

II

The Social Fabric of Stories

FOREWORD

---◆●◆---

THE THREADS OF MYTH

If philosophy is the art of finding a black cat hiding in a dark room, then mythology is the art of discovering a dark dragon in a black cave. The search for wisdom and the quest for powerful stories have been inextricably connected since at least the era of classical Greece. In *The Metaphysics*, Aristotle wrote, "The devotee of myth is in a way a philosopher, for myth is made up of things that cause wonder." More recently, the musician Tom Waits remarked, "There's a deficit of wonder. When I ask people questions now, they get out their phone. I say, Nooo! I don't want to know the answer. I just want to wonder for a while."

Speaking of being wonderstruck, I grew up "on the knee of Homer," as we used to say. After our old Philco television spluttered and died, my father initiated a practice of reading the classics out loud together as a family every Friday night, then later traveling to museums and historical sites to help illuminate the wider meaning of the stories. I felt my young heart grow strong as we followed the timeless adventures of Odysseus and Penelope, Hermes and Aphrodite, and later, the exploits in *The Hunchback of Notre Dame*, *The Adventures of Huckleberry Finn*, and *Frankenstein*. Years later I came to appreciate what a brilliant pedagogy he had developed: Read first, then travel, then read again. It is a regimen I have relished ever since.

In *The Way of Myth*, the culminating book of the prolific Dennis Patrick Slattery's career, I find an abundance of wonder and a plenitude of what the poet-astronomer Rebecca Elson called our "responsibility to awe." For him, mythology is everywhere if only we develop "the mythic slant," the ability to see its wild wisdom all around us. What vitalizes his writing is how he encourages the reader to venture beyond theory to experience one of the least appreciated aspects of mythology—the sheer joy that can come from identifying with its characters—to the point where we no longer feel alone in our own struggles.

The sheer range here of essays, poems, reminiscences, reviews and retellings underscores Slattery's ardent belief that mythmaking is one of the constants in cultures throughout history. I especially value his uncanny awareness of what he calls the "weathervanes of the soul," the cultural devices, if you will, found in art, literature, theater and cinema, as well as in sports, religion, psychiatry, nature and our romantic lives, which indicate the direction of our mythologically-inclined minds. His determination to convey the omnipresence of our mythological heritage to his students and readers is admirable.

I was so moved by the luxuriant variety of his approaches in this collection that I was inspired to go back to my own compilation of descriptions and definitions of myth that clever poets and scholars have conjured up over the centuries. One of my favorites was uttered by the fourth-century Roman philosopher Salutius: "A myth is something that never happened—but always is." The English historian Marina Warner said in a 2012 interview in "The Rumpus," "I have always argued that we can't live by or be made to exist outside of mythology, and that every group and nation has, possibly unacknowledged to themselves, some myths by which they live." The scholar of world religion, Huston Smith, once blithely remarked to me that a debate he had with Joseph Campbell about the role of myth in religion inspired him to compose the aphorism, "Myth is to religion as physics is to math. A picture language that reveals what is otherwise beyond words."

Still, as far as gnomic utterances go, it would be difficult to beat what a seven-year-old boy told the psychologist Robert A. Johnson after a lecture on the Grail Quest: "A myth is a lie on the outside and a truth on the inside."

The Way of Myth explores many of these aspects of our inheritance of folklore. While reading it, I was often reminded of a conversation I had with the Humanist psychologist Rollo May, at his home in Tiburon, California. During his years of offering psychotherapy, he confided, he detected a "cry for myth," a *cri de coeur* to experience in a world threatened by meaninglessness, one of our oldest efforts at meaning-making.

So, too, with this book, which reveals a wealth of stories worthy of the Alexandria Library, such as the dark woods of Dante, the great white whale of Melville's *Moby-Dick,* the haunted farmhouse in Toni Morrison's *Beloved.* The tone-feeling here is often reminiscent of the soul-stretching revelations in Van Gogh's letters, which I had been synchronistically reading in the days before encountering this work. The visionary Dutch painter wrote, in a letter to Emile Bernard, "I want others to feel what I am feeling under the hot sun of Provence."

Likewise, I sense the artesian depths of Slattery's desire for his students and readers to go beyond theory to feel the profundity of our sacred narratives, as the folklorist Alan Dundes described myth. Why, the reader may ask, should we bother to pay attention to stories so old they sometimes appear to be preserved in amber? As if anticipating the concern, Slattery cites the author and memoirist Tim O'Brien, who wrote in his war novel *The Things They Carried*, "Stories are for joining the past to the future . . . stories are for eternity, when memory is erased, where there is nothing to remember except the story . . . I want you to feel what I felt. I want you to know why story truth is truer sometimes than happening truth."

To help guide the reader, Slattery often uses the mythologems of threads and weaving to help us visualize the way our stories help connect us with each other and our deeper selves. Our mutual friend and colleague, Robert A. Johnson, would have been proud. In his poignant memoir, *Balancing Heaven and Earth*, Johnson employed the archetypal image of "slender threads" to evoke the seemingly disparate incidents of his life that were tied together by the story-forging forces of his own inward life.

The Way of Myth invites readers to consider the paths marked by the sacred stories in the author's rhapsodic collection and decide for themselves if they point to a greater meaning. Significantly, our word "rhapsodic" derives from the Greek *rhapsodos*, the reciters who stitched together epic poems for spellbound audiences across the ancient world. As if echoing those wandering bards, Slattery writes, "My story is a stitching of the past to where I am headed. I paused just long enough to recollect all of the above. Recollection is itself a form of deep imagining, a striving to get the narrative right. It is as close as I can get to a narrative truth, those verities that live within the weave of the yarn, those universal patterns that punctuate the plot at various moments of illumination."

This eminently refreshing approach is evocative of the vertiginous energy in the mystic painter Mark Tobey's 1940s painting, "The Way." The Northwest artist's calligraphic style of "white writing" on canvas invites viewers to find their own interpretation. Not unlike Tobey's unswerving belief in the truth of his own "frenetic rhythms," Slattery encourages his students and readers to find their own in and out of the labyrinth of world myth.

As if to clinch his argument, Slattery cites the Swiss psychiatrist and psychoanalyst C. G. Jung, who once commented that myths point to "a secret, a premonition of things unknown. It fills life with something impersonal, a numinosum. A man who has never experienced that has missed something important."

"The soul is entangled in myths," Slattery writes, evoking the threads again. Knowing this does not make us virtuous or superior, but it does reveal mythmaking is as natural as breathing, and as necessary.

"Traveler, there is no road," wrote Antonio Machado, "you make your own path as you walk." To my lights, the Spanish poet is saying that there is no one road to the truth of your life, no one path, no one method. There is only the way that is forged by walking and thinking your own way. Is it any wonder that myth, dream and art are royal roads to the land of the soul?

Phil Cousineau
Author of *Once and Future Myths*
San Francisco, Summer 2021

INTRODUCTION

◆●◆

Like that statue, a book gives physical form to invisible presences, gives to the angels in words a local habitation and a name. May both the readers and the angels be pleased to linger a while longer.

~ James Hillman, *Revisioning Psychology*, xiv.

We read stories, listen to stories, watch stories on screens, tell our stories and recall our stories because all of these forms of being nested in narratives shed light on our identity, our purpose and our reason for being in this precious life of ours.

Stories define us; some of them try to deny us; others bolster our sense of ourselves and our relation to others. Pay attention to the kinds of stories that draw you into them, as into an interactive field, and you will garner indications of who you once were, are now, and aspire to be. Stories aid us in remembering ourselves as well. How often in reading a story—ancient, classic, popular or modern—a long-forgotten memory will suddenly loom up with such insistence that you may stop reading the current plot on the screen or in your hands, and pivot into this personal slice of your history to contemplate it through the prism of the story you are presently attending to.

A fascinating article in *Harper's* magazine entitled "The Story of Storytelling" suggests that "the story of storytelling began so long ago that its opening lines have dissolved into the mists of deep time. . . . We know that by 1.5 million years ago early humans were crafting remarkably symmetrical hand axes, hunting cooperatively and possibly controlling fire. Such skills would have required careful observation and mimicry, step-by-step instructions and an ability to hold a long series of events in one's mind—an incipient form of plot" (38).

The author, Ferris Jabr, speculates that at such an early age of our species, plots of stories may have already been expressing themselves through outward forms of making. I recall the Greek word *poiesis,* meaning a making or shaping of something into a coherent form so it can be shared. My sense is that we all have this deep universal drive to create, to make simulacra, correspondences, analogies of ourselves through myriad forms of expression and to be acknowledged by others. We are, in all of our narrative complexity, communal beings-in-relation to others.

Jabr explores further how we as a species moved from making cave drawings, jewelry and burial rites such that these artifacts revealed "creatures no longer content to simply experience the world, but who also felt compelled to record and to reimagine it. Over the past few hundred thousand years, the human character gradually changed. We became consummate storytellers" (38). And consuming listeners of these stories because we find in any story some rich analogies to our own plot.

So many other rich insights grow from his article, but the above is enough to let us feel into the rich, primordial and universal impulse to create our world and ourselves through forms of imaginative expression; in the process our ancient ancestors were creating myths, both personal and collective. Mythmaking and creative expressions leading to story constructions eventually assembled into a whole. Our stories became our myths in narrative formats. It is no accident or happenstance that even within the early years of an infant's life, there is a pull toward stories— their fascination, their wonder and their mythic power—as one may learn in their later years. I believe that we each convey these ancient stories in our cells and in that part of us that is linked to our ancient ancestors. We each plot timeless adventures forward.

I have always been drawn to the autobiography of the father of analytical psychology, C. G. Jung, *Memories, Dreams, Reflections.* In the "Prologue" he helps us grasp the connective tissue between story and myth: "My life is a story of the self-realization of the unconscious. . . . What we are to our inward vision, and what man appears to be *sub specie aeternitatis,* can only be expressed by way of myth. Myth is more individual and expresses life more precisely than does science" (*Memories* 3). What follows is approximately 360 pages in which Jung recollects his personal myth and, in the process, remythologizes his story into a coherent whole.

Fascinated, we track our own narratives through the blueprint of his history.

But in the "Prologue" he is not done with describing what journey he is about to embark on: "Thus it is that I have now undertaken, in my eighty-third year, to tell my personal myth. I can only make direct statements, only 'tell stories.' Whether or not the stories are 'true' is not the problem. The only question is whether what I tell is my fable, my truth" (3). The idea of *fable* comes from something fabulous, meaning in the 15th. century, "mythical, legendary; from Latin, *fabulosus*, "celebrated in fable;" also "rich in myths," from fabula, story, tale." I do not doubt that Jung meant to resonate these meanings when he chose that particular word.

Every life is fabulous, most especially when it is recollected, i.e., reimagined, mythologized, embellished with associations, connections and a host of other webbings, for the text of our lives is laced with lattices; remembering a life includes finding the threads that create a fine yet sturdy web of associations within, while at the same time connecting through an imaginal world-wide web to stories from other countries, cultures and associations to something universal, timeless and permanent. Then we see the rich patterns enwebbed in the plot of our own lives and that of others. What connects us most forcefully and poetically and aesthetically is the interlaced patterns of our plotlines.

John Scheid and Jesper Svenbro have produced a masterful text, *The Craft of Zeus,* exploring the threading, webbing and weaving of a life in their study of Greek and Roman expressions of weaving. I will only touch on their thinking here, so vast and interlaced is it. They focus at one point on the mythic figure of Klotho, who spins the thread of one's destiny in life: "This representation of the individual, who is born a thread and dies a fabric, is in keeping with the political 'weaving'" (*Craft* 159) that they introduced earlier. "For it is by the crossing of threads— of opposite directions and sexes—that the fabric of society is created, starting with the elementary interlacing that is the sexual union of two individuals" (159). None of us is not part of the "elementary interlacing" as well as, to various degrees, part of the social fabric into which we are woven.

The Truth of a Story

Another source is worth mentioning here: Tim O'Brien's magnificent *The Things They Carried* is as much about story's structure and purpose as it is of his recollecting the horrors of the Vietnam War he found himself entangled in decades earlier: "Forty-three years old, and the war occurred half a lifetime ago, and yet the remembering makes it now. And sometimes remembering will lead to a story, which makes it forever. That's what stories are for. Stories are for joining the past to the future . . . stories are for eternity, when memory is erased, where there is nothing to remember except the story" (*Things* 38). O'Brien's fine and painful insight allows one to entertain the idea that it may be the stories we remember, tell, hear and metabolize, that invite us to weave profound connections to what is eternal and everlasting. Stories then become a form of prayer, a petition through the elegance of their plots.

A few pages later O'Brien asks a provocative question: "Does a story bring one to relive the event, or relive the event, then relieve the event?" (*Things* 57). Yes, I would respond, because we know how reliving certain stories can crush us *now* by means of a remembrance of *then*. But O'Brien speaks another truth here. Telling our own most painful traumas or reading/watching a performance of the tragedy of Oedipus or the agony of a young Russian student who murders an old pawnbroker and her younger pregnant sister, Lizaveta, can evoke a moment of healing. Raskolnikov, whose name means "split, divided," in Russian, is crushed with remorse until an 18-year-old prostitute, Sonya Marmeladov, recites to him the story of Lazarus rising from the dead in Dostoevsky's *Crime and Punishment*. By imagining the biblical story through Sonya's recitation of it "by heart," the young murderer begins his road to redemption and wholeness. We are also reminded of the young mother, Sethe in Toni Morrison's *Beloved,* who in order to spare her four children from repeating her life as a slave, attempts to murder all of them but succeeds in killing only one. Her daughter, Beloved, returns out of the water eighteen years later both to haunt and to heal her mother's guilt for her murder.

Once more to Tim O'Brien on the truth or falsity of stories: "I want you to feel what I felt. I want you to know why story truth is truer sometimes than happening truth" (*Things* 180). He follows with examples of each kind of truth, each of which points us back to the illustrations above.

Beloved mixes story truth with happening truth because it is based on a historical woman, Margaret Garner, who did literally and historically try to slay her four children. O'Brien and Dostoevsky lean more into story truth, as does Dante in his *Commedia*, which is set up for us to believe it actually happened in history. As readers we buy into its fiction "as-if" it were a recollection of Dante's literal history. Certainly, the creation of it was. The point here is that to judge a story's validity by whether it is a memory of an historical event is to risk suffocating the story's essential value and purpose.

O'Brien frames it this way: "The thing about a story is that you dream it as you tell it, hoping that others might then dream along with you, and in this way memory and imagination and language combine to make spirits in the head. There is the illusion of aliveness" (*Things* 230). But there is no illusion about its truth, I want to follow with. We identify ourselves on a much deeper level than the one we walk around in during the course of one day. On what gradient we relate to the story truth of a narrative indicates accurately the depths of our own understanding, our self-awareness and even our capacity to feel compassion and empathy for others, not just those in the narrative.

I have been thinking lately how reading great stories from a variety of cultures and historical periods aids us in our capacity to forgive both ourselves and others. The above is true in part because my responses to stories mirror what I believe, don't believe, perhaps even should believe, but am as yet incapable of making that pilgrimage.

In the process, my own narrative, lived and revised daily in small and large ways, is deepened by the stories I meditate on, whether in a book, a play, a film. They reveal in complex ways where in my story I am stuck, frozen, prejudiced, resentful, joyful, needy, selfless, selfish—you fill in other pockets of prose that have a story attached to them. In his *Power, Intimacy, and the Life Story*, Dan McAdams writes: "This book encourages the reader to think about identity as a life story and to think about the person formulating identity as a story writer—a biographer of self" (19). His words spur us all on to see how we can, or should be, the author of our own lives before someone else writes our story for us.

Earlier he cited writer Jerome Bruner who "speaks of this story writing as the making of myths. Bruner writes that the 'mythologically instructed community provides its members with a 'library of scripts' against which the individual may judge his or her own 'internal drama.'" He concludes, 'Life, then, produces myths and finally imitates it'" (qtd. in *Power* 18). We have the authority and capacity to edit our own narrative; what can help immensely is to read and learn of powerful stories that are beneficial to our own mythmaking impulses. Our created narratives may be the most original work we do in life; the aesthetic product, really a process, aids us in shaping a coherent identity which, though not blister-free, nonetheless has a through line or thread that helps us sense a life of coherence.

Know the Narrative That Guides You

Early on McAdams suggests that "identity is a sense of sameness and continuity which ties together our days anew. By integrating past, present, and an anticipated future, identity provides human lives with unity and purpose" (*Power* 28). Experiencing others' stories in a multitude of venues is in fact a way of self-creation, of cultivating one's personal myth through seeing by means of analogy—metaphor, symbol, correspond-ences, relationships—all of which can free us from the cocoon of our own self-absorption. We can experience a sense of joy, of equanimity, of peace, solace and serenity through the stories of others and through con-tinually returning to our own stories for revision, for enhancement. We may in this return begin to discard those stories whose shelf-lives are years old and whose value for us now is little-to-none. Needed, however, is a faith in the power of imagination itself to guide us, like a guru or shaman, into the forest of *our* fables.

The international musician, Yo-Yo Ma, was asked in an interview with Alison Beard, "What do you think about when you perform?" He re-sponded: "You have a responsibility, one, to know what the narrative is and make sure you're telling the story and people are receiving it, and two, if anything impedes the narrative, to fix the problem. It's the biggest thing and the nanomoment, and you have to have both in your head at all times. The main goal is to be memorable" ("Life's Work"). He under-stands that myth is central to our narrative, to our work, because it pro-vides a luminous and numinous mucilage that binds the entire work into a coherent whole. By implication, it also brings joy, which is not a by-product of learning and performing but one of its most valued contributions.

Reading, I have thought about for years, is a form of pilgrimage, an adventure, often with no stated goals in mind. The journey is itself the destination. It is a voyage towards apprehending patterns of one's soul life. Metaphors behave like transport vehicles. In *Thou Art That* Joseph Campbell affirms the path of poetry to carry us beyond categories of thought: "Here we sense the function of metaphor that allows us to make a journey we could not otherwise make, past all categories of definition" (9). Metaphors have their origin and their potent energy in the movements of the imagination in its entirety. Stories—be they told, heard, overheard, read, reread—liberate us from ourselves in order to see more, not less, of what our experiences and those of others contain, cultivate and anticipate.

In my professional life I have spent many delicious years reading, pondering, teaching and discussing classics of literature as well as contemporary novels with others who love stories. Not only do these activities challenge us, they afford great joy. Every work of fiction is a mythological journey into a fuller and deeper consciousness *if* we are willing and able to yield to its reality, not use it to buttress our own narrow interests. The pilgrimage, the migration in a story, is away from ego and towards a more imaginal shared soulful experience of reality that shifts my angle of vision enough to see from other points of view.

Phil Cousineau, one of the most mythically-attuned people I know, writes in his own book on stories: "This much I know: Unless we search for ways to become aware of the myths that are unfolding in our lives, we run the risk of being controlled by them. . . . in this book I will tell you things I myself have lived and learned about myth" (*Once and Future Myths* 7). In that last sentence we can feel a story or series of stories warming up on the front burner.

Kevin Bradt, the insightful writer of *Story as a Way of Knowing*, entertains images which contains optical illusions. At one moment we see the image of a rabbit, for instance, and at another we see a duck. Both are present simultaneously but the viewer must make a shift in optics to see one, then the other. When one figure appears, the rabbit, the other figure, the duck, becomes ground, unseen. He uses this "Gestalt diagram" (45) to reveal how "the mind, accustomed to seeing and imagining the possibility of only one reality at a time, now is forced to contain two alternative images, two different interpretations or constructions of reality. It finds the simultaneous coinherence of contradictory alternative images disquieting . . ." (*Story* 43-44).

He develops what the "'modern' mind, preconditioned to a single view of nature, forgets is that neither image that appears, neither the duck nor the rabbit, is *more* real than the other" (44). But they are both real, I underscore. So too in reading. Over the years I have shifted my perspective on how I read and interpret, for example, Sophocles' *Oedipus Rex* and *Colonus*, Homer's *Odyssey,* Melville's *Moby-Dick*, Dante's *Commedia* and Toni Morrison's *Beloved.* Were my previous ways of reading wrong? No, they were reflections of my capacity to read and understand them from that mythic point of view that I cultivated at the time. With subsequent re-readings, I came to see more, saw the duck when before I saw only the rabbit in the readings.

How I read earlier and how I read now comprise different "ways" of reading, ways in, down and through the work, to emerge at the other side of this complex and challenging and joyful experience changed, transformed and somehow more in touch with myself and others in their joys, aspirations and sufferings. As we read and especially reread over years and decades, we continue to remythologize ourselves anew from new pockets of understanding we come to know. All of the above applies as well to films, sculptures, paintings, music and other forms of creative expressions, including what we ourselves have made but did not understand fully, what we have birthed with pen, brush or clay or musical instrument.

Rereading's Unique Journey

I like to think that my discoveries of new ways of reading these and other works comprise an on-going development of mythopoetic consciousness. It is more than optics; it is closer to ontology and to epistemology, a way of being as a way of knowing from richer and deeper vantage points. Added to this is the cultivation of an imaginal consciousness, of seeing what is invisible but present if our optical focal length is sufficient to sense its reality. Such a poetic way of apprehending the rich reality in plots of fiction allows for ambiguity, nuance, indirection, paradox, multiplicity and complexity to become themselves ways of understanding. Reading then becomes a creative pilgrimage towards grasping the deep and universal patterns of soul life.

Reading imaginatively is akin to reading mythically. It is a form of field work. When we read, we both construct as well as enter an interactive field, a field of confluence as well as one of influence. Once the field of reading is established, one may sense a transfer of psycho-mythic energy between the plot of the fiction and the contours of the reader's story as one allows the "as-if" quality of the world we enter to assert its authority. We affirm our belief that this "as-if" world is as real as the one I journey through each day; I allow it its reality.

Writing not about reading per se, but about psychological experiences, James Hillman's insights in *Revisioning Psychology* can, by analogy, be applied to reading poetry, a term I use to designate any work of imaginal literature. What I am interested in relating here is the "mythical pattern" that may arise in us, a discovery of sorts, from out of the field we have given ourselves over to. What he means by this term includes the following: "Again, consciousness is not heroic and fixed to one point, but seeps as if through mystical participation in a processional of personifications, interfused, enthusiastic, suggestible, labile" (*Revisioning Psychology* 35). There is a growing awareness that "there are archetypal patterns at work, Gods affecting our styles of consciousness" (35).

Being fixed to one point of view, as Bradt earlier described it, signals a paralysis of optics, a sclerosis of imaginative possibilities, debilitating stances towards our experience. Hillman implicates in his discussion of personifying that keeping consciousness arrested in the personal when reading, both limits and suffocates because it is ego-managed; then personalism literalizes, whereas personifying imagines (47). I find this insight very helpful in the act of reading: "Personifying not allowed as a metaphorical vision returns in concrete form: we seize upon people; we cling to other persons. . . . Without metaphorical persons, we are forced into desperate clutching literalisms" (46). Imagination is frozen out of the reading field; figures in the fiction may then be atomized into concepts; now their assassination is complete.

Hillman's focus on the imagination as a personifying way of understanding is directly connected to myth: "Mythical consciousness is a mode of being in the world that brings with it imaginal persons. They are given with the imagination and are its data. Where imagination reigns, personifying happens . . . we do not invent the persons of myth and religion; they, too, happen to us. . . . To *mythic consciousness, the persons of the imagination are real*" (17).

The quote above seems essential to reading imaginally from a mythic slant. Otherwise, ego steps in with its management playbook and reduces all to some literal and univocal way of understanding, which is too limited in its range and affect and almost never fair to the stories in front of it. This condition may make us feel more comfortable, even as it drains away new ways of understanding a richer field of meanings.

And it is not unrelated to Dan McAdams' exploration of one's life story and their identity that is cultivated and explored through the stories that comprise us: "It is an individual's story which has the power to tie together past, present, and future in his or her life. . . . This book examines the proposition that, beginning in late adolescence, we construct stories to integrate the disparate elements of our lives" (*Power* 17-18).

In reading works of fiction we encounter a wide range of others' stories from around the world; we can enter them even though the culture that birthed them through their respective poets may be, and we hope are, different from our own. Yet, even as we read their stories within the context generated by the fiction, their own "as-if" world, we read them as well through the aperture of our own personal and collective myths. From the stories we read we may revise and reconstruct elements of the myth we are living at the moment. McAdams suggests that "when the person finds (creates, constructs) a personalized life myth or story, he or she no longer 'deceives' the self and world. The story provides a coherent narrative framework within which the disparate events and the various roles of a person's life can be embedded and given meaning" (*Power* 19).

Now one is open to grasping a framework that allows the yet-unassembled fragments of one's narrative to cohabitate without being absorbed into or canceled by one another. Such a moment of recognition is extremely liberating because one senses the original gift of their story within the infinite stars of the vast narrative universe in which we all live. I believe this action is a form of soul retrieval, of homecoming, of harvesting the orphaned parts of ourselves into a bundle called the self or the selves, that while never fully complete, are always enormously engaging.

Stories contain their own wisdom not dependent on our finding that wisdom and including it as an additive; no, the stories have an autonomy and an objectivity that must be honored, not judged as good or bad, weak or strong. The stories are to be contemplated imaginally, not sliced into slivers of explanation. The story itself is a representation, a mimesis, of consciousness itself. Reading from that belief will shift largely the attitude in which we read and how we interpret what arises in the exploration while avoiding exploitation of the plot. When we agree to enter the field of particular and cosmic patterns, we open our hearts to a form of knowing that is both mindful and heart-felt. The way in is through indirection, obliquely, out of the corner of our eye, so we can be active participants in the poem's co-creation and in the process allow our own stories to be edited with a benevolent, even compassionate hand.

Works Cited

Bradt, Kevin M., S. J. *Story as a Way of Knowing*. Sheed and Ward, 1997.

Campbell, Joseph. *Thou Art That: Transforming Religious Metaphor*. Edited by Eugene Kennedy. Joseph Campbell Foundation. New World Library, 2001.

Cousineau, Phil. *Once and Future Myths: The Power of Ancient Stories in Our Lives*. Cornari P, 2001.

Hillman, James. *Re-visioning Psychology*. HarperCollins*Publishers,* 1975.

Jabr, Ferris. "The Story of Storytelling: What the Hidden Relationships of Ancient Folktales Reveal About Their Evolution—And Our Own." *Harper's Magazine*. March 2019. 35-41.

Jung, C. G. *Memories, Dreams, Reflections*. Translated by Richard and Clara Winston. Edited by Aniela Jaffe. Random House, 1963.

"Life's Work: An Interview with Yo-Yo Ma."
    https://hbr.org/2016/06/yo-yo-ma.
McAdams, Dan P. *Power, Intimacy, and the Life Story: Personological Inquiries into Identity.* The Guilford P, 1988.
Morrison, Toni. *Beloved.* Alfred A. Knopf, 1992.
O'Brien, Tim. *The Things They Carried.* Houghton Mifflin, 1990.
Scheid, John and Jesper Svenbro. *The Craft of Zeus: Myths of Weaving and Fabric.* Translated by Carol Volk. Revealing Antiquity Series. G. W. Bowersock, General Editor. Harvard UP, 1996.

PART I

MINING THE MYTHS ANEW

1

---✦●✦---

TENDER MERCIES AND THE QUEST FOR WHOLENESS OR, LOVE IS A MANY-SPLINTERED THING*

My lady is desired in highest Heaven.
Now let me tell you something of her power

~ Dante, *La Vita Nuova, 33.*

If you think about a topic for a while, something will lead you to *a* source or even *its* source, as if the topic becomes its own magnet, drawing to it what is needed for further inquiry. Think, and ye shall receive. When my wife flew out to Santa Barbara to visit me some years ago when I was teaching, we headed north to San Luis Obispo, then on to Cambria to Route 46 through the rich wine country and on to Paso Robles, which we had never visited. There, on a Monday morning, while walking around the main square, we spotted a small used bookstore. I can never pass these little gems up no matter where they appear, so in we went.

We entered and walked between row-after-row of dog-eared wrinkled and bent covers of hundreds of romance novels. Love was indeed in the air and on the shelves, with only grudgingly-relinquished space for any other reading. Far in the back corner, however, and invisible to customers, was a set of two bookshelves with several titles on mythology and

** Originally published as *"Tender Mercies:* Love, Oatmeal and the Quest for Wholeness." *Psychological Perspectives: A Journal of Jungian Thought,* 59. 109-119. Spring 2016.

psychology. One particularly pitiful cover, bent back and slightly abused, was a copy of Robert Johnson's *We: Understanding the Psychology of Romantic Love.*

Now, after reading it, I believe that each of the hundreds of romance novels should have had a copy of Johnson's book taped or rubber-banded to it as a guide to the plot inside. I knew several of his other works, but not this one. I bought it for $3.00. As many of you know, it is a depth psychological and mythological treatise on the origin of romantic love in the West. Those who have escaped such an experience could be counted on one hand.

His utensil to explore this well-worn topic is the 12th. century romantic epic, *Tristan and Iseult,* which he reads deftly and provocatively as the mother story of this form of love; it remains a dominant shaping force in Western culture that feeds us consistently in various iterations through films, novels, news stories and an infinite stream of episodes of *Dateline.*

Johnson wastes no time in proclaiming in his Introduction that "Romantic Love is the single greatest energy system in the Western psyche. In our culture it has supplanted religion as the arena in which men and women seek meaning, transcendence, wholeness, and ecstasy" (xi). Rather than exploring it as one of many forms of love, he asserts that romantic love "is a whole psychological package—a combination of beliefs, ideals, attitudes and expectations" (p. xi), making it, to my mind, a full-bodied myth. He himself will attest to this truth when he writes a bit further that "a myth is true; it is not true in the outer, physical sense, but it is an accurate expression of a psychological situation, of the inner condition of the psyche" (p. 2). I would add to his clear-headed definition that a perception is a way of seeing from the outside in; a myth is a way of seeing from the inside out. Our western myth, believes Johnson, gives us a painfully accurate picture of romantic love" (p. 3) and is indeed, as I have conjectured, a many-splintered thing, for its shards can spin off into myriad forms of love's often exasperated expressions.

He also suggests that romantic love acts like a mask; behind it is a powerful array of new possibilities hiding, waiting to be integrated into consciousness" (p. 4). He chose the myth of Tristan and Iseult for his major focus of study because he discerns through its details and plot arc that it is more like a "symbolic blueprint of our Western psyche at a critical turning point in our psychological development" (p. 5). By means of this mytho-poetic narrative, the wounds, joys, paradoxes, sufferings and losses that it harbors is both a place of vulnerabilities and viabilities existing side by side in a rich symbolic arrangement and with an erotic charge that has the capacity to shift our consciousness towards unconscious contents long left slumbering, out of sight.

C. G. Jung's observation on love is no less insightful. In *Civilization in Transition,* he offers that "Love is always a problem, whatever our age may be. . . . Love is a force of destiny whose power reaches from heaven to hell" (1964, ¶ 198). He further suggests that fewer instinctual and emotional impulses in the human being can surpass those that love adumbrates and witnesses. Love, believes Jung, is "not confined to any particular province but covering every aspect of human life. It may be an ethical, a social, a psychological, a philosophical, an aesthetic, a religious, a medical, a legal or a physiological problem, to name only a few aspects of this many-sided phenomenon" (1964, ¶ 198).

Yet Love in its fullest expression is an umbrella huge enough to cover all the landscapes from heaven to hell, as Jung suggests above.

He then gravitates to a writer who influenced him repeatedly in his work, the German poet, botanist, and philosopher Johann Wilhelm von Goethe, to allow another voice in verse to convey Love's complexity and ubiquity:

> Let now the savage instincts sleep
> And all the violence they do;
> When human love stirs in the deep
> The love of God is stirring too. (1964, ¶ 199).

The Power of Mythopoetics

Now while the above remarks and poetic insights presage Johnson's deeply insightful psycho-mythic exploration, I was led in another direction. I had a second bookstore experience that I want to honor for a brief moment. My Tristan and Iseult couple emerged slowly in a more contemporary venue: the 1983 film, *Tender Mercies,* written by Horton Foote, directed by Bruce Beresford and starring two young and low- key actors,

Robert Duvall and Tess Harper. For his screenplay Foote won his second Academy Award; the first was for his earlier screenplay, Harper Lee's *To Kill a Mockingbird.*

I have several reasons for choosing *Tender Mercies* to entertain several forms of love, each with variations of intentions and expressions. One is professional: I want to use more films in my writing, having defaulted for many years to privileging texts. I also think that its rich, understated, almost quiet presence on the screen, except for a few intermittent emotionally volcanic eruptions, allows us to witness a handful of love's infinite options of expression.

On its face, the plot is simple in design. It opens onto the plainest and most common of Texas settings: some forty miles south of Dallas, just outside the town of Waxahachie, Texas on a quiet farm road where sits a two-pump gas station, and a small store which doubles as a house, around which is a set of five free-standing motel with few occupants. Then, beyond the perimeter of this oasis on the highway stretches the flattest, most barren land reaching to the horizon. Behind the small structures the expansive land has been tilled, ready for seeds to be planted. Rosa Lee (Tess Harper) lives there with her ten-year-old boy Sonny (Allen Hubbard). Widowed because her young husband was killed in Vietnam in 1971 at the age of twenty, Rosa Lee has raised her son alone from the beginning.

The film quickly introduces us to two silhouettes fighting behind a gauze curtain in one of the motel rooms. Two drunken men scrap with one another over a bottle of whiskey, hurling mutual shouts and curses at one another between blows. Like figures in a Punch-and-Judy show, they are shadows, not substances, of individuals. One of them is Mac Sledge (Robert Duvall), a former Country/Western singer who has lost his now-popular singer ex-wife, Dixie (Betty Buckley), his young daughter, Sue Ann (Ellen Barkin), all of his impressive fortune and his own increasing stardom, to his alcoholism.

Next morning, rather than simply skip out without paying, as did the man he fought with, Mac admits to Rosa Lee he is broke but is willing to work around the place to pay for his room and meals. He has hit bottom, stripped of all vestiges of his past wealth, talent and fame. But he has not despaired.

They both agree to the business arrangement, which, in a slow and invisible way transforms easily and quietly into a comfortable love between them. Mac fixes what is broken around the home and the motel rooms: a screen door, a porch, and motel room abuses; the house too is modestly transformed into a place of order, because he brings to it what order each part needs, even as he begins to reorder the parts of himself strewn along roads and singing gigs stretching to the sterile horizon. His psychological and emotional life finds a perfect mirror in the barren but promising landscape that he has made a decision to cultivate.

These simple tasks of mending, joining and readjusting parts into a greater wholeness begin to knit his own addicted soul into a coherent formation. His simple chores inaugurate him back into the world of normalcy and out of the infernal chaos and shame of his alcoholism, as well as the loss of his love for his profession as composer and singer. If addiction is a form of fixated love frozen in ice with no choice left for the addict, then the generosity of Rosa Lee initiates for Mac an opening to shift his desires towards the best part of his past as a songwriter and to a future that promises a glimmer of wholeness through a revived love for another.

The name of Rosa Lee's establishment is "The Mariposa Hotel: Clean, Quiet, Comfortable." We may recall that "Mariposa" is Spanish for butterfly. The butterfly in antiquity was understood as an image for the soul; this modest oasis on an empty highway is a soul habitation, where the addicted and afflicted Mac will begin to recover a soul he lost in the bayous of alcohol soaked in a world of excess; his recovery will also assist mother and son to reclaim a life lost when her husband, and Sonny's father, was killed. Both Rosa Lee's deceased husband and Mac have died to lives exhausted by war, addiction and violence. Rosa Lee and Mac's implicit desire is to help one another reclaim themselves in a loving relation.

As they dig together one morning in their little plot of a garden close to the highway, Mac tells Rosa Lee how he feels about her and asks if she would consider marrying him; her reply is that she *might*. And they *do*. No courtship, no sex, no passionate displays, no sweet talk; we are also not allowed to witness the marriage ceremony. But the sense of their love for one another is potent and sustained in every scene through their quiet speaking tone, relaxed gestures and soft affectionate facial expressions. Cultivating their shared garden is a rich metaphor for the simpler, earth-connected love they cultivate between themselves; it is a love without bravado, love without fanfare or endearments, and a love expressing only the subdued remnants of the passion of romance; it is rather a love as deep companionship, connectedness and relatedness in a mutual respect for one another and a tender acknowledgement of the wounds each one carries. Courtship is present, moreover, through Mac's slow return to the deep loves of his life: writing, scoring and singing country/western songs, most all of which, as you know, hover around the lyrical refrains on the theme of love—lost, dismembered, remembered, yearned for, retrieved, suffered, nostalgically lived through heartbreak, heartache and displacement.

Further, through Rosa Lee, Mac's love as a father increases for her ten-year-old Sonny, who brightens up considerably in Mac's presence, for the young boy is in search of the love of the father he never knew. This small family unit's idea of a night out consists of sitting together in their humble but clean and inviting living room watching very fuzzy images on a television fatigued by age and use; but as the camera reveals, not from close-ups but more from its position at the threshold peering into the living room, love is blossoming through the silent spaces of quiet voices asking one another about their respective histories. They tell one another stories of themselves and reclaim their identities torn by suffering and loss. What pervades the early scenes is an atmosphere of generosity and mutual regard as well as great affection for the well-being of the others, couched, however, in very spare and simple prose delivered in quiet tones. We could say that an atmosphere of mercy pervades the mutual regard they hold for one another.

"Because love is an archetype," writes Johnson, "it has its own character, its own traits, its own 'personality.' Like a god, love behaves as a 'person' in the unconscious, a separate being in the psyche. . . . Yet love is something or 'someone who lives within me" (1983, p. 189) allowing me the possibility of enabling "my ego to look outside itself, to see my fellow humans as something to be valued and cherished, rather than used" (p. 189).

Stories Rediscover Myths

The futile and destructive love that addiction expresses—Mac has now been sober for over two months—has migrated into a fuller sense of its disparaging potency, even its pornography, in its inability to deliver what it promises. From futility Mac's love is nourished toward a growing fulfillment. The understated energy of these early scenes is conveyed by the common speech to one another as well as by simple human acts of maintenance such as Rosa Lee's ironing clothes in the kitchen, fixing simple meals from the modestly-stocked refrigerator, and letting love enter as part of their lives, while not despotically taking over.

What a dramatic contrast this love, quietly glowing in the hearth of their hearts, and carrying a sense of a full relatedness to one another as individuals, is to the more flamboyant and drama-laced romantic love of Dixie's life, Mac's former wife and singing partner. Freedom may truly begin when one is open to love's power and presence; it provides texture to our suffering while not allowing our afflictions to command all our attention. Love as addiction as well as addiction to love are both responses to expressions of desire stemming from love's more impotent expressions.

Mac slowly retrieves his music muse and begins to compose new songs as well as play older ones to Sonny; he sits in the kitchen with the young boy and demonstrates various cords of the guitar, sharing in the process the most important creative impulse lying dormant for so long within him. The kitchen is the most used room of their modest home; it is also often seen as the place of comedy, from the Greek word *komos,* originally meaning a wedding song or country song; it is the genre of inclusiveness, or where the fire of a family's *communitas* has its clearest voice and presence. The kitchen is the psychic space of nourishment, of cooking things up, of tossing salads and ideas around, of sharing the events of the day, and of serving and being of service to others. Talk is spare. Words are not in abundance but the three of them sharing a simple habitation as love for one another develops is. The silences are full of love and caring; less chatter but more charity towards one another, seeing and hearing one another as they are, without impediments, projections or illusions of who one another is—well, almost.

Together they visit the grave of Carl Herbert Wadsworth (1951-1971), Sonny's father and Rosa Lee's husband who died under suspicious circumstances in Vietnam, perhaps from an overdose of drugs. Sonny and his mother express their love for him and perhaps for the first time put him to rest so that Mac can assume that vacated position in the family. Mac stays in the truck, not wanting to encroach on that former lover who brought Sonny into the world. An authentic love knows when to remain in the background, respecting the former love and its memory and its new placement within the cosmos of a growing eros sprouting from the former's fruitfulness.

One morning, a van with members of a local country-western band in a nearby town drive out to the Mariposa Motel to meet the former music star; as a formative group of musicians they seek mentoring from him— what to write, how to play, and what tips the former celebrity whose music they greatly admire, can bequeath to them. Most of all, they come to show how much they love him and his achievements and to express his strong influence on them as musicians. They seek the originality of a creative leader so they treat Mac as a legend who can guide their own development.

"We love your music," they tell him when Rosa Lee fetches him from the house to greet his new public and to enter, however modestly, a former familiar public arena; this miniature version of his famous past Mac allows himself to step into in slight increments. He is very tentative about such a retrieval, for the memories of a former fame have been pushed deep into his past and, for a time, out of reach of his soul. When they ask him if he will join them and sing again, his brief response is "I've lost it; no more singing." As they prepare to leave, disappointed, in their old van they ask Mac if he has any advice for them; he at first says, "not really." Then before entering the house, he turns to them and offers: "Sing it the way you feel it." He knows that if they truly love what they sing, it will be conveyed to their audience for them too to love it by feeling it. Love is indeed a form of musing, an expression of music.

His loving relation with Rosa Lee allows him to write his first song in many years; but his intuition is tainted by an earlier form of love: his desire to visit the Grapevine Opry House to hear Dixie perform, to see his daughter, Sue Ann and to give Dixie the new song to sing. She will have none of it. Mac, within the confident support of his new love, attempts for a moment to retrieve an old one, but unbeknownst to him, that tune has become both thin and worn out. It no longer holds a spot on the top ten music chart. The beatings Dixie suffered when Mac was drunk wounded her deeply; now, his attempt to reconnect with her fails; he in turn is injured with equal intensity by his vulnerability towards her when she spurns him.

A part of Mac still loves the earlier world of excess, with its sassy glitz, overly-bright lights, sequined costumes, Dixie's talent, full houses of adoring fans and the smoldering eros of sexual passion. Mac returns home downcast and enraged. I believe he has experienced, as did Odysseus as he snaked his way home to Penelope, the lure of the sirens of romantic love back into its turbulent waters and mutilating desires. Romantic love can also be an addiction as it assumes the trappings of fame, success, money and a life of excess.

Mac's relapse into a love excessive, violent and misdirected, which now reveals itself in his estrangement from both Dixie and their eighteen-year-old daughter Sue Ann, overwhelms him. He emotionally attacks Rosa Lee as she irons clothes in the kitchen. If we play with the metaphor of Rosa Lee's action, we might say that Mac's own love is still wrinkled, crumpled, shoddy, not ready yet for the heat of her iron. In the background as Mac drives home wounded by Dixie, his ex-wife sings on the radio one of *his* most famous songs: "I am still going crazy over you" which ends in the line "I'm still here for the taking."

His attitude is still in romantic love's den of seduction, yet another and for him new form of love's expression has been seeded and is pushing its way into his emotional landscape, to be born out of the chrysalis of his former addictive violent life and love. Mac, Rosa Lee and Sonny all seek nourishment from one another; as love nourishes the needs of others, the kitchen becomes the psychic and emotional container of such rich nurturing. Some jealousy on Rosa Lee's part towards Dixie Scott, however, finds its way into this healing space. Even though Mac tells her that "Dixie is poison to me," Rosa Lee wishes to be part of that earlier love, for she is not without her own yearnings for previous fantasies of love.

Fiercely disappointed with himself for being abused by Dixie as well as his obsessive desire to see her, he speeds off in their old pickup truck, once again the angry and violent Mac of his earlier life; he sheds all boundaries wherein love careens into libidinal license and expresses itself in a wild addictive abandon, an erotics without limits married to a rage that threatens to bring the house down. Sober now for more than two months, he nonetheless drives to a bar, sneers at people, picks a fight with someone playing a song on the jukebox written by him, is impatient and surly, projecting all his green bile onto whoever steps into his path. Impatient, he tries to pass a truck carrying bales of hay and almost slams into the side of another vehicle. Cursing at them, he squeals the tires back onto the highway in the direction of home.

In the middle of the night, he returns to an awake and anxious Rosa Lee who fears the worst; both she and Sonny wonder if he is going to return drunk and violent. His demons all surface at once in his heart as he attempts to speed in the old pickup truck fast enough to outrun them; he has taken on impossible odds. His heart can easily forget to remain open enough to see the intrinsic beauty and goodness of Rosa Lee's deeper love for him. Torn between two forms of love, Mac is very close to heartbreak at this juncture of his reentry into life.

Love's Calls One Home

When he returns home, he walks from the darkness of the kitchen to the light of the bedroom and proudly proclaims: "I came back. I bought a bottle of whiskey but poured it all out on the ground." His love, however, is still knotted in his transition from Dixie to Rosa Lee. They sit on the bed and Mac pulls out the song he took for Dixie to sing and asks Rosa Lee to sing it. She cannot and will not because she senses Mac's motives: to transform her into Dixie's former role. She further realizes that if Mac cannot have Dixie, he will transform Rosa Lee into her surrogate, so she wisely rejects even trying to sing the new song.

I sense Mac experiences a breakthrough at this moment; he holds Rosa Lee and kisses her for the first and only time in the film. It is a crossing kiss, a kiss that allows him to cross over from his fantasy of Rosalie as Dixie, to Rosa Lee's own goodness in her own right. The moment is a pivotal one, for it signals a change in Mac's attitude towards her, one which allows him to relinquish his efforts to shape Rosa Lee into someone she is not; he becomes through this song capable of allowing Rosa Lee to be fully present to him as she is in and for herself. We might say he crosses the Rosa/Dixie line for good and never retreats into his earlier angry, violent existence.

Johnson is helpful here: "When guided by love," he writes, "one is more concerned with her needs and her well-being, not fixated on his own wants and whims" (1983, p.191). And to the question: can the love FROM another person allow one in time to engage the love OF another? Yes, as Rosa Lee's presence testifies to. Johnson further observes that human love, not romantic love, "affirms that person who is actually there—not the ideal we would like him/her to be" (p. 190). In time, love causes us to value that person as a total, individual self" (p. 191). It is indeed a form of "tender mercy," a term Rosa Lee uses to express her love for God and God for her, based on an unconditional acceptance of the other.

Only now in the film does Mac's daughter, hearing her father attempted to find her, visit him in his home. They meet in the living room but do not approach or embrace one another; too many years apart looms between them. The first words from Sue Ann are uttered across the room: "Momma says you tried to kill her." Mac admits to his behavior and tells her his drinking made him do terrible things. She in turn wants to bring her new husband by to meet her father; he is, like Mac, a country-western singer and an alcoholic who will soon kill her in a driving accident while driving drunk; he, however, will survive.

The daughter searches for the father's love through the distorted figure of her husband, with all the traits that made her father absent emotionally and physically to her. It is the only father she knew and she loved him as he was. Mac agrees to meet him but the car accident kills Sue Ann before they can visit him. She asks as she is leaving, in an attempt to connect with him on a loving level, if he remembers a song he used to sing to her as a child when he called her "Sister," his fond nickname for her; he tells her in an even, quiet tone that he does not.

When Sue Ann drives off, Mac walks to the living room window and watches her; he then begins to sing: "When Jesus went down to the waters that day/He was baptized in the usual way. /When it was done/ God blessed his soul. / He sent Him His love/ on the wings of a dove. / On the wings of a snow-white dove/ He sends His pure sweet love; / a sign from above, on the wings of the dove" (*Tender Mercies*).

Then a quick and immediate cut to Dixie on stage under the bright lights and cheering fans belting out her romantic love song, full of the eros of romantic enthusiasm; one feels in this musical juxtaposition the shallow quality of romantic love sitting beside Mac's spiritual awakening through the daughter's yearning for her father, and through Rosa Lee and Sonny's unconditional love for him. The contrasting scenes are a bit heavy-handed; nonetheless, they successfully underscore the potent difference between human and romantic forms of love; the latter is the one we are constantly being persuaded to pursue while the former seems to hold the most authentic feelings and more ample sustainable relations in familial love.

The above meeting between father and daughter is followed by a worship ceremony at Rosa Lee's church, where she sings in the choir every Sunday. It is a special ceremony because it includes first Sonny, then Mac, being baptized through total immersion in a pool of water behind a curtain that is pulled open for each of their baptisms to be witnessed by the congregation and a beaming Rosa Lee. If the beginning scenes reveal Mac's incarcerated world of addictions as the infernal dimension of the plot, then the baptism signals its purgatorial genesis where the transgressions of the past are washed from his soul.

Mac's bottle of whiskey gives way to the small tank of water into which first Sonny and then Mac are submerged. One might surmise that Mac is trying to please Rosa Lee in this ritual, but the film argues otherwise; Mac realizes it is a necessary part of his conversion from romantic to human loving, where one serves more than the ego's fascination with itself and its constant, often self-absorbed promptings to be satisfied.

Towards the last pages of *Memories, Dreams, Reflections,* C. G. Jung writes eloquently in first citing Paul's letter to the Corinthians—"Love 'bears all things' and 'endures all things'"—then adds: "For we are in the deepest sense the victims and the instruments of cosmogonic 'love'" (1963, p. 354). He explains further that he puts the word "love" in quotes because he wishes "to indicate I do not use it in its connotations of desiring, preferring, favoring, wishing . . . but as something superior to the individual, a unified and undivided whole" (p. 354).

Mac's pilgrim's progress through several stages of love in the film reveals this move to a participation in something beyond him, while still including him. His shift in attitude towards himself and his first family observes this recognition that something beyond him is at work within him. Rosa Lee is the very active Beatricean presence leading him to a fuller love that includes a more authentic presence of relatedness which excludes nothing of who and what the individual is.

Mac is now ready to become a public performer again. He sings for the first time with the band that initially sought him out as mentor and artist. He performs communally with them at the Cedar Creek Plowboys' Club; after his baptism he retrieves the best of himself and performs the first song written since his sobriety. The song is his creation: slow, melodious, hopeful, and a joy for the audience to hear and dance to. Incidentally, Robert Duvall wrote two of the songs for the movie and performed several himself. His talent is both gracious and grand as he makes his singing debut.

Love's Landscape

Though a small plot of earth, mentioned earlier, the garden outside their modest home is an important locale where big decisions are made and authentic deeply-rooted feelings are unearthed to flower. Mac digs in the garden once more with Rosa Lee and in so doing seeds, cultivates and brings to fruition deeper uncultivated parts of himself that have lain fallow as he loves his way back to a fullness of himself. Gardening occasions a reclamation of earlier seedings. Not far from the garden sits a coke machine on the porch, which stands like a sentinel to refresh passers-by; on the red paint is an oracular sentence painted in white: "Here's the real thing." It captures what Mac in his loving quest, his quest to love, awakens to with Rosa Lee and Sonny's assistance; they in turn are revived by his presence in their lives.

Love allows for a clear vision; it is a new attitude towards knowing. Through his love of Rosa Lee, Mac begins to reclaim and to love parts of himself he had discarded along the side of his road to fame and addiction. He suffered an acute alienation through shame, rage, resentment, addiction and failure. Now he has gathered the pieces and gardened them back into his organic self, like the seeds he cultivates tending the land, whose produce nourishes the entire family. He has succeeded in letting the glamorous life dissolve by yielding to the quotidian, the common, the ordinary and to see in these simplicities a sacred quality to life that one can assent to. Human love allows us to yield to another, not in self-service but in giving oneself without conditions to the beloved.

His inner world begins to yield fruits and vegetables in the form of songs that he composes afresh and sings outwardly in a generous spirit, not one attuned to profits or a lust for fame. His muse-laden insights that emerge in the lyrics marry the interior life to the public world that is touched and enjoys his creative expressions because they connect to the deep emotional life of his audience. His coaxes his creations into organic living entities that nourish him and others.

Singing also brings Mac back more fully into the human order of being; Rosa Lee and Sonny sit at their table in the club where he likes to perform, and they enjoy others enjoying Mac's new voice and talents. In the latter section of *We*, Johnson shares an image offered to him by a wise friend, as he calls her: "Stirring the Oatmeal" (1983, p. 195). What could be more mundane on one level, and simultaneously more profound as an analogue to enjoying the simple pleasures of life, on another, than stirring the oatmeal on the stove. "Stirring oatmeal is a humble act—not exciting or thrilling. But it symbolizes a relatedness that brings love down to earth. It represents a willingness to share ordinary human life, to find meaning in the simple, unromantic tasks" (p. 195). What it is we learn to relate to in love is where the value of a life survives and flourishes. One place is in the inherent goodness of small things. Johnson cites C. G. Jung who observes: "feeling is a matter of the small" (qtd. in *We*, 195).

The film's last scene depicts Sonny returning from school on the bus. His mother tells him Mac has left him a gift on his bed. He finds the new football lying there and takes it outside to Mac, who is sitting across the highway looking out at the land that expands to meet the horizon. Together they pass the ball to one another. Rosa Lee stands at the front door and gazes after them. She enters the home, still enjoys watching them through the screen door; she remains there as the camera fades to dark. If love is expressed less by words than by the gaze, then Rosa Lee is a first prize gazer; she is like Athena, overseeing the love growing between her husband and son. Her love is given such elegant form through the gaze, like Beatrice's gazing at Dante, as the clumsy pilgrim tries to gain a fuller sense of loving as a way of knowing the world in its particulars.

Like a young man, Mac catches and runs with the football, reclaiming something of himself from decades earlier; Sonny is his instructor, running with the ball directly opposite the garden flourishing in the Texas heat just off the highway and across from where they are playing and communing with one another; both are held by the deep love gazing at them through the screen door of their modest but abundant home, full of oatmeal stirrings. They are not involved in what Johnson calls a cosmic drama or in an extraordinary intensity in everything (p. 195) but in a slow stirring of the pot, which is the beginning of the word "pot-ential" and that is what love offers in its beingness: a promise of potential, also a word that harbors the word "potency," for there is no stronger energy in the world than that of human love, of *agape* in the human soul.

A love with its roots deep in the *Tender Mercies* that life and the sacred bestow can offer to those in touch with it what Jung labels "a secret, a premonition of things unknown. It fills life with something impersonal, a *numinosum*. A man who has never experienced that has missed something important" (1961/1963, p. 357). It may just be the richest form of affection and makes pale by comparison the bells and whistles of romantic love—lots of drama but so often amidst little more than tinkling cymbals.

Works Cited

Alighieri, Dante. *La Vita Nuova.* New Edition. Translated by Mark Musa. Indiana UP, 1973.

Foote, Horton. *Tender Mercies.* Directed by Bruce Beresford. Lionsgate Studio, 1983.

Johnson, Robert. *We: Understanding the Psychology of Romantic Love.* HarperSanFrancisco, 1983.

Jung, C. G.   *Memories, Dreams, Reflections.* Translated by Richard and Clara Winston. Pantheon Books, 1963.

C. G. Jung. *Civilization In Transition. The Collected Works of C. G. Jung.* Vol. 10. Translated by R. F. C. Hull. Princeton UP, 1964.

2

— ◆●◆ —

PATERSON: WHERE THE POET BECOMES A CITY*

Stated another way, all creative acts are potentially spiritual.

Jennifer Leigh Selig, "All That You Do is Sacred."
Deep Creativity: Seven Ways to Spark Your Creative Spirit, 262.

What urge brings each of us to create, or at least to yearn for the ability and the courage to make something for the world to acknowledge and appreciate? Creating is a calling. Do we answer the call, shove off on an aesthetic adventure, then return at some point to share the fruits of our travels and travails? Or do we refuse it, preferring the ordinary status of a less original renewal? Jennifer, one of two coauthors of a book the three of us worked on for years and finally published, *Deep Creativity: Seven Ways to Spark Your Creative Spirit*, wrote the following in one of her essays when she was musing over her own creative urges: "So why do we do it? We do it because it's a spiritual calling for us, creation" (260). I use her fine insight to launch us into a film that highlights and excavates the creative spark in a bus driver and his wife who creates in her own space at home when he is working.

---

* Originally published as "*Paterson*: Where the Poet Becomes the City." Review of the film, *Paterson*. Written and directed by Jim Jarmusch. *Psychological Perspectives* 60: 2017. 505-10.

A long epic poem rests behind director Jim Jarmusch's 2016 film about a man, his wife and the city he drives a municipal bus through daily. The poet and physician, William Carlos Williams, created five books of poetry between 1946 and 1958, all on the city of Paterson, New Jersey that sits along the Passaic River; eventually they were gathered into the poem we know as *Paterson*. The character named Paterson, (Adam Driver) both poet and city bus driver, retreats frequently to a park bench along the river to write in his poetry journal. At the same time, during the day, his lovely wife Laura (Golshifteh Farahani) feeds her own soul by creating stunning fabric designs, baking exotic black and white cupcakes and reinventing herself as a Nashville country-western singer. Her continual metamorphosis reveals the complexity of soul that all of us have within us, waiting for a chance to spark.

Paterson and Laura have found the mold that allows them to create themselves in the world and to fashion the world in new forms, both poetic and fabricated. For Paterson, if the bus is the vehicle for his life, then the river is the metaphor that guides his creative muse.

The man named Paterson, the city named Paterson and the epic poem named *Paterson* weave themselves together in a quiet but strong trinity of creative synthesis.

Williams writes at the beginning of his epic poem: "That is why I started to write *Paterson*: a man is indeed a city, and for the poet there are no ideas but in things" (4). Paterson the bus driver embodies this insight from the film's inception to its end, which, I suspect, harbors a new beginning. A creature of habitual punctuality, he wakes between 6:10-6:15 each of the seven mornings of the film, wrapped in the embrace of his wife. He eats his small bowl of Cheerios, showers, then dresses in the industrial uniform of the city, packs his lunch and walks to the bus barns tucked into the maze of factories now abandoned along Market Street. As he drives his eight-hour shift, he listens to and watches his passengers, each creating their own lives through conversation. Paterson sweeps up the bits and pieces of their adventures and fantasies and creates composites from them, including poems he works on while sitting in his bus before his shift begins. It should be noted that all of the poems in the film were composed by Minnesota poet, Ron Padgett, who was commissioned by the director. There Paterson's inner life is given a form and a destiny; his own myth develops in these moments of quiet inspiration, saving him from a life of quiet desperation.

As he eats breakfast one morning, he plays with a box of Ohio Blue Tip matches; when he walks to work and enters his bus, we hear his voice and see on the screen words that create something from the most ordinary object: "We have plenty of matches in our house/we keep them on hand; naturally/we used to prefer Diamond Brand" he writes in his small journal just before pulling out from the bus barn with mechanical regularity. On his lunch hour he sits on a bench in a park by the Passaic River and composes his thoughts further: "Here is the most beautiful match in the world/its one-and-a-half-inch soft pine stem capped/by a grainy dark purple head so sober and furious" (*Paterson*).

When he gathers his lunch remains and notebook, he sets them in his lunch box, which contains a portrait of the medieval Italian poet, Dante Alighieri. Both nourish Paterson's soul as he performs his routine round in the world, a world he transforms through his love poetry, a central interest he shares with Dante throughout his own 14th. century poetic creations.

Poems, Person and Place

Paterson seems such a whole and content person as he walks the same path home in the evening, there to be greeted by Laura and their grumpy bull dog, Marvin, the latter always impatient for an evening walk. Laura is always excited to see him and to share her own creative work generated during the day inside their tiny, tidy bungalow. She speaks of her dreams and shows him what muses visited her during the day to encourage her work with fabrics. In one vivid dream, she tells him, she is in ancient Persia; there she witnesses Paterson riding an ancient elephant. And as his muse, she encourages his poetry writing and insists he copy them for future publication; she believes his poetry is magnificent and worth duplicating.

After dinner, Paterson slips into his other routine: walking Marvin through his neighborhood to a local pub, where he ties him outside, enters and allows himself one beer and social conversations with neighborhood characters, most especially with "Doc" (Barry Shabika Henley), the tavern's proprietor burdened with his own addiction to gambling. One neighbor in particular, Everette (William Jackson Harp), is hopelessly in love with Marie (Chaston Harmon) who he has known since childhood; while sympathetic, she is increasingly annoyed by his constant advances. Love has no soil to be requited. Everette's anguish is palpable and sets the darkened mood of the tavern when he is present.

One evening, and pushed to desperation, he enters with a fake pistol and threatens to blow his brains out in front of all the customers unless Marie accepts his love. Paterson, without thought, leaps into action, pulling Everette to the ground and taking the pistol from him. The owner sees him thenceforth as a hero who saved the young distraught man from himself. Toward the end of the film Paterson will meet Everette on the street one early Sunday morning; there Everette will confess: "Without love what reason is there for anything?" (*Paterson*).

The tavern itself is a rich psychological space; it is akin to the soul of Paterson, the city. On the wall behind the bar are dozens of photos of celebrities who lived in Paterson at one time: Iggy Pop, Lou Costello, the singing duo of Sam and Dave, and a host of others. The legion of photos of famous people have fed and continue to nourish the soul of the city, and they in turn were nourished by it. Paterson, we see, is a poem, a person and a place, but it is also an attitude and a mindset, a way of imagining oneself in place. Paterson the city is an anchor grounding its inhabitants; its river provides its life line, its motion, and its psychic energy. While so much of the city is constant, some might call it dull, it is also rich soil when the imagination is invited in to reshape and reformat it.

There is a certain beautiful monotony in the seven days we enter each morning, with the camera looking down on Dante and Beatrice from the ceiling, enveloped in one another's bodies and souls. At the bus barn, the poem about Ohio Blue Tip Matches begins to transcend its particularities through analogy: "Or, I'm the match/blazing with kisses that/smolder toward heaven." Often his poems will be called simply, "Another One": "I knock off work, have a drink at the bar. /I look down at the glass/and feel glad" (*Paterson*). I think his poetic utterances, grounded in the soil of William's epic poem, securely stitches the entire plot together.

One night, before dinner, Laura asks him to buy her a guitar. She has had a vision of a new future, one in which she becomes a famous

Nashville country-western singer. The expense is more than Paterson feels he can afford, but he says yes to her dream and orders it. When it arrives, Laura spends part of the day designing an appropriate wardrobe and hat to create the appearance of a unique singer; she also learns part of a song guided by the DVDs that accompany the guitar and performs it for him when he returns from work. Paterson applauds her efforts, absorbs the cost of the guitar, and encourages Laura to pursue this new dream of a musician.

Love's Desire to Create

Their deep love for one another is nurtured by the profound commitment they both have for their own creative work in the world. They share their respective soul work with one another and grow more deeply into their relationship. The film continues to assign prominence to the way each of us takes in the world in creative ways rather than just settling for some mundane version of another's reality. Propelling creativity is desire, eros, and a love of the new as it grows from the familiar. I like how my other coauthor, Deborah, explores one avenue of creativity: "Along the creative's path, the smallest of things demand our gasp, our loving attention, our fixed gaze, and our compassionate noticing" (*Deep Creativity* 15).

On a Wednesday night as Paterson walks Marvin to the tavern, he passes the open doors of a laundromat where a rapper practices his rhythms and lyrics; his desire is to create a persona through his rap patterns. Paterson stops to listen, then encourages him to keep at it. It made me think of what each of us does to make our mark in the world through some creative endeavors that our soul needs in order to fulfill itself by means of its own originality. How often we may yearn for some encouragement from outside ourselves to keep the work alive.

On Thursday morning Paterson begins his routine journey to the bus barn and notices perhaps for the first time in a while the city's "Lou Costello Memorial" in homage to one of the its most famous citizens. Remembering who came before us and who can inspire us is part of history's task and imagination's future; it reveals a continuity between our own lives and those who have been memorialized—and so mythologized—

to aid us in remembering ourselves into the future out of a grounding tradition we can be proud of.

A poem called "Glow" begins to shape itself into his early morning musings as he prepares for work: "When I wake up earlier than you/.... I tie my shoes and go downstairs to/put the coffee on" (*Paterson*). Paterson's poems always begin with the ordinary things in the world, but as he develops them his imagination wonders the ordinary into new forms and shapes. This is true not just for his own poems, but also extends to the writings of a young ten-year-old girl he comes upon as he walks home one evening. She is by herself waiting for her mother and sister to return to the car. She sits with her journal as Paterson pauses to ask her if he can join her until her mother and sister return.

She soon confesses to him that she writes poetry in "her secret notebook" and whether he would like to hear her read one. He of course encourages her. It is called "Water Falls": "Water falls from the bright air. . ." (*Paterson*). The line haunts him, so he shares it with Laura when he arrives home. Paterson's generous imagination is as excited about the young girl's poem as he is about his own. Perhaps it is less the poem itself than the soul of the one who yearns to give form to what might simply remain monotonously mundane. In fact, the creative imagination, nurtured for love of the world, as is true of Dante's own writing, seems at certain moments the most ambitious character in the film.

Love Invites a New Beginning

The action takes a dramatic turn one Saturday night. Laura has taken dozens of cupcakes with black and white frosting to the Farmer's Market early in the day and sells all of them, earning $286.00 for her creative efforts. She tells Paterson she wants to treat him to dinner and a horror movie. He is excited to go out, so much so that he leaves his poetry journal on the couch instead of returning it to his study in the garage. Now it is open game.

Vulnerable now, it is soon torn to shreds by the cantankerous canine, Marvin, who most surely has his own frustrations. When they arrive home, they find the journal scattered throughout the living room and one guilty Marvin hiding in the next room. Paterson is devastated. He trivializes losing his poems by telling Laura: "They're just words." But he knows these words define and mirror his soul. Their loss is devastating, especially when he recalls that Laura has repeatedly suggested he make copies of them.

Sunday morning, he walks to the bench by the river where he would compose his poems; but now he is empty-handed and simply sits by himself, despondent and defeated, absent energy and purpose. At this moment he is visited by one of the most destructive presences in the act of creation: the Cynic. Jungian analyst Linda Leonard informs us that "whenever I commit to a creative project, I know that sooner or later I will encounter a character inside myself who I have come to call the Cynic" (*Call to Create* 59). The Cynic is a heavy and relentless partner whose negative response to creativity is corrosive.

Shortly, a Japanese man joins him, a poet from Japan who happens to carry in his satchel a bilingual copy of Williams' *Paterson;* the Japanese poet has made the pilgrimage to Paterson to learn more of this famous American writer and the city of the poem's title. When he asks Paterson if he is a poet, the latter responds: "No. I'm just a bus driver" (Paterson). He has been defeated not by Marvin's destructive action but by the potent presence of the Cynic, who has the capacity to reduce any of our creative pursuits to confetti, then sprinkle it on our head.

The pilgrim, a poet in Japan but whose own work has not been translated, gets up to leave; after taking a few short steps, he returns to Paterson on the bench, opens his satchel and offers him a blank journal with the observation: "Sometimes an empty page presents more possibilities" (*Paterson*). Counter to the Cynic is the Guardian or Guide who keeps the light of imagination burning and one's creative energy glowing. With his perfect gift he seeds Paterson's creative impulses to be-in-creation. Perhaps the Japanese guide is the muse of poetry, or a messenger from that dimension of the soul that creates and enjoys itself in creation, or that guide Leonard refers to as the Sower (*Call to Create* 52). He may be the impetus or the desire to create. Whichever is true, some correspondence has passed between them, offering Paterson hope and a fresh beginning. One feels a resurgence in the distraught poet, a reclamation of sorts, of a new level of poetry not yet formatted. Perhaps Marvin too has helped

Paterson to move to a new level of poetic inspiration by shredding his past creations.

As the film draws to a close, Paterson remembers a poem titled "The Line" that rises out of his past: "There's an old song/my grandfather used to sing/that has the question—/Would you rather be a fish?" The poem asks us to remember what it is we strive to be and whether it is the path of wholeness we authentically seek.

I end with a memorial of sorts, with lines toward the end of Williams' *Paterson* poem that resonates with the end and beginning of bus driver Paterson's new page as a poet: "You will come to it, the blood dark sea/of praise. You must come to it. Seed/of Venus, you will return to/a girl standing upon a titled shell, rose/pink" (*Paterson* 236). The aesthetic hero begins, then begins again in a rhythm that sustains him/her during dark times. When we can recognize that creation always harbors seeds of destruction and break-down, we can pursue our calling *within* and not *outside* of the risks every creative act will harbor at any step in the process.

Works Cited

Jarmusch, Jay. *Paterson*. Directed by J. Jarmusch, 2016.

Leonard, Linda. (2000). *The Call to Create: Celebrating Acts of Imagination*. Harmony Books, 2000.

Padgett, Ron. (2013). *Ron Padgett: Collected Poems*. Coffee House Press, 2013.

Quibell, Deborah Anne, Jennifer Leigh Selig and Dennis Patrick Slattery. *Deep Creativity: Seven Ways to Spark Your Creative Spirit*. Shambhala, 2019.

Williams, William Carlos. *Paterson*. New Directions, 1963.

3

────────── ◆●◆ ──────────

THE LIGHTHOUSE: PROTEUS' PLAYGROUND[*]

I have to think of hell where there are also cinemas for those who despised this institution on earth and did not go there because everyone else found it to their taste.

~ C. G. Jung, *The Red Book*, 265.

Mythology is like the god Proteus, "the ancient one of the sea, whose speech is sooth."

~Joseph Campbell, *The Hero with a Thousand Faces*, 329.

C. G. Jung's observation from *The Red Book* cited above occurs when he confronts a shaggy traveler who begins to relate to him the miraculous events that can happen in a film that transcends our daily lives. His companion's passion changes Jung's mind on the value of cinema because he now grasps how this medium can open up dimensions of life's possibilities that often remain under the floorboards of daily existence. Perhaps only in dreams can human and divine expressions defy the borders of our waking consciousness.

In Robert Eggers' *The Lighthouse,* vistas open that we may have witnessed in other forms, wherein people are transported to a deserted

─────────────

[*] Originally published as *"The Lighthouse"* (2019). Directed by Robert Eggers. *Psychological Perspectives,* 63:2, 2020. 310-314.

island, or a forest outside the city, and in this borderland are awakened to their deeper selves and transformed in such a mysterious, unfamiliar and temporary setting. One thinks of Odysseus isolated from life for seven years on Calypso's Island, or the confluence of nobles and peasants who find themselves entangled in an enchanted forest in *A Midsummer Night's Dream* or on Prospero's Island in Shakespeare's magical land of *The Tempest.* More current is Chuck Noland (Tom Hanks), a time-management consultant for Fed-Ex washed up on a Fiji island, who after four years makes his escape across the barrier reef in *Castaway.* He is aided along the way by a whale whose exhaling spout awakens him in just enough time to wave down a passing freighter. Not surprisingly, the home he desperately seeks to reclaim is no longer there.

Robert Johnson offers this mythical description in his *Inner Work:* "In dreams and myths the conscious mind is often symbolized by an island. Like an island people in an island world, the ego sets up a little world of its own—a system of order and a set of assumptions about reality" (9). We might also claim the whaleship Pequod as an island world that Ishmael and his other-worldly companion, Queequeg, board that becomes the try pot of the soul. Elements of their identity will be dissolved in the alchemical fires of the cauldron that melt whales into barrels of oil. I have personally discovered that monastic or other forms of retreat settings can also serve as places in which one can journey into the deepest recesses of one's self.

In a similar archetypal situation, two men are ferried onto a spit of land with a lighthouse where they will tend it for four weeks. Thomas Wake (Willem Dafoe), a wizened career veteran of the lighthouse, is accompanied by a new apprentice, Ephraim Winslow, a younger, more robust employee as well as a drifter from Canada looking to set down roots somewhere and become captain of his own destiny. With more than one reference to Herman Melville's *Moby-Dick,* the film asks that we recall the inner drama of Captain Ahab and perhaps a less naïve Ishmael rehearsing itself on the island. Some storylines insist on being retold in a host of new venues.

Within the grooves of Melville's masterpiece, I question if the luminous white light at the top of the lighthouse may be a new form of the white whale that Wake selfishly keeps locked up for his own pleasure and that Winslow wished to covet as the film unfolds. Perhaps the seeker Winslow awakens for the first time in his life on the tiny island in the wilderness of the ocean. Screenwriting consultant Christopher Vogler writes in his revised 25th. anniversary version of *The Writer's Journey* that "The Call to Adventure," first proposed by mythologist Joseph Campbell, "may simply be a stirring within the hero, a messenger from the unconscious, bearing news that it's time for a change" (120).

Like the other stories mentioned, Eggers' film cultivates a series of threshold crossings, where one chooses or is forced to swap one set of normative terms that structure life for a new angle or complete revision of the old story. This new terrain unsettles and dismantles the familiar. When the steamer drops the men off at the small island off the coast of Maine, the seagulls are everywhere, surrounding the tiny skid mark of land and its prominent white lighthouse. In the film's finale, the seagulls once more soak the screen; they frame the entire action as active participants rivaling in importance to the two men.

When Conflict Reigns

Wake and Winslow could not be more opposite and oppositional: Wake is a hard-bitten storyteller who, like a merciless father, with the caustic bite of an Ahab, dominates and abuses his "new son" from the outset. When Winslow asks him, what happened to his last apprentice, he is told the young man went insane after seven months in his new role. Wake spews a stream of stories and thereby coerces Winslow to be more like him, especially in dinner conversation. The grizzled old man of the sea seeks a duplicate of himself in his new apprentice but was burdened with his opposite.

Eggers uses the power of black and white film as well as constant music and noises that sound at once like a moaning whale, the foghorn of the lighthouse and the ship's horn to create a mood that is somber, menacing and kept me on edge throughout the many threshold crossings that frame the film's forward motion. The characters make do in their small dining room, sitting room, and their tiny bedroom reached by walking up a spiral staircase. As Winslow settles into his bunk, he notices a hole in the mattress; from it he removes a tuft of stuffing and pulls out a small statue of a mermaid, which he hides from Wake.

To continue up the spiral staircase, which is the geometry C. G. Jung finds central to growth—"Psychologically, you develop in a spiral" (*Analysis of the Dream Seminars, 1928-30* 100)—takes one to a locked metal floor, the key for which Wake hordes, giving the film a fairy tale atmosphere. The coveted key, the secret space above that forbids entrance to Winslow, as well as the brutish Wake's abuse of his increasingly frustrated charge, creates the morbid and increasing tension in the plot. Wake records in his large daily ledger all the mistakes and shortfalls he believes Winslow makes daily: he is too slow, doesn't complete all tasks, is sloppy, careless and lazy. Wake employs shame and guilt to keep Winslow off-balance, distraught, and under his thumb.

The film's story, however, reveals that Winslow works without ceasing during the day as Wake sleeps. He hauls coal by wheelbarrow to the fire that turns the wheels that rotates the slowly-revolving brilliant white light that warns ships in night and fog. He cleans, scours, paints and does all of Wake's biddings, only to be pilloried with abuse for his exhausting efforts. It is easy to recall the tyrannical and often maniacal Ahab on the deck of the Pequod pushing his crew to exhaustion in pursuit of the white whale, the source of Ahab's dismemberment and his outrage.

Wake tells Winslow over dinner that he is married to the lighthouse, his feminine desire. He spends his "watch" up by the luminous, even numinous, light within the constricted space of the magnificent, otherworldly brilliance. This otherworldly space comprises another threshold crossing forbidden to the apprentice. At one point Winslow stands by on the spiral steps and listens to the erotic groans of Wake above; he watches in wonder at the slime (jism?) that seeps down through the metal mesh floor and drips past him. On one occasion he observes in disbelief as a large tentacle, like that of a squid or octopus, squirms across the metal floor above him. His desire to witness the light increases immensely at this moment. He has awakened to and intensifies his pursuit of the one forbidden thing that defines so many narratives and often shapes the destiny of the pursuer.

The world they have entered begins to reveal its other-worldly dimensions while at the same time the relationship between the two men

oscillates between friendship and hostility, contest and desire, cooperation and violence. One day, as Winslow takes the contents of filthy pots
out to the rocks by the sea to empty, he notices something lying there
wrapped in seaweed. When he bends down to uncover it, he exposes a
mermaid and jumps back in horror as she begins to scream like the gulls.
Later, he imagines he makes love to the enchanting creature, but the film
shows him self-gratifying his lustful desires while holding his mermaid
statue.

The Power of Wonder

Earlier, while transporting a wheelbarrow of coal to a storage shed, Winslow is confronted by a seagull blocking his path. He throws a lump of
coal at it; the bird responds by attacking him violently, then flying off.
He relates this incident to Wake who responds: "Bad luck to kill a gull;
they are the souls of sailors." Later, a major turning point in the action,
as Winslow pumps water into his cup, it gushes black as oil. He checks
the cistern and notices a seagull resting inside, perhaps dead. The gull he
attacked earlier appears and attacks him a second time. Winslow snatches
it from the air and in a rage beats it into tatters against a rock. Its death
signals a dramatic drop in barometric pressure as the wind shifts to the
north, a clear sign, warns Wake, of intense treacherous weather. Yet another threshold is crossed.

Eggers is brilliant in conveying the breakdown of two realities: the
outer natural order loses all boundaries and containment as waves and
wind break into their living quarters. The other melt-down occurs in the
psyche of both men as they turn violently against one another, with Winslow ascending to the alpha-male and Wake dropping into subservience.
Their now constant and excessive drinking creates its own line of thun-
derstorms of chaos between and within them as all social conventions
collapse and thresholds become tenuous and frequent.

On what is to be their last night before being picked up by the ship,
they seem possessed. After binge-drinking, they awake but have no sense
of how long they have slept. Time itself seems to have melted away.
Watching his apprentice turn on him, Wake accuses him: "You're so

mad, you don't know up from down . . . I'm probably a figment of your imagination; this rock is a figment of your imagination too" (*Lighthouse*).

Disgusted by Wake's abuse and his foul breath, constant farting and accelerating decay, Winslow speaks in low tones: "I'm tired of your farting and of your yarns in your Captain Ahab voice. Your stories are bullshit." Wake's response: "You lied to yourself but don't have the sauce to see it" (*Lighthouse*). Such an accusation prompts Winslow to blurt out his desire: "Let me into that light," he pleads and demands at once. Here, the object that has been denied gains in force and desire; it gathers the energies of an obsession to obtain the small enchanted space at the top of the lighthouse that holds the numinous revolving light. Perhaps Winslow has become the new Ahab in his maniacal quest for the white whale.

When they fight shortly after, Wake, on his back, appears to Winslow first as the mermaid, then as the god of the sea—Proteus or Poseidon—with large octopus tentacles writhing behind him, his face covered with shells. Winslow ties him to a leash and walks Wake on all fours to the hole dug earlier to retrieve a cache of supplies, including alcohol. He throws Wake into it and begins to bury him; with dirt thrown in his face, Wake continues in a mad reverie about the god Proteus: "that Protean force that serves up from men's minds" (*Lighthouse*) all forms of shapeshifting illusions. It seems that another threshold has been crossed, one that separates consciousness from the unconscious so that all the figures and desires of the latter are unleashed.

Winslow takes the key from Wake, who up to now has been the threshold guardian of the light and of transformation. But before he can begin his final journey, Wake appears from the grave to attack Winslow one last time. Winslow kills him on the spot, then rushes to unlock what C. G. Jung has termed "the treasure hard to attain" (*CW* 12 par. 442). He rushes up the spiral stairs to satisfy his desires. It is his grail, the numinous, the treasure he has made it his mission to confiscate and possess. He now ascends to the illumination he has yearned for.

There, as the light turns, we see on the carved lens of the glass what looks like an alien creature with large eyes. A door opens to invite Winslow into the inner sanctum of the light's source; in a final threshold crossing, he is fully embraced and absorbed by the light's mystery, a beacon and anchor to his wandering life.

The last scene reveals a naked Winslow on the rocks of the tiny beach, facing up, as the gulls peck at his flesh to integrate him into themselves. The fog closes over this final scene where the "souls of sailors" take Winslow into their bodies.

The Lighthouse is a mesmerizing mythic film about the imagination, the gods, the immortals and the feminine figure of legends, sought by mortals for millennia. It also tells the hero's journey, seeking one's own path, and the desire to find one's own grail, whatever the price. Winslow may have at one moment realized that he has apprenticed himself to the old man of the sea, a primordial presence, shape-shifter and life-changer. Perhaps only the audience is able to tell if he was worthy.

Works Cited

Campbell, Joseph. *The Hero with a Thousand Faces*. Bollingen Series XVII. Princeton UP, 1973.

Johnson, Robert A. *Inner Work: Using Dreams and Active Imagination for Personal Growth*. HarperSanFrancisco, 1989.

Jung, C. G. *Dream Analysis: Notes of the Seminar Given in 1928-1930*. William McGuire, editor. Bollingen Series XCIX. Princeton UP, 1984.

---. *The Red Book: Liber Novus. A Reader's Edition*. Sonu Shamdasani Ed. Mark Kyburz, John Peck et. al, translators. Philemon Series. New York: Norton, 2009.

---. *Psychology and Alchemy. The Collected Works of C. G. Jung* Vol. 12. G. Adler & R. F. C. Hull Eds. & translators. Bollingen Series XX. Princeton UP, 1970.

Vogler, Christopher. *The Writer's Journey: Mythic Structure for Writers*. 25th. anniversary (Fourth) edition. Studio City, California: Michael Wiese Productions, 2020.

4

◆●◆

SHADES OF THE GROTESQUE: *VICTOR FRANKENSTEIN, THE MONSTER, AND THE SHADOWS OF TECHNOLOGY**

> *There are many good reasons to undertake cross-disciplinary studies, but one compelling justification is that a problem one wants to solve cannot be adequately addressed with the tools of one discipline alone.*

> ~ Paul B. Armstrong, *How Literature Plays with the Brain: The Neuroscience of Reading and Art* 1.

One writer who has known and integrated Armstrong's observation deep in his bones through his own writing over the past thirty plus years is Robert Romanyshyn. I have been reading his vast inventory of thought, insights and innovative angles on culture for at least that long and share his love for an imagination that is not afraid to roam playfully across disciplines and subject matter, but always with a serious intent. He is also fearless in his ability to dream and to take the dreaming imagination seriously, especially when it dreams in that shadowed arena of what is between the vast terrains of psyche and world.

---

* Originally published as Romanyshyn, R. (2019). *Victor Frankenstein, The Monster and the Shadows of Technology: The Frankenstein Prophecies.* Routledge. In *The Journal of Humanistic Psychology*, 2020. 1-6.

In this new study, which has its roots in soil decades old that he has been cultivating and tending, like a farmer, with one eye on the weather and the other on the seeds he has just planted, he engages two tasks: gathering up dozens of ideas he has been brooding over for the lifetime of his professional career, and pushing them forward in *The Frankenstein Prophecies* into discussions of, for instance, the internet, techno-culture generally, cyborgs, the Promethean impulse in human beings to create gods of themselves for themselves as well as for self-justification, and the various structures of human embodiment or their dramatic absence.

As I read his book, I felt the gravitational pull of a homecoming; his recent study is, for me, a homecoming text, for it echoes so many themes that he wrote about and taught for decades, as well as a host of new insights gleaned from one 19th. century novel created out of a waking dream. So, the geometry of the work is in keeping with Jung's idea that "Psychologically you develop in a spiral, you always come over the same point where you have been before, but it is never exactly the same, it is either above or below" (*Dream Analysis* 100). One must, then, be content with traversing the same field one has worked before but with little chance of engaging the same furrows of other visits. That is at it should be, to encourage a fresh footprint to trod the familiar/unfamiliar land-scape.

In this far-ranging and deeply analogical study comprised of eight questions surrounding Mary Shelley's brilliant and quickly-created gothic novel, *Frankenstein, or, The Modern Prometheus* (1818), he centers on various situations and figures in her creation in order to cull from them intimations of our current technological age, with many of its attendant anxieties and potentials. I use the word "analogical" above to depict Romanyshyn' s mythodology; he works like a poet with enormous respect for the power of metaphor, symbol and story, including their healing properties as well as a rich genesis for deep psychological reflections. From C. G. Jung's observation that "since analogy formation is a law which to a large extent governs the life of the psyche . . ." (*CW* 9, ii. par. 414), we as readers can readily observe how Romanyshyn apprehends Mary Shelley's classic as an intricate, complex and prophetic poetic expression of our own cultural terrain.

A Misguided Quest

One of its main mythic figures, Victor Frankenstein, sets out on a quest to improve on nature by eliminating "Death the Spoiler" (*Prophecies* 12). In his pursuit, coupled with his adoration of science as source of his genius, Frankenstein creates a Monster from the dead flesh of corpses. In its deformed presence on the margins of the central narrative of Mary Shelley's tale, the story that Frankenstein relays on his death bed to Captain Walton, Romanyshyn explores both the scientist's narrative and leaves white space for the Monster's story; together, through Romanyshyn's deep reading, they together convey valid and valuable insights to share with us over the expanse of 200 years.

One of the most prominent psychic sand traps in our present day, Romanyshyn reminds us frequently in this study, resides in not regarding or valuing the unconscious, both personal and collective. I recall Jung's observation that "the unconscious is a whole world of images whose range is as boundless as that of the world of 'real' things" (*CW* 6 par. 281). Not taking account of the unconscious, Romanyshyn asserts, is to place our humanity, as an often rapacious and self-indulged species, as well as the planet we inhabit, in deeper peril of self-destruction. He reveals these insights by creating a unique structure to the text.

The assembly is unique. It is comprised of eight questions, along with dozens of additional queries imbedded within each chapter title. Here is a sample to give a sense of the landscape: "Question One: Resurrecting the dead: Is Mary Shelley's story a prophecy of the dangers of acting as gods?" (*Prophecies* ix); "Question Four: Out of Africa to the moon: Is Mary Shelley's story a prophecy of creating a new species of humankind?" (ix); "Question Six: WWW: Adrift in the digital world: Is Mary Shelley's story a prophecy of the last generations of humankind?" (ix); "Question Eight: Other seeds of hope in Mary Shelley's story: Is Mary Shelley's story a prophecy of new beginnings?" (x).

These interrogatives frame the eight quests; each quest journeys deeply into Mary Shelley's prophetic fiction. Romanyshyn calls our attention to the genesis of her story at the end of his study in a statement that illuminates the depth psychology of her work: "That she claimed, therefore, that Victor Frankenstein, the Monster and their story were born in a waking dream is a curious and important detail to be noted" (*Prophecies* 113), for he has entered its devastating and at times heart-rending world, as one would a work of fiction and a descent into the unconscious, as Dante did hundreds of years earlier, as Ishmael dared in Herman Melville's *Moby-Dick* and as C. G. Jung willingly yielded to the spirit of the depths in *The Red Book*. It is worth noting what C. G. Jung observes about "visionary fiction" and its origins: "It is something strange that derives its existence from the hinterland of man's mind, as if it had emerged from the abyss of prehuman ages, or from a superhuman world of contrasting light and darkness. It is a primordial experience which surpasses man's understanding . . . " (*CW* 11 par. 141)

On his journey, epic in size and atmosphere, and ending in a hopeful vision, Romanyshyn confronts and converses with dozens of characters and impulses in the soul, including the following: technology, embodiment and its absence, the spectator, astronauts, margins, creativity, history, Prometheus, gods and goddesses, shadow figures, genetics, cyborgs, the homeless, refugees, the marginalized, zombies, shopping malls, computer bodies, abortion, the disposables, the forgotten, the oppressed, the migrants and a host of others. The ultimate tensile strength of his study, I suggest, is in his continual journeying back in history from the mother ship of Mary Shelley's novel to explore the abandoned body that begins with the invention of linear perspective vision and the telescope of Galileo, then forward to our increasingly disembodied, astronaut-inflected space where communion with our own nature and the natural order's miracles continue to grow more feeble, leaving just the slightest green blip on the heart monitor of culture.

Multiple Forms of Mimesis

As he explores the obsession with Victor Frankenstein's fantasy to absolve humankind of aging and dying, and the subsequent Monster he creates as a prototype of a new form of humankind, Romanyshyn holds the tension within a trifecta of disciplines: history, psycho-somatics and mythology; yet undergirding that structure is a keen eye for the poetic, or better-said, the mythopoetics of culture, as it is given shape both in historical perspectives and in prophetic envisionings.

I found each of his quests to comprise a series of related journeys that nonetheless stand on their own as perspectives that reveal Mary Shelley's imaginative vision of how energy could be harnessed to create new life. But within the hubris that may attend such a desire in science and scientists resides a destructive component, a shadowed underbelly, that can be easily buried in the unconscious by the shovels of technological achievements.

Such is the case, he believes, in citing the sixteenth century visionary, Francis Bacon, whose brutal image of humankind against nature is disturbing: "the new sciences were to put nature on the rack to torture her secrets from her" (*Prophecies* 23). With the rise of the tendency to objectivity and measurement, Romanyshyn asserts, a humus-inflected mankind begins to lose its place in the world as human, instead to metamorphose slowly into a specimen, an object, to be shed of its humanity as it is studied objectively and controlled absolutely. In this process, he asserts, we become a further version of Victor Frankenstein's Monster. But he is quick to remind us that we both are capable and have an ethical imperative to be able to listen to the Monster's story told on the frozen and uninhabited margins of society where sympathetic listeners comprise a modest population.

Reclaiming the Dispossessed

As I watched Romanyshyn's brilliant and provocative web of relationships whet our own imaginations to dream his work further, I asked myself: what metaphors are we living out personally today? Which are silenced and which are we asked or coerced to forget? Which are dominant and persuasive to unreflective minds? For what we recall and reference become our reverence points; what we casually or violently forget become gaps in our narrative that breeds a shattered story line as well as sense of homelessness; our stories are the transport vehicles that take us home and offer us a sense of belonging in a world that has infinite correspondences with our own nature. Homelessness in Romanyshyn's study is a center piece, here and in his earlier writings. The orphan is the archetype that inhabits homelessness. Its natural family is the earth and all the rest of us.

Because, apropos of what I just wrote above, I want to step back and survey the entire book, which actually contains three stories: 1. The novel written by the young and brilliant Mary Shelley; 2. The stories that emanate from Romanyshyn' s imaginal involvement with each particularity of the novel; 3. The footnotes that I sense are another story unto themselves, however much they have threads attached to the second story.[†]

I have not, in this review, as is now apparent, rehearsed the plot of Mary Shelley's novel; one can do that for oneself. My interest has been on the imaginal methods by which Romanyshyn has seen our contemporary world *by means of* the Frankenstein novel. That is how myths work. As such, *Frankenstein* became the mythopoetic ground by which to become more fully aware of our current world that seems intent on divorcing itself from the natural rhythms of nature, including those tempos and intimacies that the marginal Monster in the story exhibits in his "unnatural" creation. As Romanyshyn makes clear in a footnote in the sixth chapter, "For Victor Frankenstein, the Monster he has made is a thing, a thing with no name and never to be seen in any other way. But the essential point of *The Frankenstein Prophecies* is to see the Monster in another way, as a being with his own agency whose tale is told from the margins, from his place of exile" (*Prophecies* 85, fn. 5). He goes on to tell us in a subsequent insight that the Monster's deepest education has been "by the book of Nature," so that "even in its disfigurement, and the charms of Nature" (108), he is realigned with the natural order's magnificence, if not its healing impulses.

When the voices and narratives of the dispossessed are given space and loving attention, they may usher in hope, at times even a promise of a new way of seeing and of responding to what haunts the margins of society as well as the edges of consciousness. In the face of the disfigured and exiled, repelled and tossed to culture's waste bin as they often are, their presence allows us all to dream of another way, a renovated myth, one less monstrous toward the environment, the earth with her limited resources, and the ravages of consumption. In the Monster's presence,

---

[†] A side bar to Routledge: Have pity on us ripening mortals who struggle as I did with the font size of the notes! I kept my magnifying glass close at hand because I did not want to miss their revelations.

in whatever form, there is a story we have not yet heard; that is our loss, not its.

Romanyshyn's rich metaphorical exploration that slices into the wounds of our cultural exhaustion, offers nutrients of another order, one which asserts the primacy of the imaginal and the wealth of the human spirit that is hardly ever satisfied by acquisitions and spasms of achieving more power. Reading it as a therapy of journeying into the unfamiliar, each of our personal quests will yield further questions, which is one of the goals of the knight errant's project. Hardly a quest energized by illusion but rather by the desire for illumination and community.

Works Cited

Armstrong, Paul B. *How Literature Plays with the Brain: The Neuroscience of Reading and Art.* Johns Hopkins UP, 2013.

Jung. C. G. *Psychological Types,* Vol. 6 *The Collected Works of C. G. Jung.* R. F. C. Hull, Herbert Read, Michael Fordham, et. al, editors and translators. Princeton UP, 1990.

---. *Aion: Researches into the Phenomenology of the Self.* Vol. 9, ii. *The Collected Works of C. G. Jung,* R. F. C. Hull and Gerhard Adler, editors and translators. Princeton UP, 1959.

---. *The Spirit in Man, Art and Literature,* Vol. 15. *The Collected Works of C. G. Jung.* R. F. C Hull, translator. Princeton UP, 1966.

---. Jung, C. G. (1984). *Dream Analysis: Notes of the Seminar Given in 1928-1930.* Bollingen Series XCIX. William McGuire, editor. Princeton UP, 1984.

Romanyshyn, Robert. *Victor Frankenstein, The Monster and the Shadows of Technology: The Frankenstein Prophecies.* Routledge, 2019.

5

—◆●◆—

QUEST-IONING THE WOUND: THE KNIGHT'S QUEST FOR WHOLENESS*

The "lapis exilis" may correspond to the "lapsit exillis," Wolfram von Eschenbach's name for the Grail.

~ C. G. Jung "On the Rosarium Philosophorum"
(1976, *CW* 18, par. 1783).

Some images which can haunt the imagination of cultures for millennia, refuse to fade with the passing of time. We may think of the shield of Achilles in Homer's *Iliad,* the figure of Satan frozen in ice in the deepest terrain of Dante's *Inferno,* the white whale of Herman Melville's *Moby-Dick,* and the haunted house at 124 Bluestone Road in Toni Morrison's *Beloved.* Tucked in time between these titles is the Holy Grail, sometimes depicted as a chalice, a cup, a bowl, or a stone. As powerful archetypal images, these and others continue to define and circulate through civilizations, leaving their traces anew as crucial weather vanes of the soul. At times they function on an unconscious level, but occasionally they abrupt onto the surface of consciousness and help to transform an entire people.

---

* Originally published as "Quest-ioning the Wound: The Knights Quest for Wholeness." Review of Evans Lansing Smith's *Romance of the Grail. The Jung Journal: Culture and Psyche.* Vol. 11, 2017, Issue 2, 86-90.

Evans Lansing Smith's excellent research and editing of one of the most prominent mythologists of the past and current century, Joseph Campbell, focuses on his writings and epic narratives of the Grail legend. As he outlines in his "Foreword," Smith had the marvelous advantage of traveling with Campbell on several occasions, most notably to a host of cities in France and Brittany, ending with a pilgrimage through Chartres Cathedral (*Grail* x). One of the delights of traveling with Campbell, Smith informs us, is that he laced so many of the sites with stories of Merlin, Lancelot, Galahad, Gawain, Feirefiz and Parzival, a host of heroic figures who populated the Grail trail.

Such direct, personal connections with Campbell on this, as well as other journeys, both in story and geography, adds immensely to the texture of his editing as well as to the vitality of Campbell's presence when he engaged these medieval masterpieces of the Grail's history and their lasting influence on troubadour and romantic poetry. At the same time, it underscores the durability and flexibility of an archetypal image as it haunts the mythic spine of so many dramatic narratives over time.

As Smith spent years pouring through boxes of rich material from the Campbell Collection in the Archives of Pacifica Graduate Institute in Carpinteria, California, he had his own moments of remarkable discoveries about the mythologist and his scholarly pilgrimage through Grail lore.

The Collection revealed to him Campbell's "shift from Celtic to Oriental mythologies in his understanding of the Arthurian material, a shift that catalyzed the emergence of Campbell's truly global, comparative perspective on myth in general and on the Grail romances in particular that has become the signature of his unique genius of creative synthesis" (*Grail* xvii). Clearly, the Grail material became Campbell's own grail quest, which led him to form an entire worldview for understanding how myths have their genesis and evolve over centuries, retaining something core in their nature while morphing to the demands and pressures of history's insistence.

Structuring the Search

Smith divides his study into three parts, ending in an appendix that contains Campbell's master's thesis from Columbia University, entitled "A Study of the Dolorous Stroke," which he submitted to the English faculty in 1927. It compares the weaponry of the lance and the sword used by Balin in wounding the king, effectively bringing three kingdoms into poverty and waste before healing could occur in both king and kingdom.

When I read it, I grasped more clearly the early seeds of one of the most famous comparative mythologists in our history. In Campbell's thesis was born a methodology, or perhaps a *mythodology,* which rested on comparison, likeness, correspondence, accords and resonances that became a signature of his writing during his lifetime and further references Smith's key keen insight just cited.

The other sections are worth mentioning as roadmaps for an abundant amount of material that comprises just under three hundred pages of text: "Part One: Foundations and Backgrounds of the Grail Romances," "Part Two: Knights in Quest," "Part Three: Themes and Motifs." I found this chronological vessel an effective program for tracking the mystery of the Grail Legend across time and territories, gathering in its cumulative progress a host of heroes and heroines as it processed through some of the richest literary epics Western culture has produced.

Campbell explains to the reader at the beginning of his thesis that he plans to follow a route seldom taken: "The path which I propose to follow lies aloof from the main road, and no one has ever pressed it to conclusion" (*Grail* 171). It is, therefore, more than appropriate that Smith ends his volume with Campbell's scholarly beginnings at age twenty-three when he submitted his thesis. Anyone who knows even a few of Campbell's writings, or his *Power of Myth* conversations with host Bill Moyers on PBS, will soon discern his birthing and developing a method by which to cross-reference various works across time and space based on their common core imagery and parallel plot structures as well as recurring archetypal images that stitch the works together. We watch throughout the thesis as Campbell creates a comparative anatomy of stories by mixing a blend of analogy and homology in his own quest toward a mythopoetic discovery of meaning. Words like "resemblance" (214), "parallel traditions" (216), and "curious parallels" (21) form the lexicon of this new comparative approach, mentored in part by the works of Sir James Frazer as well Campbell's guide at Columbia, Roger Sherman Loomis (1981).

To address the order and arrangement of this very convincing and thorough study and edited volume, I first draw attention to the role of an editor. An editor serves a volume of work much as an orchestra conductor serves the music she or he will elicit from its members. An editor must align and assign an assemblage of moving parts into a harmonious and melodious whole, while not losing the rich musical notes that each instrument adds. Editing can be an unappreciated art form; one must map the territory of the symphony into chapters, akin to the symphony's movements, that congeal into a melodic form. Smith's sure hand as editor gives this volume a fine coherence, replete with pages of notes to guide us through each epic he presents as well as sources that will keep any interested reader of the Grail Quest busy for years excavating one of the richest archetypal journeys history and poetry have bequeathed us.

On a personal level, my own work and teaching of Dante's *Divine Comedy* was enriched and deepened in knowing the Italian poet's tradition as well as the rich relations between the Grail and the evolving Christian mythos; I would, however, argue strongly against Campbell's assessment that begins Chapter 4: "Wolfram von Eschenbach's *Parzival*": "Parzival by Wolfram von Eschenbach is a truly magnificent work—in my opinion, the greatest of the Middle Ages, surpassing even that of Dante" (*Grail* 35).

Commenting on the various texts themselves that Campbell cogently, and with great vitality and love, both summarizes and frames in mythological terms would not serve the readers of this essay. Instead, I want to focus on what I, and many others, study Campbell for: his insights into the human condition in all its nuanced complexities through the apertures of literary classics, as well as his explicit and implicit remarks on the relationship between history and myth, which I have written about elsewhere.

Concrete and Literal Understandings

In these writings, I offer the possibility that myth serves history as its consistent inner sleeve, which remains invisible but no less important as the outer sleeve. Although the visible outer fabric is, to my mind, history, the tabulated events of the past, the invisible lining of the inner sleeve, is what gives history its shape, its form, and, ultimately, its meaning. That is its myth. Without the inner sleeve of myth, history remains inert, deadening and incarcerated in literalisms. It then offers no insights into the present through a wisdom informed by myth in previous histories. I am using the metaphor of fabric in its inner and outer qualities to capture some measure of the *fabrication* that all stories enunciate.

I mention this relationship here because Campbell's belief, repeated throughout his writings spanning over sixty years, is that a harmful misunderstanding persists in confusing the concreteness of a myth, or scripture or a poem, for a literal reality, thereby infusing an individual or an entire people's beliefs based on a persuasive fiction. In exploring the travels of the Celtic figure Brendan, for instance, he pauses in his summary to affirm: "It is one of the prime mistakes of many interpreters of mythological symbols to read them as references, not to mysteries of the human spirit, but to earthly or unearthly scenes and to actual or imagined historical events—the Promised Land as Canaan, for example . . ." (*Grail* 14). Here is Campbell's strong suit: to make the literary work a living myth as it becomes "affectively present" as an aesthetic expression, according to Robert Armstrong (*Presence* 4), to the reader as a lived experience, not as historical data.

Campbell always has his sights less on *in-formation* than *trans-formation;* the poem, myth, fable or tale must cohere on a deep level with the reader's own life quest so that the form of the myth that gives the narrative its shape informs the myth of the reader's own life quest. One might venture that "the quest" itself is the main character in the medieval poems Campbell turns his attention to in Smith's collection: von Eschenbach's *Parzival,* von Strasburg's *Tristan and Iseult, Sir Gawain and the Green Knight,* as well as interpretations of "The Waste Land" that include both Asian and Western approaches. Appendix B, "Works on the Arthurian Romances of the Middle Ages from the Joseph Campbell

Collection," offers an exhaustive array of titles that together comprise an entire library of the medieval cosmos (*Grail* 237–244).

Campbell goes on to suggest that one of many virtues in the Celtic tradition is its fertile and clear imagination as it retranslates religious themes "from the languages of imagined fact into a mythological idiom, so that they may be experienced not as time-conditioned but as timeless. ..." (*Grail* 14). The result is that we do not read them as historical realities *back there* but "miracles potential within ourselves, here, now, and forever" (14). His description and insight here I would call one of Campbell's most fundamental motifs in the entire canon of his writing.

Myth and History

What we are offered is an angle of vision, a way of perception that is itself mythopoetic and mythohistorical; it accounts, to my mind, for one of the most familiar attractors for the millions of people who have read and been affected by Campbell's writings and lectures: the direct connection of ancient stories to our contemporary consciousness. The substance that brings these two worlds into coherence is comprised of analogies in the form of symbols, metaphors, homologies and similes—everlasting correspondences between worlds and worldviews and between the conscious and unconscious dimensions of our being.

The interface of history and myth is richly illustrated in Campbell's discussion of Wolfram von Eschenbach's *Parzival* quest, where he pivots to the Orient to amplify a key quality of this epic. He praises the Celtic imagination for highlighting "the inward, mystical aspects of a story" and "the outward, historical aspect" (*Grail* 81), while combining both with the Gospel legend that undergirds the Medieval epics' exploration of not only human but also divine love. His insight at this juncture is germane to his entire outlook on mythopoiesis, that is, making or shaping a myth into a new form: "It is not on the importance of historical events that may or may not have taken place, but on the requirement that something should happen, here and now, in one's mind and will" (81).

He then claims that the entire subject's importance hinges on this crucial discovery: "that of the radical distinction between the esoteric (mystical) and exoteric (historical) ways of reading mythological symbols:

as references, on the one hand, to powers operative in the human heart as agents of transformation, and, on the other, to actual or imagined historical events" (82). I want to end on this illustration because Campbell's insight proposes another iteration of what the Greeks discovered at least as early as the fifth century BCE, namely what Aristotle was to call in his *Poetics* "mimesis" (*Poetics* 7). Smith's research reveals in what rich ways Campbell is a mimetic mythologist because he intuits how the stories we read or hear and are drawn to have an attraction to the deepest narratives that guide our own imaginal existence. They reflect the oldest part of who we are as a species.

In writing of Sophocles' masterpiece, *Oedipus Rex,* Aristotle claims that the tragic drama—and I think his discovery applies to all genres of literature—is an outward depiction or representation of an action, carried through its plot, of a dramatic psychological (e)motion within the spectator, wherein discovery of one's essence comes through a wound, an affliction. As we watch or read poetry, we *mimetically* participate in the action, not "vicariously," a term I have never liked or thought appropriate to this deep psychological, emotional and mythic experience. Rather, we experience Oedipus' action by analogy so that it resonates with our own lives as richly as do the actions of Parzival, Lancelot, Gawain, King Anfortas or any other of the Medieval epic heroes that Campbell never tired of exploring. We might recall C. G. Jung's observation in *Aion*: "Since analogy formation is a law which, to a large extent, governs the psyche …" (*CW* 9ii, ¶414)—to draw a direct line from the aesthetic rendering of Oedipus' discovery of himself through his own wounding to our potential for discovery through our own afflictions.

In this basic sense, Campbell is Aristotelian in temperament; his entire professional and personal life was devoted to this mimetic play between the outer reality of these magnificent creations that Smith has researched and assembled in this luxurious addition to Campbell's canon, and the interior dramatic stage that exists in each one of us. Having Campbell's research and insights cluster in this volume is a service to all who wish to deepen their understanding of the power, the potentials and the poetics of myth.

Works Cited

Aristotle. *The Poetics.* Translated by S. H. Butcher. Introduction by Francis Fergusson. New York: Hill and Wang, 1989.

Armstrong, Robert Plant. *The Powers of Presence: Consciousness, Myth and Affecting Presence.* U Pennsylvania P, 1981.

Campbell, Joseph. *Romance of the Grail: The Magic and Mystery of Arthurian Myth.* Evans Lansing Smith, editor. New World Library, 2015.

Jung, C. G. "On the Rosarium Philosophorum." *The Symbolic Live: Miscellaneous Writings, Vol. 20. The Collected Works of C. G. Jung,* R. F. C Hull, translator. Princeton UP, 1970. 797-800.

---. "The structure and dynamics of the self. *Aion: Researches into the Phenomenology of the Self. CW* 9, ii. Second Edition. *The Collected Works of C. G. Jung.* R. F. C. Hull, translator. Princeton UP, 1970.

Loomis, Richard L. 1991. *The Grail: From Celtic Myth to Christian Symbol.* Princeton UP, 1991.

Slattery, Dennis Patrick. "The Myth of Nature and the Nature of Myth: Becoming Transparent to Transcendence." *Harvesting Darkness: Essays on Literature, Myth, Film and Culture,* iUniverse Publishing, 2006. 288–307.

---. "Mystic Faces, History's Traces: Joseph Campbell, Mystic." *Bridge Work: Essays on Mythology, Literature and Psychology.* Mandorla Books, 2015. 47-68.

6

---◆●◆---

MOBY-DICK AS FIGURE IN THE FIELD: MYTHMAKING AS SOUL-SAVING

I would also include Melville's Moby-Dick, *which I consider to be the greatest American novel, in this broad class of writings* [visionary fiction].

~ C. G. Jung, *CW* 15, par. 137.

For the past sixteen years I have been taking my Mythological Studies students whale watching in the Santa Barbara channel in Southern California. It accompanies the last meeting of our Epic Imagination course in which we read Homer's *Odyssey*, Melville's *Moby-Dick* and Toni Morrison's *Beloved*. The whale watch is not mandatory, but most all of the students sign on board the Condor Express to enjoy five hours at sea spotting a variety of whales. We also frequently sight thousands of bottlenose dolphins, sea lions, seals and a host of other marine life. In all these years I have felt each boarding was my first outing. I say this early on in this presentation because with every launching into the blue waters of the Pacific, a new mystery unfolds; when whales are sighted by their vapory blow hole as they exhale, the lives of all on board quicken. Whales seem to have mastered the capacity to evoke wonder by simply being themselves.

Many of the students see their first whale on this voyage. For me, after so many years and hundreds of whale sightings—usually greys, humpbacks and blues, with an occasional minke whale or a rarer Orca darting along in the traffic of hundreds of bottle-nosed dolphins, the thrill never abates. Why is this, and why does the thrill of reentering Melville's magnificent epic never become rote or routine when I enter its seas of mystery each year?

Once, a pair of humpbacks swam up alongside the Condor Express when we were miles from shore; one playfully cut across her bow performing an energetic barrel roll; then its partner, not to be outdone, cruised up slowly and bumped its forehead against the bow, not once but three times—love taps from the deep; affection from fathoms down. All on board were giddy with excitement and awe.

When several impassioned passengers leaned over the bow to see it more closely, it blew hard through its blowhole the most rancid nauseating smell of decaying krill. One student and two other passengers vomited on the spot. One is naïve not to think the whale knew exactly what it was doing. It was socializing!

Breaching is of course another of its favorite show stoppers. Various theories have been put forth as to why whales, most especially humpbacks, perform this acrobatic move: shaking barnacles off of its massive body when it slams back to the water's surface; getting a bird's eye view of the surroundings; simply playing. I don't think it really matters; the experience of all those tons of blubber hurtling vertically into the air, then crashing in a splendid display of white foam, is a wondrous spectacle. That and a camera to record the event.

When the whales are spotted, behavior of those on board alters immediately; all strangers to one another become more friendly, more talkative, even helping one another spot the next sighting or sharing binoculars with those who failed to bring a pair. The whales create a *communitas* on board that will usually begin to evaporate when the captain turns the bow of the ship towards the Santa Barbara harbor. But in these moments, even hours, something mythic occurs between people and between them and the natural order abrupting itself into our midst through the sea and the whales' splendid displays of themselves in their vapored blows and in their often friendly and curious showmanship. I think that on a very tangible level, they are curious about us as much as we wonder about them.

The Power of Mythopoiesis

I want to use Melville's epic to explore how a myth finds soil and soul to grow. What makes it at first an event and then a psychological and emotional experience, while other events or literary works never lift beyond the mundane and remain consistently unmemorable? What does memory perform on the past to make those events present in a new way, where the familiar is rendered unfamiliar because of a new angle of vision? Myths might be understood as much as angles of vision or as new imaginal attitudes towards what we see that develops and deepens with time and through revisioning or rereading. So there appears to be a progression of effect: from event to expression of that event, to a story, to a reality shared, to a myth evoked and to a consciousness made more aware. Now the briny waters begin to churn with the energy of archetypal images; something primal and primordial begins to pattern itself on the waters to create a world as much as a world view. I would call it a developing mythopoetic consciousness.

Moreover, in teaching *Moby-Dick* for so many years to hundreds of mostly curious students, I have never seen the same white whale breach twice in the classroom. It is always a different creature, changed, in large measure by the group of myths that gather around it to read passages closely and to brood over the deep fathoms of significance out of which the epic emerges. Entering the Pequod as a ship and as an interactive field can be both risky and revitalizing. Risks revitalize us more often than not. After all, the ship, made of many parts of the whale, is itself one of the most interesting characters populating this sea tale.

Here is an analogy that might assist us in exploring the above questions. It is from Jungian-oriented D. Stephenson Bond's fine study of mythology, *Living Myth*. In it he relates how human experiences, like burials, may have grown in consciousness by ritualizing themselves into a myth. Of course, saying it this way opens up the complex argument of whether myths happen first, then ritual, or rituals begin and myth follows. Nonetheless, Bond imagines that at one time in history, a woman buried her young infant or child as an instinctive response to her grief. No one told her to bury the young one; she performed it through an inner necessity or sense of rightness, or because of a deep connection to life and death and to the earth herself. Then she told others, perhaps in her grieving condition, the story of that event, the death of her child, and her experience of burying him or her. Now her experience is doubled through the narrative to become an experience for others. I want to speculate that right here it also achieves the level of mimesis for it *re-presents* and may certainly evoke in others a similar urge or impulse to bury one's young. Her remembered event becomes their future way of treating their own dead family members. It may rouse in them a desire to honor the dead person and so sustain the one who died's continuity through the memory of that ritual action. I would add here C. G. Jung's insightful remark from his autobiography, *Memories, Dreams, Reflections*: "My life is a story of the self-realization of the unconscious. . . . What we are to our inward vision, and what man appears to be *sub specie aeternitas*, can only be expressed by way of myth" (1963, p. 3).

The event of burying her child has undergone a doubling; the event has been doubled into an experience and given language so it may be shared with others. The narrative is not simply a double of the original event but the story of how that event was imagined into an experience of grief to be shared in community.

But doubling itself is an archetype and one of the strongest and most consistent leitmotifs in *Moby-Dick*. I have considered, given the first chapter, "Loomings" wherein we are led back to Ovid's depiction of the Narcissus-Echo myth in *Metamorphosis* as well as the doubling that appears in myriad forms in the epic, that Melville was offering us a way in which events become experiences through the doubling imagination. And if doubling feels too literal, then let's call it an analogical imagination for it is through analogies that we learn in powerful ways by connecting what we know with what is unfamiliar. It is also close to James Hillman's insight at the beginning of his own white whale narrative, *Revisioning Psychology*, how soul making, or imagining, "transforms events into experiences, is communicated in love, and has a religious concern" (*Revisioning Psychology* xvi) Any work that is soulful implicates depth. *Moby-Dick* is a depth-oriented epic on several registers at once.

Perhaps Melville's other intention among many was to reveal how the creative process takes events and shapes them into a coherent form to be shared, in an act called mythopoiesis, or a making or shaping of a myth into a new form of awareness. At the heart of such an enterprise is analogy formation, where form is tapped, discovered, invented—and more. Myths may be understood as both personal and collective; how is then each given birth? Further, did Melville, in crafting his masterpiece, discover a unique way to shape events into experiences that created a white whale out of the soul's depths that lives in our collective lives with the force of a divinity? Let's sail close to the shores of the epic's ending and consider for a moment Chapter 133, "The Chase—First Day." The men have gathered into their whale boats as Moby Dick makes its first appearance after we have anticipated its arising for 586 pages:

> Like noiseless nautilus shells, their light prows sped through the sea; but only slowly they neared the foe. As they neared him, the ocean grew still more smooth; seemed drawing a carpet over its waves; seemed a noon-meadow, so serenely it spread. At length the breathless hunter came so nigh his seemingly, unsuspecting prey, that his entire dazzling hump was distinctly visible, sliding along the sea as if an isolated thing, and continually set in a revolving ring of finest, fleecy, greenish foam. . . . Before it, far out on the soft Turkish-rugged waters, went the glistening white shadow from his broad, milky forehead, a musical rippling playfully accompanying the shade; . . . (586)

Fathoming a New Myth

Recall that Ahab began the myth-making process on the quarter deck hundreds of pages earlier by outlining the malignancy that is the white whale as he conceives it through the aperture of his dismemberment. Ishmael gives it another form of language that shapes the whale into a mythic presence on the sea by a series of analogies. What we have only heard about for almost 600 pages now emerges into presence to become a power of what Robert Armstrong refers to as "affecting presence" (*Power* 16). What we have only heard about and been given shape through words, now becomes incarnate through words but in its living presence. Mythmaking occurs right here in the language-evoking presence. The white whale now gains an energy and a value absent previously; what we have heard has been hearsay; what we witness now is a living presence, a living myth, with all the vitality and energy that attends a myth that is still alive and vibrant, and most importantly, practically useful.

In a section of her rich and thought-provoking essay entitled "Myth in the Modern World," literary theorist and mythologist Louise Cowan writes of the relation between "Myth and Poetry." Focusing primarily on the literary genre of epic, which would certainly include Melville's masterpiece, she suggests: "The epic, then, gives the myth symbolic form, establishes it in the communal mind, makes it available for contemplation. . . . For it is the epic perspective on life, as distinct from tragedy, say, or comedy, that establishes in imagination the cosmos implicit within the myth" (13). Two words in her rich insight are "perspective" and "contemplation." The poem is the vehicle that carries the myth as its cargo as a symbolic expression that has resonances that reach deep into the soul of the reader or listener. And, just as crucially, the poem is not to be analyzed and explained so much as it is to be contemplated with a porousness and openness that allows it to work its deepest layers into the imagination of the reader. Let's return to Ishmael's methodology early in the voyage and how this form of quantification and measurement will fall short of capturing the whale.

Up to now, Ishmael has spent his time and efforts in classifying whales, describing them, measuring them, explaining the process of dismantling them, boiling and barreling them, noting their continual historical presence—all processes that finally prove unsatisfying. Now the whale appears and conjures a particular language to double its presence and its affect. My sense is that we are watching the creation of a symbol that has energy, multiple meanings, as well as a grand majesty, as he writes soon after the quote above:

> A gentle joyousness—a mighty mildness of repose in swiftness, invested the gliding whale. Not the white bull Jupiter swimming away with ravished Europa clinging to his graceful horns; his lovely, leering eyes sideways intent upon the maid; with smooth bewitching fleetness, rippling straight for the nuptial bower in Crete; not Jove, not that great majesty

Supreme! Did surpass the glorified White Whale as he so divinely swam. (586)

The analogies stack up one after another in a *neti, neti* fashion: not this, not that, but the genius here is that all these analogies do count in fashioning the whale for our imagination to contemplate. Such a rich transfer of worlds is operative; the whale is lifted from its natural presence to an imaginal, supernatural reality whose energy is fierce in repose.

Let me return for a moment to Armstrong's book and an observation that seems appropriate here. He draws an analogy early in his study with persons and the work of art. His intention is to locate those aspects in which processes of the work of art and persons are the same. "Since these identities are neither physiological nor anatomical [though they could be] they are to be seen as psychological." He goes on to draw this conclusion: "The work of affecting presence (AP) sometimes seems as much to apprehend its witness as the witness apprehends it," . . . making "the work of art a phenomenon of consciousness" as well as "a testimony to the nature of this power that both man and work own" (*Power* 16).

I would add that the descriptions of Moby Dick above are mimetic, aesthetic and affective; they conjure in us as witness-whaler-readers kindred set of feelings or affects. The mimetic act doubles an action or an image from what appears outside us to a correspondence within us. We may therefore in fact touch and recognize something of the divine within us that the whale exhibits through the graceful prose-poetry of Melville: "For an instant, his whole marbleized body formed a high arch, like Virginia's Natural Bridge, and warningly waving his bannered flukes in the air, the grand god revealed himself, sounded and went out of sight. Hoveringly, halting, and dipping on the wing, the white sea-fowls longingly lingered over the agitated pool that he left" (587).

Melville makes present the myth of the divine through a language that is both lyric and epic in tone and in scope. Its intention, I believe, is to help us enter the space of what the Sufi scholar, Henri Corbin, describes as the *mundus imaginalis* in his essay, "Mundus Imaginalis, or, The Imaginary and the Imaginal." I want to call it instead the "mimetic imaginalis" but will refrain. It is an essay that might best accompany any reader's pilgrimage through Melville's epic. There Corbin claims that "the imagination is neither the sensible world nor the world of abstract concepts, yet is a cognitive power in its own right. Its mediating faculty is to make us able to know without any reservation that region of Being which, without this mediation, would remain forbidden ground, and whose disappearance brings on a catastrophe of the spirit (7). I believe that this mediation is the role of analogy formation, to link different worlds through likeness, correspondence and confluence.

The Quest in Liminal Space

Melville achieves the mediating world between the sensible world and that of the intellect, a space in which symbols are generated, divine presences are evoked, a cosmos created, as Corbin calls it, a place in which divinity is manifested, and the space in which Sophia, wisdom, the "world of soul" finds its habitation: the mundus imaginalis. It is the space of poets, artists and creatives of all kinds; its difficulty lies in one's learning to dwell between the sensible world of the world's flesh and the realm of spirit, spiritual bodies and what cannot, finally, be known. Melville's genius in creating *Moby-Dick* is that he was gifted with the ability to inhabit that space so much more fully and authentically than most other successful writers. He discovered that the whale, inhabiting the deepest fathoms of the created world, yet needing our world of air to continue to breathe and live, was the perfect symbol for entering the mundus imaginalis as a mediating image.

The mundus imaginalis is also the play of mimesis, of representation and of the richest analogies that mediate entire cosmoi. I offer in my introduction to *Our Daily Breach* in reflecting on Melville's work as well as other classics of literature: "These powerful tales were not a substitute or a replacement for something; they were life itself in a shaped, organic, living imaginal form and in their formative structure re-formed my own narratives with a profundity that had been absent" (9). I want to highlight again Louise Cowan's essay where she writes: "A shared spiritual response to a revelation given to a people at the time for their becoming a people—this is, finally, the way in which I should like to define myth" ("Myth" 14). Not only does myth contact our spiritual nature, it reveals to us how our developing as a person or as a communal body is progressing and is revealed to us through the mythic portal of awareness. Having said all this, let me return to our whaler-writer, Ishmael, to develop this and other themes a bit further.

The whaling voyage places Ishmael in the intermediate space between land and ocean: the Pequod. On it and through his experiences of hunting for the white whale, he writes himself through the corridors of memory into his personal identity and destiny. It is of course a remembrance that guides him, by way of the Greek goddess, Mnemosyne, where memory imagines and where imagination recollects. Ahab as well suffers his wound into his personal identity, swallowed by the whale that is the deeper affliction. In this way, by analogy, we can all relate to what swallows us whole and spits us out days, months or years later on a shore we may not recognize as home. I am already now into metaphor, myth and memory—the three capital Ms of consciousness.

James Hillman's further observation is worth noting here: "the primary rhetoric of archetypal psychology is myth" (*Archetypal Psychology* 31). He goes on to suggest that "by relying on myths as its primary rhetoric, archetypal psychology grounds itself in a fantasy that cannot be taken historically, physically, literally" (31). As soon as we settle into one or the other of these arenas, we have just demythologized and emasculated the fantasy, that being for our present discussion the white whale. I mention here that Hillman was deeply influenced by Corbin's thought shared above and understood him as one of the founders of Archetypal Psychology.

At the end of the teaching day when *Moby-Dick* has been our text for seven hours of class time, I bring the session to a close by springing on my students this question: what is the white whale in *your* imagination? I push them a bit to respond without much hesitation so they have little time to think it through; each is encouraged with some speculation. The results are astonishing in their differences and in their overlaps. I ask them at this juncture in order to get a glimpse of the mythic field they are seeing by means of, a way of gauging what determines or influences the myth guiding each of them. My own hunch has been that Melville is instructing us in "Loomings" that the mythic lens that would most enrich one's reading of the epic is the Narcissus-Echo story. Part of its doubling strength is that it includes each of us readers as doubles of the action as well as the doublings that permeate dozens of scenes in the epic. The myths themselves are understood as metaphors. Joseph Campbell was very clear about this relation when he posited: "There can be no real progress in understanding how myths function until we understand and allow metaphoric symbols to address, in their own unmodified way, the inner levels of our consciousness" (*Thou Art That* 8) "Metaphor," he offers in this same volume, "is the native tongue of myth" (6).

Melville is the supreme metaphor-maker. I believe he asks us readers what is needed for an historical event—personal, collective, fictional or factual—to rise and deepen to the level of a mythical reality. We pay close attention as Ishmael recounts his voyage on the Pequod and chooses a language to transform it into a soul journey towards divinity, into the heart of life itself with all its attendant breachings and deep dives, its ambiguities, if not outright dismemberments. And as many have written before and after him, the divine is within; the white whale swims in the interior waters of our own souls first and foremost.

As an archetypal psychologist, Ishmael would find the following idea from James Hillman compatible with his own development as he remembers the whale hunt: "The role of myths in archetypal psychology is to open the questions of life to transpersonal and culturally imaginative reflection. We may thereby see our ordinary lives embedded in and ennobled by the dramatic and world-creative life of mythical figures" (*Archetypal Psychology* 31). I would ask if this insight helps us to see how Melville's work advances or raises to an epic level of consciousness as an analogy of being, itself.

Who has not been wounded by the pursuit of a white whale? What do we think of when we consider the outlines of the phantom of life itself? *Moby-Dick* as an epic narrative has as one of its main concerns, itself as a great mythic vessel; it is an epic narrative about the imagination itself when it enters the oceanic fields of the human soul and the world soul. Melville does civic work by offering to us an American recollection of the *Anima Mundi,* the world soul with a Parliament grand enough to take on a vast host of interpretations and points of view.

Its features include ambiguity, paradox, uncertainty, threats of annihilation, the ineffable, wonder and awe, and the divine as it accommodates the four literary genres in their specific language of lyric, tragedy, comedy, while epic serves as an umbrella under which all genres cluster, as Louise Cowan has shown. But more: All this is to say that, with the help of the gods, the epic poet makes a cosmos within which a hero, following the guidance of prophecy, can lead a people forward on their journey into an unknown future" ("Introduction: Epic as Cosmopoesis" 22).

Less a gene pool than a genre ocean. Each by itself is able to create an entire cosmos, an entire world, but epic is most cast as the congregation in which each participates. We cast about for a narrative to give these life presences a mythic frame of coherence. Our narrator lays the ground in his potent three words: "Call me Ishmael" (3). The implications are wide in their suggestibility, for they implicate:

> To be called
> Is to be called out
> Is to be called forth
> Is to be called to account
> Is to be called to recall

Embodiment's Permanent Residence in the Action

Moby-Dick reveals the role of the guide, the shaman, the wise soul in silence and in action through the figure of Queequeg. He serves Ishmael as a witness and as a life buoy floating in the deep waters between life and death. His body is tattooed with his tribe's entire cosmology; Ahab's body is dismembered and scarred, while the white whale's lower jaw is crooked and Ishmael the scribe's is tattooed with measurements of a whale. He is also the tattooist-in-residence, struggling to scratch the white page with the inky hieroglyphs from his pen across paper to slowly and enigmatically coax to the surface, to make appear, a world that is mythic, philosophic, quantitative, measured, spiritual, aesthetic, economic and symbolic, to name a few.

Since the words he inscribes on the flat surface of the paper carries both surface and depth as its cargo, writing becomes whale-like, moving constantly with admittedly long pauses, between surface and depth. The entirety of the work is full of inscriptions folded into the written action of the hunt. Each person's history is encoded and inscribed on their bodies to reveal a narrative that is at once fixed and on-going. I have considered this theme, a central lynchpin in the work, in earlier writings, that I represent here. Hunting for the white whale and seeking the blank page on which to scar its virginal surface with significant scribblings are the same action; the pursuit of what wants to remain a phantom; bringing the phantom to life through the interplay of sounding surface and depth. Melville is a willing participant, ready to risk it all by sinking into the ocean of words to find just those living organisms to process his vision in the try pots of the imagination.

The question I propose is this: how do these elements that implicate both the human and the world's body, writing and whaling, wounds and words, conjoin in *Moby-Dick* to outline in general form the prevailing myth of America? Is there something distinctly American in the action of this epic that seems to be intrinsic to us as a nation and as individuals, a mixture of tribes and peoples that intertwine, a symphony of world myths that gather round the activity of industrialism, humanism, *communitas,* and otherism (specifically, hunting the whale) and commerce as the central action we share? Perhaps we are less a melting pot or a mixed salad than a confederacy of myths lined along a guiding keel; these myths swirl around and through the American psyche with an undeveloped unifying image that will, or can in time, give them all a coherence not sensed before.

Further, what place do we give the scarred, scored body of Ahab? Is he our emblem of the cosmic wound, the originary affliction that each of us carries inscribed on our own souls? (*The Wounded Body* 13). The body is the locale which allows mimesis, metaphor and memory to find a home in which to mingle and melt into one another. Analogy comprises the skeletal structure and their habitation. If we think of the expression that Ishmael forms out of his journey as a mimetic rendering of a series of events that transforms him, then the body is the genesis of such an imaginal process. *Moby-Dick* illustrates that the physical, tangible body is a second-order or narrative presence, indeed even a phantom presence: first words, then presences. Words have the ability to conjure an absence into presence; the trace of such presence is the epic itself, inscribed with enigmatic meaning always around the body of Queequeg, Ahab, Ishmael and the whale. Words remember what is absent into a presence because they allow us to imagine what is there through their verbal simulacra. The body is then, as Peter Brooks writes, "the ultimate field from which all symbolism derives and to which it returns . . . the primary source of symbolism (*Body Work* 6).

Russell Lockhart has likened Melville's novel to "an alchemical oven" wherein our souls are made to desire deeper imaginings when the normal answers for our collective psyche are no longer adequate ("What Whale Does America Pursue?" 80). I add that the white whale offers a rich symbol for life itself, the ultimate phantom, which we pursue to conquer at times and scurry from when it turns to hold us to account. The white whale may also be the life that our stories bring us, a double of our life events and heritages that find a new form, one that coheres in the stories we tell and the stories we read. Mythologist Phil Cousineau reminds us of the wise Black Elk's sense of stories: "This they tell, and whether it happened so or not, I do not know; *but if you think about it, you can see that it is true*" (qtd. in *The Oldest Story in the World* 49)

We can never see the entirety of the whale, Ishmael informs us, only a glimpse; occasionally a breach will reveal its greater contours and its massive mystery. The same may be said about some stories. Because, like the whale, our lives become stories, a making or shaping of what seems disconnected, even desperate, into a coherent form; that same form gives us a context and a content, one as necessary as the other. We may then discern the figure in the field and the field in the figure. But there is no doubt in my mind that we each seek the white whale's form.

All stories have as their intention, going to *see*. Ishmael's singular drive is to go to see, and to be seen, then heard. The see-scape he enters raises the level of his conscious awareness by myth-making his seeing into meaning. Melville, I sense, came on the most perfect symbol to capture the see, to impart new ways of seeing, to see the invisibles by way of the visible, always by doubling, by analogy, and thereby crafting a work that teases us to find our Pequod wherever it is harbored, and signing on board, no matter the distant and often inadequate lay we are assigned by those who make such determinations. The symbol he chose, or which chose him, to lure us to sea, comprises the brilliance of his instincts and the grace of his intentions. One could hardly choose a better metaphor to be guided by.

Works Cited

Armstrong, Robert Plant. *The Powers of Presence: Consciousness, Myth and Affecting Presence*. U Pennsylvania P, 1981.

Bond, D. Stephenson. *Living Myth: Personal Meaning as a Way of Life*. Shambhala Publications, 1993.

Brooks, Peter. *Body Work: Objects of Desire in Modern Narrative*. Cambridge UP, 1993.

Campbell, Joseph. *Thou Art That: Transforming Religious Metaphor*. New World Library, 2001.

Corbin, Henri. "Mundus Imaginalis, or, The Imaginary and the Imaginal." http:/hermetic.com/bev/mundua imaginalis.htm.

Cousineau, Phil. *The Oldest Story in the World: A Mosaic of Meditations on the Secret Strength of Stories*. Sisyphus Press, 2010.

Cowan, Louise. "Myth in the Modern World." *Texas Myths*. Robert F. O'Connor editor. Texas Committee for the Humanities. Texas A&M UP, 1984. 3-22.

---." Introduction: Epic as Cosmopoesis." *The Epic Cosmos*, edited by Larry Allums. The Dallas Institute Publications, 2000. 1-26.

Hillman, James. *Archetypal Psychology: A Brief Account*. 1997.

---. *Revisioning Psychology*. 1975. HarperCollins Publishers, 1975.

Jung, C. G. *The Spirit in Man, Art and Literature. Volume 15. The Collected Works of C. G. Jung*. Translated by R. F. C. Hull. Bollingen Foundation. Princeton UP, 1966.

---. *Memories, Dreams, Reflections*. Aniela Jaffe editor. Translated by Richard and Clara Winston. Pantheon Books, 1963.

Lockhart, Russell. *Words as Eggs: Psyche in Language and Clinic*. Spring Publications, 1983.

Melville, Herman. *Moby-Dick; or, The Whale*. Collector's Edition. Introduction by Clifton Fadiman. The Easton Press, 1977.

Slattery, Dennis Patrick. *The Wounded Body: Remembering the Markings of Flesh*. SUNY Press, 2000.

---. *Our Daily Breach: Exploring Your Personal Myth Through Herman Melville's Moby-Dick*. Fisher King Press, 2015.

7

◆◆●◆◆

REMEMBERING ONE'S SECOND LIFE: A JOURNEY TOWARDS MEANING

But don't be satisfied with stories, how things/ have gone with others. Unfold/your own myth, without complicated explanation . . .

~ Rumi, "Unfold Your Own Myth," 41.

I have yet to discover anything in the world more mysterious, grand, challenging or fascinating than a human life. I also do not think there is any gap whatsoever between an individual life's meaning and that same life's story. For to tap into either or both is to confront the myth that guides one. Without our story I do not think we have an identity, neither a past nor a future. But that story needs to be recollected periodically and for each of us to ask: Is this the story that I believe is mine to pursue, to continue to develop the plot to its resolution?

Taking this notion as my guide, and with the belief that my plotted life is my personal myth with a narrative line, I offer these "moments," or perhaps, these thresholds, recollected in a life that to date I have found to be both a challenge and a treasure to have lived. Dan McAdams reminds us that "Stories help us organize our thoughts, providing a narrative for human intentions and interpersonal events that is readily remembered and told" (*The Stories We Live By* 31). Such is my goal in this chapter.

I am, finally, interested in the imaginal life of my story, but to get to that dimension I need some literal historical matrices to work with. From a depth psychological point of view, the literal is a uni-dimensional expression of the imaginal; the latter marks where soul making takes place, as James Hillman informs us. I wonder as well about my story: Do requirements to change the narrative of our story reorganize the myth we live by? Let's see.

Some mythologists believe that a myth is not authentic unless it begins with tales of origins, be it of a person, a tribe, a culture or a civilization. I don't clench tight around that belief, but I grant that remembering when something was born in us, when it happened for the first time as a signpost that pointed us in a specific direction, has immense value for discerning the stirrings of a personal myth. These thresholds have such value because I think they are callings to meaning through an awareness of our destiny. They are moments when we emerge from the dark wood, the *selva oscura* of Dante's beginning when he begins to be guided through the territories of his own life, when he chooses to step out of his ego-driven life and initiates that painful and exciting trek towards the Self, as C. G. Jung refers to it, to the totality of the psyche's reality and not our fantasies alone that guide us. Learning to trust the reality of the psyche is one of the most important tutorials any of us can engage. The grade assigned may range from "Pass It On" to "Try Again."

History is Destiny

I grew up on the east side of Cleveland, Ohio in a tiny one-bedroom apartment on St. Clair Ave. with two brothers, a caring mother and an alcoholic father. He was my first introduction to the pain and suffering that pathology can inflict on oneself and others. Ironically, he also set the compass for my life's work. Years later there were five of us.

When I was four, we moved to a suburb in Euclid, Ohio. During the week my father dutifully attended Mass, rode a bus called "The Blue Flyer" because it made few stops between Lake Shore Blvd. in Euclid to downtown Cleveland, where he worked at a menial job entitled "Personnel" (later renamed Human Resources). Heading home on Friday evening, he would stop at Lokar's Tavern at the end of our street for a few beers. From then until Sunday morning those of us who had not scattered to friends' homes were once again prey to the headwinds of his rage, destructive behavior and mad howls of pain such that we found other places to be when fortune smiled on us.

My mother suffered the most from his rage; but it poisoned us all, as any member of a home laden with addictions bears out. That was the experience that defined all of our mythologies most profoundly. But gifts were imbedded in it, as you will see, and perhaps as you have discovered from your own experiences. My father carried the shadow of a life not lived in its fullness. He inhabited this shadow region and archetype which, if one can muster the courage to peer into it, can reveal treasures, even opportunities. One of its benefits is that I was able to observe the pathology of the psyche from a vulnerable first-row seat and became interested in that kind of story, as I hope to show. I learned that it was primarily a story of shaming.

In his periods of sobriety my father was a sweet but timid man. Once, when I was nine or ten, he brought home a gift for me, a Scripto fountain pen, along with a packet of four little transparent tubes of ink that one would insert at the end of the pen when the ink in one was used up. I immediately sat on the arm of a chair in the living room and, like a good Catholic boy, I wrote out from memory a Hail Mary, an Our Father, and A Glory Be or two. Then, still wanting to write, I thought to compose a story of my two brothers and me on an adventure; later a third brother would follow the two of us, then a sister.

I remember now how I loved creating both the prayers as well as the story. I said no to my parents' call to dinner; I was too engrossed in my story. Looking back for more understanding, I believe that somewhere in my ten-year-old self was a sense of the healing power inherent in stories, either ones I read or those I might write. In creating my first story, I felt whole, complete, far less anxious and fearful. It was less an escape than a voyage to the world of make-believe, of imagining an alternative and more favorable land to inhabit. This threshold on the arm of the living room chair, you see, and unbeknownst to me at the time, was my initiation into the magic of words and to the writing life as a psychological and emotional reality. A gift from my sober father was the origin of this career. Another gift, this time from my weekend raging alcoholic father, attracted me to the pathology that is coiled in each of us and can seep out in myriad forms of addiction, bad temper, bullying, as well as domination and control of those one professes to love. James Hillman reminds us that we can do without therapists but not without our pathologies, birthed so often in our fantasies, for "The soul sees by means of affliction" (*Revisioning Psychology* 107).

Spirit Inhabits the Wound

This time was also when I began serving Mass as an altar boy; what intrigued me most was memorizing the Mass in Latin, my first exposure to a foreign language. When, during Mass we recited our parts in response to the priest's words and gestures, I felt a mystery unfolding in this strange language as well as a power inherent in uttering these ancient prayers. I loved serving Mass for this and other reasons, not the least of which was the birth of my spiritual self through the rich and mysterious rituals of the drama that comprises the story the Mass holds and reverences.

Another gift entered my life: I began working small jobs when I was eleven—cutting grass, sorting bottles at Clark's Delicatessen on E. 222nd. Street in Euclid, shining shoes in Cleveland bars with my friend Mike Aspinwall on Saturday afternoons, and a few years later, washing and waxing mobile homes in Euclid Beach Park when I was fourteen or fifteen. When I was sixteen, a friend helped me land a job in a major supermarket chain working in the produce department, a job I kept for years to pay my tuition through St. Joseph's High School, directed and taught by the Society of Mary brothers and priests as well as lay faculty in Cleveland. I also purchased my own used cars, all in service of breaking from financial restrictions posed by an unhappy home life and general scarcity.

One day, after work, and there were multiple incidents like it to follow, I drove home on a Saturday night after a 12-hour day at the supermarket, weary and seeking some repose. There I found, not surprisingly, my father drunk and enraged. He saw me come in, came downstairs in his underwear and began yelling at how worthless I was, how I would not amount to anything, that I was a failure, and other such wounding words that deflated me and my sense of achievement. How could this be? I asked myself. I was doing well in school, paying my own tuition, working to support myself, buying my own automobiles, and I was still worthless? The confusion in such a condition haunted me because I was prone to believe the alcoholic and not my own sense of myself, which was very fragile to begin with.

These incidents repeated themselves for years, where all of us were emotionally lashed by his drunken rages; they taught us all a graduate curriculum in how to live within the emotional pendulum of rage and shame, two emotions that had tyrannical holds over us. No room for others. These two destructive affects became the defining building blocks of our personal myths. But—and this is so important for you to hear— it was my opening into *wonder*. How could I be these things he accused me of while I felt I was doing more than my share, since *never enough* was the ruling tyrant in our family because only one meager income was all we had to work with. But we were *never enough* in his blurred drunken vision because *he was never enough*. I was not to learn until years later how both projection and transference worked in the psyche and inter-psychi-cally. So, I became interested in psychology without even knowing it. But I also felt in a way that I have wrestled with my entire life: I am not doing enough; I am not good enough; so, do more; be more; exhaust yourself more. I did not know that with this attitude I had taken on the burden of my father's deep wounds *he received* at the hands of a tyrannical mother.

In addition, as was true of the other members of our family, I would look desperately for ways to avoid the house as much as possible on the weekends. My savior at this time was a sweet young woman, Anna Marie, who attended Regina High School cross town and was my faithful com-panion on weekends. Rarely did my father drink during the week, but we knew, when he switched from beer to Mogen David wine on the week-ends, that we were in for an avalanche of abuse as his addiction acceler-ated and then locked in cruise control. But Mogen David?!

Fate Has Two Wheels

I also discovered that where there is one negative action, there may ap-pear a contrary reaction or response. Here is how I discovered how fate works on an existential level: a good friend, Rick, both of whose parents

were alcoholics of a more benevolent brand, had the first tattoo of anyone I had ever known except for two uncles who sported tattoos when
they came home from WW II. He also rode a 650 BSA (Birmingham
Small Arms) motorcycle that he taught me to ride. The first time I rode
it, something trip-wired in me—a sense of unconditional freedom. I
made it my life's mission to own one, which was not to happen for another five years, when I married my sweet wife, Sandy, fifty-three years
ago. I have owned and ridden motorcycles for all of those fifty-three
years, often with her as my passenger.

They have been critical instruments that helped shape my personal
myth in its need to be free of abuse by doing more and more. Motorcycles helped me to believe that I lived such freedom "as-if" it were true.
Writers like Dan McAdams and others have revealed to me that perhaps
our greatest creative urge is to construct our own biographies. McAdams
writes: "The created identity per se—is a dynamic evolving *life story*. Beginning in late adolescence, we become biographers of self, mythologically rearranging the scattered elements of our lives—the different
'selves,' . . . into a narrative whole providing unity and purpose. Thus,
identity is a life story" (*Power* 29).

Out of the blue one hot and sticky Ohio evening, Rick said that he
wanted to visit Long Island, New York to see where he had grown up.
We were both seventeen at the time. He said he wanted to leave in two
days and was I interested in riding as a passenger on his BSA to New
York? I remember zero hesitation. We packed a small backpack which I
would wear because his bike had no saddle bags, and two hot late afternoons later, we headed south to the Ohio Turnpike in white t-shirts,
Levi's and tennis shoes. No helmets, rain gear or jackets. Rick then
pointed the handlebars towards New York City, 550 miles east.

We rode the 550 miles for two days, arriving in Manhattan drip drying
from a thunder storm that caught up to us in New Jersey and pummeled
us for over an hour; we then continued out to Long Island. I remember
growing tired on the turnpike section of the ride, gazing obsessively at a
black mole on the left side of Rick's neck, and fell asleep to the sound of
the engine moaning below us. I woke multiple times with a start; afraid
of falling to the pavement at 65 miles per hour, I suggested that we tie
our belts together or buy rope so we could tie ourselves to one another

in case I began to fall off. He refused the idea; later we learned of two other motorcycle riders who had done this and the one who fell asleep pulled them both to the concrete highway to their deaths.

My life-long interest in both travel and motorcycles was born on that ride. I have been riding a various assortment of motorcycles since 1968. They played a major role in my growing interest in monasteries that began in 1972. Again, the major reason for my saying "yes" to Rick's offer was to travel far away *from* something; I did not care what *"to"* was. That something was the scourge of my father's disease and its consequent violence to us all. The ride with Rick was and is one of the happiest memories of my life and a major calling to make mythically permanent both travel and motorcycle riding.

Destiny is Always in the Process

Our myths, the ones that shape our psyches, are an amalgam always, a confluence of choices and destinies; when they match up, they give one a sense of wholeness and being in accord with something bigger, as Joseph Campbell observes in *The Hero with a Thousand Faces*: "The adventure of the hero normally follows the pattern of the nuclear unit above described: a separation from the world, a penetration to some source of power, and a life-enhancing return" (27-28). In short, the adventure gives life meaning and purpose. It was a calling to the unknown, to the new and to the unexpected; this trip began to quench a deep thirst in me for the Hero's Adventure, to give up and step away from the familiar and secure so to embrace what is unknown and therefore risky. It seemed to infuse my life with meaning. I felt vitally alive in thinking that I was making the calls in my life, little knowing that other presences as well were shaping my destiny in their image.

C. G. Jung, father of analytical psychology, which would later be labelled depth psychology, writes at one point that "Meaninglessness inhibits fullness of life and is therefore equivalent to illness. Without meaning, *everything* becomes painful; with meaning we can survive and flourish" for it allows for what he terms "spiritual enlargement," which he suggests is a necessity in life, not a luxury (*Memories, Dreams, Reflections* 340).

When I began my freshman year at Cuyahoga Community College in the fall of 1963, which was the year they opened their doors to the first community college in Ohio, I majored in both psychology and sociology. But the psychology was more behavioral—B. F. Skinner and the like, and I found it unsatisfying. But the sociology teacher, Harold Gaines, was another shaman in my development. He was a black man versed in literature and psychology and had us reading the novels of James Baldwin almost immediately. I loved his style in combining psychology with literature to open both fields with one discipline leveraging the other.

As life continued to unfurl, often with surprises that kept my future interesting, I found myself in the second year at "Tri-C" while also working as a deputy bailiff in the Municipal Court offices in Euclid Ohio during the week and on Saturdays continuing at the supermarket. I had just bought a new Pontiac Tempest (1964), was taking classes at night and dating the police chief's secretary, Jan. And . . . I was bored out of my skin with my new wealth, car and female companion. In one sociology night course in the spring of 1965, I met a fellow who would be my best man at my wedding four years later, Denny Collins. He too had a new car, wrote for the sports pages of the *Cleveland Plain Dealer*, was pursuing a degree in sociology and suffering ennui intense enough to rival mine. My own father had stopped drinking after being fired from his job, so the home situation had improved because his violent outbursts had ceased, but not their destructive repercussions. My own inner chaos, by contrast, had its source in sheer restlessness.

Taking to Sea

One evening after class, and on a whim (watch for those whims that surface in your life; they are loaded), we wandered down to the Cleveland docks where ships from around the world docked to unload and load goods for other countries. We inquired of the station master if there was a chance to book passage on board a cargo ship, which often took a few passengers, to Europe; *where* in Europe we were less concerned with, but Ireland would be our final destination. Our goal was to make it to southern Ireland to visit relatives from both our families who lived there.

The station master told us that a German freighter currently docked in Detroit was short-handed in their crew and was due at the Cleveland docks in nine days; if we could be at the docks on June 16th., we could work our passage to Bremerhaven, Germany. Excited, we began the process of acquiring passports, talked to our very enthusiastic sociology professor, who moved our final exam up ten days, finished the class, stuffed army sacks with clothing and other essentials, and showed up at the dock at 8 pm on a warm breezy June evening.

We were both twenty at the time. Two hours later, we shipped out on the HMS Transamerica, a freighter owned by Poseidon Lines, named after the mythical brother of both Zeus and Hades, and sailed into Lake Erie, up the St. Lawrence Seaway, stopping during the next week in the ports of Toronto, Montreal and Quebec, before heading out to the North Atlantic and Europe. Our time on the water was ten days. The ship was an old tramp steamer filled with German men of various ages serving their two years of military obligation by working on the steamer. Our adventures through storms, iceberg fields, whales sleeping on the surface that required the ship to change course several times, our travels hitchhiking through Germany, England, Wales and finally to southern Ireland's coast, could be a book in itself. We stayed with relatives in two counties. Neighbors of our relatives in County Mayo loaned us their bicycles to travel around the region. The poverty of so many rural Irish was both common and depressing. Many of their cottages had dirt floors, laundry hanging from the ceiling in the main room of their tiny homes, and in the back of their domicile, peat bogs provided the natural organic fuel for the bitter winter months.

At the same time the United States' engagement in the Vietnam War was increasing. Denny's parents telegraphed that he was reclassified 1-A and to return quickly in order to join the Coast Guard and avoid being shipped to the war in Southeast Asia. Because so many of Ireland's youth were emigrating from the country for jobs abroad, we could not book passage on any ship sailing out of Belfast. I do remember a man who gave us a lift one day when we were hitchhiking to Belfast and who spotted the string of my scapular: "Take it off," he told me, "And let no one know you are Catholic," which I did immediately. In time we flew home from Shannon to La Guardia and hitchhiked from there to Cleveland and home. But in a sense the real journey was to begin after arriving back to our familiar domestic life.

During the voyage across the Atlantic, when the weather was good, I would sit each evening on the ship's aft where seagulls slept after following us all day for the food scraps we threw overboard after each meal; there I would write in my journal of what had occurred that day that was worth recollecting. It was my first attempt at such a sustained way of remembering. This habit became a necessity for me as a way of understanding the inner journey I was also exploring and I looked forward to this time in solitude at dusk each day. My writing life was now moving into another stage. I had not yet discovered or formulated the idea that writing is indeed a form of healing, as Louise DeSalvo has so eloquently explored this form of soul expression. She observes that "writing is a form of meditation . . . writing cleanses the mind and enables the writers to achieve serenity, for it purges us of tangled emotions" (*Healing* 70). Her work revealed to me how much writing is a form of ritual, that we rite our passages as a form of journeying inward towards coherence. I have made journal writing an essential part of my life for the past 45 years, so certain do I sense that some deep aspect of me is completed in the act of writing.

One more discovery here that bears mention. In a rich chapter on St. Augustine's writing his *Confessions,* James Olney entertains the metaphor of weaving enjoying a long tradition in life-writing "for the operation of memory" (*Memory* 20). He writes of the weaver's "shuttle and loom [which] constantly produce new and different patterns, designs and forms, and if the operation of memory is, like weaving . . . processual, then it will bring forth ever different memorial configurations and an ever newly shaped self" (20). Writing, then, is a form of self-shaping, with the implied idea that it is a form of self-discovery, self-recovery and self-renewal. Writing is a rich rhetorical form of myth-making.

From Event to Experience: Creative Writing

When I arrived home and began working at an empty and soul-draining job in the shipping office of J & L Steel in Cleveland's Flats before school began, this time at Cleveland State University, on days off I would head east to Mentor Headlands along the shores of Lake Erie with my small portable Olympia typewriter, which I still have. There on a picnic bench, after a swim, I would type my notes from my ship-board journal. Over weeks, I created a manuscript of about eighty to ninety pages, an epic-length writing achievement for me and the longest piece of writing I would accomplish until writing a graduate thesis for a Master's Degree in Comparative Literature at Kent State University years later.

In retrospect, I realized that the actual physical journey was one threshold; the other threshold was what it added up to, what it meant, how it changed me. I could not articulate these questions at the time, but I knew the experience had to find language to give it shape and meaning, which is what led me to the aft of the ship each evening, to recollect on the day and to offer some coherence to the events that, without such reflective writing, would remain inert and disconnected. I received assistance on what it all meant years later when reading mythologist Joseph Campbell's *Myths to Live By*. There he states that "myths help us to keep in touch with inward forces. They tell us of powers of our psyche or soul to be recognized and integrated into our lives . . ." (18). This keeping in touch occurs every time my pen contacts the paper where I tattoo my thoughts and feelings onto, first in cursive writing.

After abandoning this habit for many years, I returned to it about 45 years ago and continue to this day journaling most mornings; my writing also includes any adventures from my dream life that sailed into my world while I slept. I have two shelves of journals in my study that contain over 9500 cursive writing pages. Someday I may pull them down and see my development in them for the first time. But I doubt it. What I had intuited is something C. G. Jung writes about our dreams. "We have here a question: 'How is it that we create symbols in dreams? How can we be sure that the interpretation is correct, especially when there are no associations?' That is, of course, a very practical and fundamental question" (*Analysis* 16). Nonetheless, we must try to give our dreams their own language. I think the same is true of any book I read and any experience of note that I or any of us engages; it begs to be given its own language, its own lexicon, as one searches for the psychic energy imbedded in it that can continue to nourish us on our pilgrimage through life.

I like the writer Richard Kearney's observation on this part of the process of meaning-making: "In this way, storytelling may be said to *humanize* time by transforming it from an impersonal passing of fragmented moments into a pattern, a plot, a *mythos*" (*On Stories* 4). This journey to another country as my twenty-year-old soul was crying to be made sense of, found an outlet in both stories; the events of my travels and typing the manuscript from memory afterwards, shaping my life into a *mythos,* as Kearney's insight makes clear. While both helped me cohere in ways that are hard to define or defend, there was still a gap, some space between the events and their meaning that made me feel my writing was not yet adequate. What I was searching for, as James Hillman's work years later helped me see, was soul-making out of the events of the journey.

The work of soul, he tells us in *Revisioning Psychology,* is "to transform events into experiences" so they acquire meaning for us. His basic premise is that "our life is psychological, and the purpose of life is to make psyche of it, to find connections between life and soul" (*Revisioning* xvi). In other words, we need the imagination's involvement in order to find our bearing on any depth level. On reflection, I discovered that when I arrived home, when I began to read a cargo hold of sea stories: *Two Years Before the Mast,* The *Hornblower* series, *Huck Finn*, stories by Jack London, *White Jacket, Billy Budd* and then the big Kahuna, *Moby-Dick.*

They served not as replacements for my story but rich analogies using the prisms of different stories that shared many of the archetypal patterns that comprised *my* life story. A Buddhist proverb informs us that "if we are facing in the right direction, all we have to do is keep walking." That is how I felt—I was facing in the right direction, so I kept reading and writing. Questions of success or failure faded, as into a mist on a calm day on the North Atlantic seas.

When Destiny is a Phone Call Away

I want to tell you how teaching found me; I did not find it nor did I have any desire to teach; my desires were confined to reading and writing and enjoying both immensely, for I was a passionate learner curious about a dozen areas of exploration. When I transferred to Kent State University in the fall of 1996, I had joined the staff and became over time the Poetry editor, then General Editor of *The Kent Quarterly*, a literary journal housed in the English department. I found that I loved and enjoyed my time engaging others' writing. The faculty advisor, a creative writing professor, Barbara Child, was a beacon of encouragement for me as I wrestled still with shyness and shame, but pushed on anyway with her prodding. Two years later, while still living in Kent, Ohio and working to complete a graduate degree, my wife Sandy, who I met my first quarter at the University, married. That summer, while we both took classes and worked at various jobs, I found a never-driven one-year-old 1967 BSA motorcycle in Ravenna, Ohio, east of Kent. It cost $1000.00. I asked Sandy if I could buy it at such a good price. She told me to get it. That it was the same brand, but a smaller version of Rick's BSA we drove to New York on some nine years earlier was not lost to me. I was replicating that experience in this purchase and felt good about it. The big difference, of course, is that I would be driving it.

Later that same summer, Sandy quit classes at Kent to take a position in the Ravenna school system teaching math and history to 7th. grade students. I was working part-time so we had two incomes that improved our lives greatly. Three days before the school year was to begin, the phone in our apartment rang. Now here is a literal illustration of Joseph Campbell's famous phrase: "The Call to Adventure." It was the assistant superintendent of the Ravenna school system; he asked if I was Sandy's husband. He then told me that the Special Education teacher who was to begin teaching in three days had just resigned. He asked if I was interested in the job but said nothing about requiring any training in this area of education. Now, I did not know what was "special" about "special education" but said yes anyway. Again, I was called to something I had no real inkling of but assented nonetheless. The adventure with a literal calling from this administrator; that classroom adventure is now 53 years old and still in progress.

I reported the next day at Palmyra Elementary School twelve miles east of Kent, Ohio to meet the principal. He led me into the basement of the school that sat among cornfields in rural Ohio just a few miles west of Youngstown. The room was the now-deserted band and music room since those programs had been dropped because of insufficient funding. Everything was painted light blue but the floor. There were thirteen desks in it, a shelf with ten to fifteen books on it, only a few of them duplicates, and a worn teacher's desk in front. Several small windows close to the ceiling let in natural light.

He was amiable enough and also impatient to wrap up his time with me. He said he had only two rules for me to follow: "Keep your students quiet and busy, and keep them away from the *normal students,*" he concluded as he left the room, closing the door behind him. He had never asked me what my teaching experience consisted of and if it included teaching "special" students, a code word for those with learning disabilities, discipline problems in regular classes and those with neurological challenges. I realize now that I had just crossed yet another threshold and been initiated into the field of education with a rather truncated version of a ritual of passage.

I subsequently taught this sweet but challenging group of eleven students for two years, designing curricula for grades one through four since only a few had similar learning levels. I discovered what a "lesson plan" was from a few very helpful women who also taught at Palmyra. Next to the principal and the janitor, I was the only full-time male in the school. I do not hesitate to say now, that those students, who would be in their 60s today, taught me far more than I taught them about the profession and about the mysteries inherent in teaching and learning.

Finding the Language of Soul

My introduction to the work of C. G. Jung and others in depth psychology came soon thereafter. During this time when we lived in an apartment in a large house in Kent, I met a man whose family occupied the other apartment. He was working on his doctorate in English at Kent State and we began conversations on a regular basis. At one point, Dave introduced me to a book entitled *Modern Man in Search of a Soul* by the Swiss psychiatrist, C. G. Jung. It was a compilation of several of Jung's essays from his *Collected Works*. Here, I exclaimed to myself, was the kind of psychology I had been seeking but did not know existed, a kind of angle on the human spirit that put me back in touch with the complexity of the psyche and more importantly, to the treasures of exploring the interior life as it is lived from the inside out.

Together we began reading Jung in earnest and puzzling over his concepts: the reality and autonomy of the psyche; the nature and function of archetypes like anima, animus, wise old man, trickster, and shadow; the personal and collective unconscious; active imagination; the four functions of thinking, feeling, sensation and intuition; the Self. But I also liked Jung's mystical inflection as he sought the god image throughout his life. He combined the spiritual and psychological and cited literary works often to enrich his descriptions. He also believed unwaveringly in the power of myth, as Joseph Campbell, a devoted student of Jung, was to call it in his writings. But I believe what Dave and I were hungry for was transformation by crossing a threshold into a new or at least revised, mythos.

This crossing was first inaugurated by Jung's work at this juncture; I began to grasp literary texts on a new, much deeper level of understanding, for the archetypal and mythic realms were basic structures of poetry in both pattern recognition and purpose. My Master's thesis was informed largely by Jungian thought; his writings remain a large influence to this day, along with the further addition of the enormously powerful words of Joseph Campbell, Robert Johnson, Marie-Louise von Franz, Marian Woodman, Louise and Don Cowan, and many others.

After two years of teaching these beautiful children, and with the help of an old high school friend, Mike Hommel, I took a position in secondary education at Lorain Catholic High School in Lorain, Ohio. We said goodbye to Kent State and its lovely, though war-torn city. But we both yearned for some new adventures, so we headed north to Oberlin, Ohio to live. Much later I was to read the words of Jung cited by his colleague, Marie-Louise von Franz: "Yes. If one does not constantly walk forward, the past sucks one back. The past is like an enormous sucking wind that sucks one back all the time. If you don't walk forward, you regress. You have constantly to carry the torch of the new light forward, so to speak, historically and also in your own life. As soon as you begin to look backward sadly, or even scornfully, it has you again. The past is a tremendous power" (*Cat* 129).

In the two years I taught there, I had the freedom to offer classes I desired. In the second year I established a psychology department to teach survey courses on various schools of psychological thought. I had a chance to bring C. G. Jung's perspective into classes limited to juniors and seniors. I wound up teaching more of these courses than literature and writing courses and actually welcomed the change. Such a rich and challenging project burned into me the reality of teaching: we don't know fully what we think we know until we try to teach it to others. That truth never wavered in all my years in the classroom and in workshop offerings.

Beginning a Monastic Quest

While there I approached the school's chaplain about any retreat centers that he might recommend. My desire to begin retreating into solitude had surfaced once more and I wanted to act on it. Father Bill said the only one he would recommend was Gethsemane Monastery in Trappist Kentucky, some 60 miles southwest of Lexington. I took his suggestion and made a reservation to pilgrimage there at the end of the school year. In June, 1971, I loaded my new BMW motorcycle with provisions and headed south to Columbus, Cincinnati, Lexington and on to Trappist, Kentucky.

On arrival, I checked into my small, cozy and spare room, then asked the retreat director if there was a place to park my motorcycle rather than in the gravel parking area. He thought for a moment, then suggested I park it inside in the large post office space at the side of the main building. I drove it in through the side door and unpacked. Each time I would go down to fetch something that I had forgotten, I found 2-3 monks gathered around it, conferring. I offered to take any of them for a ride, but they politely declined. They were content to simply look it over as a point of curiosity, even a bit of wonder.

It was here that I met Brother Patrick Hart, who for decades was secretary to the most famous monk of the last century, Father Louis, or more popularly known as Thomas Merton. Brother Patrick took me around to the side of the monastery to meet him. He was buried in a small cemetery plot right up against the chapel wall, in the company of many other monks. Merton's writings, beginning with *Conjectures of a*

Guilty Bystander, became an instant part of my reading which continues to this day.

In one of his journal entries, May 21, 1968, the year he will die in Bangkok, he reflects on what is not enough about monastic life: "In our monasteries we have been content to find our way to a kind of peace, a simple, undisturbed, thoughtful life." But this is no longer satisfactory for him. "I, for one, realize that now I need more. Not simply to be quiet, ... There is a need of effort, deepening, change and transformation. . . . I do have a past to break with, an accumulation of inertia . . ." (*The Intimate Merton* 331).

Gazing back reflectively on his restlessness, and because of Merton's sustained influence on me, years later, in 1998, after making many retreats to Gethsemane, I packed up my Ford Ranger pickup truck this time, and headed out from our home in Goleta, California for a threeand-a-half month pilgrimage to monasteries, retreat centers or Zen Buddhist centers in the Western part of the United States. I wrote in my journal through the entire trip; those writings came to fruition in the publication of a book, *Grace in the Desert: Awakening to the Gifts of Monastic Life,* which was revised and significantly expanded years later to *A Pilgrimage Beyond Belief: Spiritual Journeys through Christian and Buddhist Monasteries of the American West.*

The most dramatic event of that time away was that my father, who had died two years earlier, appeared to me at the second monastery on my pilgrimage, this one in Napa Valley in California: The Carmelite House of Prayer. I remember clearly that while I was sitting with the monastery dog, Rusty, outside by the fish pond, I suddenly felt his presence sitting next to me, to my right. We had a conversation so powerful that the next morning I cleared the passenger seat of my truck so that he could sit up front if he wanted to be part of my odyssey. On that pilgrimage, at age fifty-four, I reconciled with my father, his raging alcoholism, his violence and his own shame for his behavior towards all of us and towards himself. Whether they are alive or dead, I learned, it is never too late to reconcile with loved ones, estranged or not. They are not with us literally, but that does not mean they no longer exist.

But to return to my teaching at Lorain Catholic High School, I knew that after two years of teaching secondary school, I needed to be challenged more, so I began to research graduate schools in psychology. I must collapse the process here. Through curvatures of fate, I found that the University of Dallas in Irving, Texas was to begin an Institute of Philosophic Studies in the fall of 1972 and I should apply. I crossed another threshold and submitted my application, was accepted and entered with the first class of eighteen of us across five disciplines in August of 1972 when Sandy and I moved there from Oberlin.

Living Abroad With a New Vision

While I began in their program in Phenomenological Psychology, I enrolled in a class on "The Russian Novel" taught by a Louise Cowan, who was to be my and others' mentor for decades after the program, and I was converted back to literature. I minored in what was formerly my major discipline. What an ideal situation: to study poetry and Phenomenological Psychology at the same time. The program transformed every part of my life in earth-trembling ways.

After graduation in 1976, my wife, our son Matt, who was now three-and-a-half, and I crossed the next threshold together; we accepted an invitation by the University to teach on their Rome, Italy campus. We accepted this call to venture and we moved to Rome, where I taught for two years and for the last three semesters directed the program; Sandy was hired as my assistant and served the students admirably.

One of the major thresholds of our life occurred when we entered the Italian world. When we returned to the US, I taught at the University for a year, followed by a semester at Texas Christian University in Fort Worth, then seven years at Southern Methodist University. I also taught literary classics four glorious summers in The Dallas Institute of Humanities and Culture's new program teaching teachers the classics of literature in the genres of lyric, epic, tragedy and comedy. When we moved to San Antonio to begin another adventure, I also drove for five of those summers to Fairhope, Alabama to teach in a similar program directed by my good friend, Larry Allums.

We moved to San Antonio in August, 1987, where I taught at the University of the Incarnate Word for ten years, which was a period of transformation for all of us in the family; our second son was born in

1978, growing our family to four. Then for the next twenty-six years, I taught Masters and Doctoral students at Pacifica Graduate Institute in Carpinteria, California. There I was invited to teach courses exploring Joseph Campbell's thinking on myth and literature, as well as other courses I designed and taught: a course in the Underworld, in Psyche and Nature, on Dante's *Commedia,* and Creative Writing and Personal Myth, as well as others; each allowed me to continue to blend the regions of psyche with poetics and myth.

I also began to branch out from the classroom, accepting invitations to teach and offer Riting Personal Myth retreats in the United States, Canada, Ireland, Italy and Switzerland. It satisfied a deep desire in me to expand the student populations in the classroom to the larger community. The results have been immensely rewarding in such diversity of participant populations of soul-seekers.

As Distinguished Professor Emeritus faculty in Mythological Studies, I continued to teach two courses each spring: Epic Imagination and Creative Writing and Personal Myth, both affording me richly-textured courses through the apertures of myth and depth and archetypal psychology. With the invasion of the COVID-19, I resigned my position in March, 2020.

Metaphor, Joseph Campbell reminds us, is the native tongue of myth (*Thou Art That* 8). It is the primary lexicon of mythic utterances which transports us from one reality to another and finds common ground in the quality of relationships between them (*The Inner Reaches of Outer Space* 29). Moreover, C. G. Jung reminds us as well that "analogy formation is a law which to a large extent governs the life of the psyche. . . ." (*CW* 9, ii, par. 414). Both writers guide us to the presences of metaphor, symbols and the poetic language of the individual and world psyches being in accord with one another in an as-if relationship. When we pay attention to the rich stories enshrined in the perduring classics of literature through the prism of the figures that live in the psyche, we access opportunities to integrate them into our own lives. Then we are on the path of what Jung called "individuation," wherein we become as whole and as authentic individuals as our destiny invites us to be.

Tim O'Brien, author of many works of fiction, is best known for his book of remembrances of the time he served in combat in Vietnam: *The*

Things They Carried. But it is also a story about the nature and power of stories themselves. At one point he writes: "Forty-three years old, and the war occurred half a lifetime ago, and yet the remembering makes it now. And sometimes remembering will lead to a story, which makes it forever. That's what stories are for. Stories are for joining the past to the future" (*Carried* 38).

My story is a quilt patchwork of the past with where I am headed. I paused just long enough to recollect all of the above. Recollection is itself a form of deep imagining, a striving to get the narrative right and to expose more of the complexity of personal identity. It is as close as I can get to a narrative truth, those verities that live within the weave of the yarn, universal patterns that punctuate the plot at various moments of illumination. I felt its healing properties at every step of the writing journey. My hope is that you felt, at least a little, your own story resonates within the chamber of this chapter. May it have been so. Now consider writing out your own narrative; you will be surprised at many turns by what your plot-line exposes.

Works Cited

Campbell, Joseph. *The Hero with a Thousand Faces*. Bollingen Series XVII. Princeton UP, 2001.

---. *Myths to Live By*. Penguin Group, 1972.

---. *Thou Art That: Transforming Religious Metaphor*. Edited Eugene Kennedy. New World Library 2001.

---. *The Inner Reaches of Outer Space: Metaphor as Myth and Religion*. New World Library, 2002.

DeSalvo, Louise. *Writing as a Way of Healing*. Beacon P, 2000.

Hillman, James. *Revisioning Psychology*. HarperPerennial, 1992.

Jung, C. G. *Memories, Dreams, Reflections*. Translated by Richard and Clara Winston. Pantheon, 1963.

---. *Aion: Researches into the Phenomenology of the Self*, Vol. 9, ii. *The Collected Works of C. G. Jung*. Translated by R. F. C. Hull. Bollingen Series XX. Princeton UP, 1970.

---. *Dream Analysis: Notes of the Seminar Given in 1928-1930*. Bollingen Series XCIX. Edited by William McGuire. Princeton UP, 1984.

Kearney, Richard. *On Stories*. Routledge, 2002.

Merton, Thomas. *The Intimate Merton: His Life from His Journals*. Patrick Hart and Jonathan Montaldo, editors. HarperSanFrancisco, 1999.

McAdams. Dan P. *Power, Intimacy, and the Life Story: Personal Inquiries into Identity*. The Guilford Press, 1988.

---. *The Stories We Live By: Personal Myths and the Making of the Self*. The Guilford Press, 1993.

O'Brien, Tim. *The Things They Carried*. Broadway Books, 1990.

Olney, James. *Memory and Narrative: The Weave of Life-Writing*. U Chicago P, 1998.

Rumi. *The Essential Rumi*. Translated by Coleman Barks, with John Moyne, A.J Arberry and Reynold Nicholson. Castle Books, 1977. 40-41.

von Franz, Marie-Louise. *The Cat: A Tale of Feminine Redemption*. Inner City Books, 2000.

8

---◆●◆---

ENVY'S CORROSIVE POWER AS SOUL SICKNESS*

If one loves the other really, one wants him to be free, not to put him on a leash like a dog.

~ Marie-Louise von Franz, *The Way of the Dream*, 198.

The topic of love is a vast oceanic theme for anyone to row across. Envy might best be understood as one of its pricklier stepchildren. What "transport vehicle," a figure that mythologist Joseph Campbell has used to describe a metaphor, we use to navigate these waters is as crucial as the content we express by means of it.

Framing the Story

The very popular cognitive linguist George Lakoff's politically-inflected book, *Don't Think of an Elephant!* uses the controlling metaphor of the frame. Rereading his book recently, I thought of how poetry itself is a form of metaphorical and symbolic framing, not necessarily for politics but for psycho-aesthetic purposes. His insights have led me to think of the way in which poetry frames the world. It forces me to reassess that

---

* Parts of this essay were originally published in *Road, Frame, Window: A Poetics of Seeing. Selected Poems of Timothy Donohue, Donald Carlson and Dennis Patrick Slattery*. Mandorla Books, 2015.

not just windows gazing out to the world have power. The frame also resides as support for what the window glass clings to. Frames remain faithful to the worldview they both structure and contain through the boundaries they establish. Frames both bound and beatify one piece of the world's arena; the frame attends to its shaping.

A frame might also be understood as a fidelity. It is faithful to a way of understanding one thing and everything at once. It exudes certainty of one's devising. A poem like Dante's *Commedia,* which I am learning to appreciate with a more clarity in each rereading, is a frame, a beautiful, mysterious and aesthetic one, of course, absent a glass skin. Poetics may then be an aesthetic act of framing the world into a worldview. Its optional optics are infinite. Every word in a poem, each a precise structural placement, secures the frame further; it can also dismantle it, one piece at a time. It is a psychic boundary as well as an opening.

I suggest that the frame is analogous to a myth: it is a bounded way of seeing, with edges, a framed space for content to be set in, and most often, a container for something "suitable for framing." As a myth, a frame can consist of an attitude, a belief, a feeling, an insight, a prejudice, an ignorance, a moral certitude, an arresting image and even a complete vision. As such, myths as frames can support our ability to bring more focus on or perhaps even support a blurred view of the world.

The work area, its terrain or space in which frames are constructed, is the imagination. But the heart of a poem resides, like a myth, in the language that frames its design and content. With the heart at its center, it is guaranteed an embodiment that perhaps was not possible before. Poetry, if taken to heart and heard deeply, encourages new frames in us by revealing what frames are folly, as well as discerning those whose shelf-life is long expired. A poem can pose the most crucial question to us as readers and listeners and as creators of it: when does a frame need dismantling, is no longer assisting us in our development and actually arrests our awareness rather than expanding it? C. G. Jung saw the psychological value of mythopoiesis when he wrestled with the story of Prometheus and his brother, Epimetheus in "The Type Problem in Poetry":

> This bare statement of the case might leave us entirely cold
> were there no poets who could fathom and read the collective

unconscious. They are always the first to divine the darkly moving mysterious currents and to express them as best they can, in symbols that speak to us. They make known, like true prophets, the stirrings of the collective unconscious, or, in the language of the Old Testament, 'the will of God.' (CW 6, par. 321)

Implicit in Jung's observation is the power of Musing as a way to transport the imagination down, to deepen the sense of what one knows and to express it in freshets of new language. If it is true that, as he writes elsewhere, "analogy formation is a law which to a large extent governs the life of the psyche . . ." (CW 9, ii, par. 414), then Dante's poem, like all poetry, rests on the creation of analogy to offer insights for us to ponder, not to dissect or explain. No less is this true of both love and envy as one of its offshoots, as frames of perception. Envy can frame me when I succumb to its narrowing and corrosive design. Envy can also frame originality by demeaning it, trivializing it or ignoring it.

In their magnificent study of analogy, Douglas Hofstadter and Emmanuel Sander recall: "Some ancient philosophers, including Plato and Aristotle, were fervent defenders of analogy, seeing it as a fertile medium for thinking rather than just a figure of speech" (*Surfaces and Essences* 21). They also point out a bit earlier: "Analogy-making, far from being merely an occasional mental sport, is the very lifeblood of cognition, permeating it at all levels . . . " (19). Few poets use the power of analogy with greater force than Dante in his *Commedia*.

Dante's Purgatory and Purgation

In *Purgatorio* XIII and XIV, Dante explores both as pilgrim and as poet, what envy is and what medicinals are available to restore the soul from a state of being envious. In other words, what restorative qualities have the capacity to dissolve envy? For envy seems to be a fierce frame of revenge. In his own epic journey given poetic expression in his *The Red Book*, C. G. Jung suggests that, like Dante's *Commedia*, which he studied deeply, he realizes where he is in his journey: "On the second night after the creation of my God, a vision made known to me that I had reached the underworld" (*Liber Secundus* 315). Like Dante, Jung is in search of the soul's origin in love in its distortions, excesses and divine community.

Nowhere is this truer than in our attitude towards romantic love, whose origin in the West is in the 11th. entury, as Robert Johnson describes it in his book *We: Understanding the Psychology of Romantic Love*. Furthermore, he writes, "Our myth shows us that romantic love is a necessary ingredient in the evolution of the Western psyche" (*We* 3). Dante's 14,000+ line love poem operates out of a particular notion of love, ranging from the most crude, cruel and mean expressions in *Inferno* (Body), to the communal love in *Purgatorio* (Heart), then on to the mystical love in Paradiso *(soul)*. All the forms of love that are given poetic form in the *Commedia* are infinite in scope and nuance. Here is what was believed and serves as ground for this exploration of envy.

In *Purgatorio* Virgil offers his student a brief discourse on the seven sins as distortions of the soul's attempts to love. Pride, covetousness, lust, anger, gluttony, envy and sloth comprise this packet of imperfections, or limitations, in the soul. This last, sloth, is less about laziness and more attuned to an attitude of indifference towards anything and everything in life, as Dorothy Sayers helps us to understand (*Purgatorio*, note on "The Images" 170). One word comes closest to approximating the atmosphere of sloth: "whatever." These seven defective appetites or unmeasured ways of loving, are nonetheless expressions of the good, even intuiting the Primal Love, as Dante refers to it, of God, so that there is something at the heart of each to work with. And each of them has its own intelligence, its own field of thought and emotion, in one of three forms: Excessive, diminished and distorted expressions of love could be categorized the following way:

Pride = love excessive
Covetousness = love distorted
Lust = Love excessive and distorted
Anger = love distorted
Gluttony = love excessive and distorted
Envy = love distorted and excessive
Sloth = love diminished and distorted

Moreover, each of these has a virtuous psychological reality to help the individual modulate or even purge or cleanse one's self from each tether.

Pride/charity
Covetousness/justice
Lust/temperance
Anger/temperance
Gluttony/fortitude
Envy/love in forms of mercy and compassion
Sloth/hope

Another belief Dante works with is that love in all of its three forms as well as in its measured expressions, has intelligence, what Dante calls in the context of *La Vita Nuova*, "intelleto de amore," or "the intelligence of love" (*Vita Nuova* 32). This is a monumental moment in his early exploration of love, for it suggests no separation of reason from emotion, of Eros from epistemology, of psyche from affect. How one loves, its manner, condition and intensity or lack thereof—is directly mirrored in how one knows; one can know excessively, or in an impoverished way, or in a limited way, or distortedly. If, then, one's loving is not measured, or in "due measure," one's knowing is also not restrained so that what one knows, when linked to how one knows, may never be trusted or assumed to be toward the good because one's manner of loving is already distorted.

As Virgil and Dante climb to the First Terrace, the Prideful, Dante makes this observation: "When I had crossed the threshold of the gate/that—since the souls' aberrant love would make/the crooked way seem straight—is seldom used, / I heard the gate resound . . . (*Purg*. X. ll.1-4). Illusions of love confuse the moral optics of the heart, such that what is abnormal looks like normality, the straight path of due measure in love.

In *Purgatorio* we experience a terrain that is closest to the world we daily inhabit. Time exists in this realm; hope exists here as well, for hope is a temporal phenomenon. It is, however, absent in *Inferno* and *Paradiso*, except for the way in which Dante as a living being carries time into the eternal realms. Space too is a living reality since pilgrims are in motion, spiraling upward in community, not isolated from one another. Envy, then, like each of the other six shortcomings, is a way of knowing, a form and a style of apprehending that is still false because it mirrors a distorted, excessive way of loving. Envy has an intelligence, though it is gnarled, entangled, self-absorbing and self-destructive. Its "due measure" is out of proportion, even as heart and intelligence are themselves fractured. What one knows and how they know it is splintered by the forceful fear generated in the soul by envy.

In *Purgatorio*, however, each sin or defect to be erased through the penitential spiral climb up the cone of the Mount, rests in its own cornice. *Purgatorio* XIII-XIV are two cantos Dante devotes to the scourge of envy. What does he tell us about its conditions that might illuminate us today? Let's look at the landscape as a first sign of the nature of the defect, of the shades in this realm: Dante informs us that the summit of the stairs leads him and Virgil, his guide, to a terrace that "describes a sharper arc" (*Purg.* XIII, l.6). The only cornice they have already pilgrimaged through is that of the Prideful, origin of all the other violations of love; so, envy follows pride and insists on a steep climb soon after both Virgil and Dante have passed through the huge, groaning iron gates of this region. This iron threshold is guarded by an angel with two keys used to unlock the doors when souls are granted entrance.

Now both Virgil, who is a shade, and Dante, a living person, note that "the bank is visible, the naked path—only the livid color of raw rock" (*Purg.* XIII, ll. 7-8). Virgil then turns to the sunlight and asks for guidance: "'O gentle light, through trust in which I enter/on this new path, may you conduct us here,'"/ he said, "'for men need guidance in this place. / . . . your rays must always be the guides that lead'" (XIII, ll.16-18, 21). He gives the two over to the light of God's grace, or to the Primal Love that the light carries. As they continue, they hear another voice proclaim: "'Love those by whom you have been hurt'" (XIII, l. 36). Confused by this proclamation, Dante asks his guide, who responds: "'. . . the cords/that form the scourging here are plied by love'" (XIII, ll. 38-39). Virgil continues: "'The sounds of punished envy, envy curbed,/are different; If I judge right, you'll hear/those sounds before we reach the pass of pardon'" (XIII, ll. 40-43).

Envy and the Soul's Corrosion

Now we move into the field of envy as a corrosive energy field: "'But let your eyes be fixed attentively/and, through the air/you will see people seated/before us, all of them on the stone terrace'" (*Purg.* XIII, ll. 44-45). And Dante: "I opened—wider than before—my eyes;/I looked ahead of men, and I saw shades/with cloaks that shared their color with the rocks" (XIII, ll. 46-48). Dante appears to exaggerate his own seeing in the spirit of the envious. Was their seeing magnified or excessive, in taking in with some delight the sight of others in misfortune or anger over the gifts of another, while being blinded to one's own good fortune?

The translator, Allen Mandelbaum, points out that Envy, from *Invidia*, is related to the idea of seeing (*videre*) which will be the corrective measure of the envious because they cast their eyes on what belonged to others; now they are reduced to blindness and to begging (*Commedia* 659, n. 62). In addition, Dorothy Sayers, another translator and commentator on the poem, writes that "Envy (*Invidia*) differs from that of pride in that it contains always an element of fear. . . . The envious man is afraid of losing something by the admission of superiority in others, and therefore looks with grudging hatred upon other men's gifts and good fortune . . . " (*Purgatory* note on "The Images," 170). In popular Italian, *face videre* means "let's see."

Now Dante hears the shades in this region cry out: "'Mary, pray for us,'" and then heard, "'Michael, Peter and all saints'" (*Purg.* XIII. 49-50), turning to the blessed for assistance. We also notice that they are communally helping one another, because all their eyelids are not simply closed—they are sewn shut with iron wire, so they need support from one another. They now recognize and even plead for the superior qualities of others; blinded, they must seek aid. We see that their pride is lessened. Their eyes are being turned to the good through their absence of sight; in addition, their will, which at one point in life was directed to their own willing or willfulness in either seeking what others had, and not just in material possessions, which is the most trivial of one's property envied but in who the one envied *is*.

At one time reveling in the suffering of others, now in their own blind suffering, they migrate towards a more measured form of loving. Eyes wired shut encourages in-sight. Dante, eyes wide open as pilgrim, sees them and comments as poet: "'I think no man now walks upon the earth/who is so hard that he would not have been/pierced by compassion for what I saw next'" (*Purg.* XIII, ll. 52-54). A careful poet with every word, his choice of "pierced" aligns him in sympathy with the eyelids of the envious pierced by the wire that forces their closure. Dante sees that they are cloaked in coarse haircloths; each leans on the shoulder of another, while all are bolstered by the rocks.

They are compared to beggars who "on pardon days" plead for what they need. They bend towards one another, blind, yet in sympathy for the condition of the others, knowing full well that they are in the same condition. They have been levelled to equals, the very condition envy wishes to place others in who are the object or victim of this imperfect love. Now, however, pity, not envy, is their credo. They seek compassion for and from the others, in community, not in a hellish state of self-absorption. Their purgation is a form of healing the wounds that envy scourged them with in life; in the afterlife they heal-in-community.

Further, their eyes wired closed denies them the light of heaven; they are compared rather to untamed hawks in the way the birds are treated by having a small sack of leather over their eyes to tame or subdue them so they do not dart off, flying above the others, as they did as souls in their earlier flights of envy. Dante himself feels great compassion for the shades; he is at an advantage for he can see them but not they him. His wide-eyed wonder at their sight fosters a heart-felt empathy for their plight.

As he continues to converse with Virgil on this injustice, he notices further that the eyes sewn "so atrociously" (*Purg.* XIII, l. 83), did not stop the shades from forcing tears out of them that bathed their cheeks. Dante, seemingly unable to tolerate his division from them any longer, turns to address them: "'You who can be certain . . ./of seeing that high light/which is the only object of your longing, /may, in your conscience, all impurity/soon to be dissolved by grace, so that the stream/of memory flow through it limpidly'" (*Purg.* XIII, ll. 88-91).

One shade in particular steps forward to address the pilgrim: Sapia, from the wealthy Salvani family of Siena, enemy of the Ghibellines. She will give voice to another deployment of envy—not desire for what another has or is, but rather a more insidious delight in observing the suffering of others in what they have lost, surrendered, or been sundered by. She admits to the play on her name: "'I was not sapient, though I was called Sapia;/and I rejoiced far more at others' hurts than at my own good fortune'" (*Purg.* XIII, ll. 109-11). She further admits feeling this way even late in life when her enemies were routed and abused as they tried to escape. In their suffering, she confesses, "'I felt incomparable joy, /so that I lifted up my daring face/and cried to God: 'Now I fear you no more--/as did the blackbird after brief fair weather. / I looked for peace with God at my life' send'" (*Purg.* XIII, ll. 118-24).

Envy's Optics

Envy here promotes a short-sighted vision; one's optics are narrowed to see the suffering of another through the prism of pleasure. Perhaps part of its allure is that it offers the one envying a false sense of superiority over the other and may in the process camouflage the mediocrity or the unlived life of the one imprisoned in envy's wrath. It certainly separates one out from others, leaving one solitary, ostensibly enjoying the pain of another in distress. Not aiding them but eyeing them seems to be envy's insistent response. It does not give one solace, peace or comfort; the one who envies seems to suffer his/her own torment, one's own way of being in pain, even it not immediately recognized.

Sapia confesses to Dante that she eventually "'looked for peace with God at my life's end'"(*Purg.* XIII, l. 124). Now here we see the hinter side of envy. She admits that the penalty owed for her distorted and excessive love was lessened because of a fellow Sienese, "'Pier Pettinaio—/remembered me in his devout petitions'" (XIII, l. 128). His measured love, expressed in the spirit of generosity, has shortened her time in Purgatory. Otherwise, we are told, Sapia would be in a lower terrace of Purgatory, still making her way even today to the cornice of envy.

She then asks Dante: why is that your eyes "'have not been sewn, who uses breath to speak?'" (*Purg.* XIII, l. 132), for she senses he is not yet a shade. Dante responds that he is not only alive, but that he would be willing to pray for her if she so wished. Sapia seems for a moment puzzled, then realizes: "'the sign is clear—you have God's love. /Thus, help me sometimes with your prayers. I ask /of you, by that which you desire most, if ever you should tread the Tuscan earth, /to see my name restored among my kin'" (XIII, ll. 146-49). Not envy but a plea to be assisted in her current condition of rehabilitation; seeing her name restored is immensely important to her, for she is in process of purging envy for a fuller, more ample love; Dante's prayers, given in charity, or caritas, would assist that changed perception of her.

Purgatorio XIV also treats envy through two figures, Guido del Duca and Rinieri da Calboli, both political figures from the Romagna. They do not recognize him but are willing, at his request, to identify themselves. They "see" in Dante a special trait, as Guido observes: "'But since God would, in you, have His grace glow/so brightly, I shall not be miserly;/know, therefore, that I was Guido del Duca. /My blood was so afire with envy that,/when I had seen a man becoming happy/the lividness in me was plain to see'" (*Purg.* XIV, ll. 79-84). The sense of seeing, of perceiving, is a moral condition, one which blinds the envious to anything but one's own self-absorption, which is then maintained, in the irony that envy expresses, by demeaning or diminishing the status of another.

Guido freely admits that what he sowed in life he has reaped in the afterlife, that place that Dante names "animarium statem postmortem" (the state of souls after death), which brings the poet to this observation: "'O humankind, why do you set your hearts/there where our sharing cannot have a part?'" (*Purg.* XIV, ll. 83-84). Being cut off from humanity appears to be one of envy's most destructive and painful tendencies. It self-encloses the individual in his own incarceration. Loss of freedom, of a loving relationship with others except in the most debilitating manner of anger overseeing happiness, envy seems a most intense demonic condition in which one creates one's own hell. Envy seems an infernal format of love; like the shades in Inferno who are each isolated from one another except in moments of physical or verbal violence, Guido's envy prohibits him from participating in any form of benevolent and constructive love. Envy narrows one's options in life for enjoying even the simplest of pleasures, for their distorted love puts joy out of reach.

As Virgil and Dante depart from both "gentle souls" (*Purg.* XIV, l. 127), as Dante calls them—for they suffer once again in their speaking and weeping in remembrance—a voice slices into their path "as it splits/the air encountered us" to utter one sentence: "'Whoever captures me will slaughter me'" (XIV, l. 133) and "then it fled like thunder when it fades/after the cloud is suddenly ripped through" (ll. 134-35). He is identified through a note in the text as the Biblical Cain, who out of envy for his brother Abel, favored so in God's eyes, killed him in a rage and now believes that given the hideous nature of his transgression, is fair game for anyone who wishes to exact justice on him.

Like other shades in *Purgatorio* XIV, fierce and heavy remorse attends those who have envied and taken action to assuage it through assassinating the source of the envy in a confused belief that it will eliminate the debilitating and resentful feelings brought on by another's good fortune. To the contrary, it increases the hell one inhabits. Now Cain believes he is a ripe victim for any man who wishes to exact justice on such an excessive act. The thunder and lightning imagery that accompanies Cain captures something of the power and fury of envy's hostility and violence; envy is in fact a double act of violence, at once violence towards assassinating the other as well as an act of self-violence, of self-loathing, and finally, of self-murder, as one stumbles through the fog of envy with a distorted vision. Envy's fog consists of: one part pride; one part anger; and one part self-loathing.

The last figure to speak of envy is from mythology: she is Aglauros, who informs Virgil and Dante that she was turned to stone. An Athenian princess who felt envy for her sister because of the love the god Mercury showered on her, she was punished by being turned to stone by him (Mandelbaum 662, note 133). Aglauros' delivery of her plight was, like Cain's, a huge uproar—"like thunder quick to follow thunder" (*Purg.* XIV, l. 138). Through so many repeated examples, we understand the enormous energy that gathers around envy and propels it forward to destroy so much in its pernicious path. It produces its own violent energy field and creates enormous noise. Emotionally volcanic, it erupts in the soul; its hot lava of anger spills down the individual's sides and transforms into immobile rock. Envy paralyzes the soul in which it festers into a titanic hate.

Virgil then admonishes Dante for giving so much of his seeing to the envious, in part because he is being baited by Satan to draw him into the

forcefield of envy. Heaven calls you, Virgil informs him, to " 'see its
never-ending beauties;/and yet your eyes would only see the ground'"
(*Purg.* XIV, ll.148-50). Envy blinds; envy narrows vision; envy would create a form of myopic discerning, both morally bankrupt and violent. Dorothy Sayers, one of the poem's finest readers and translators, writes that
envy's source is fear; seeing another with things or situations one covets
or seeing with delight another suffering, creates insecurity, or creates in
the mind of the envious one's own inadequacy or the real specter that I
could find myself suffering like the other (*The Divine Comedy 2: Purgatory*
170). Envy runs counter to both freedom and an ability to feel compassion for another, as well as an authentic pursuit of justice.

Other Voices on Envy

As Dante's two cantos on envy reveal its corrosive nature, I offer here a
few additional reflections on this invidious disease in the soul that stops
the heart's ability to feel compassion for another and, most importantly,
for one's self.

And while he does not ever mention envy, the physicist David Bohm,
writing on original and creative individuals, does make some worthy connections to envy's presence, which are implicit in Dante's poetic formulation. Let me put it this way: envy is the tacit admission that one's response to originality and to creatives generally, is mechanical, frustrating,
as well as a signal of one's own limited and indeed sclerotic imagination.
Envy is a failure of imagination; it is both an admission and a recognition—conscious or not—of own's own mediocrity and yearning in the
soul that replaces celebrating the excellence and originality that was there
in inchoate form, but that one failed to acknowledge, much less nurture.

Given the above, I sense further that envy is a form of deep grieving
for an individual's original, creative and compassionate being that one
did not allow to bear fruit. Envy is an expression in the deepest landscape
of one's being of the creative and original response to life that nonetheless remained still-born. In other words, the originality of the person who
suffers the stings of envy shows up dead-on-arrival and remains so. Their
originality was reduced to sterility and frozen into a mechanical expression. In its invidious invective towards another, envy exhibits a blindness

to the difference between a creative and a mechanized character of a human response not just towards the other, but to one's self.

In the above lighting, envy may be the voice of a tremendous frustration in realizing that for whatever reason—for instance, in setting too safe and limiting boundaries on one's own unique and creative nature—that an individual failed either: 1. to discover that creative richness in one's self, or; 2. failed to allow it a full birthing into all the uncertainty that being creative must engage, as physicist David Bohm has written (*On Creativity* 23).

If one's unique creativity can be squashed by old sustaining and corroding patterns of one's past so that it twists, confuses and distorts, even suffocates the fresh and vital energy that companions and supports every creative act and original response to the world, a knee-jerk response can often be an angry and envious ferocity. Envy in this sense can be alchemical in the following way: it transforms creative energy, which rests on entering fully the arena of uncertainty, into the caustic caldron of envy in order to cut down, ostracize, isolate, denigrate and even assassinate the one envied. It is a painful experience, this closing of one's emotional landscape to insulate one from the absence of courage in their lives that can lead one to be creative, authentic and whole.

Thus, an envious rage towards the other's originality and authenticity is in fact a form of self-assassination by murdering the truth of the self nesting quietly, waiting to be given expression. Envy itself, if recognized as a signal or an emblem of a clash of opposing selves in the soul, can be an opportunity to wake up to one's own authenticity that begins to break down suffocating limits imposed by the desire to be: a team player; one of the crowd; one who goes along to get along; as well as other sell-outs of one's authenticity and inner authority.

Envy, as I mentioned, is a form of grieving, with all the attendant anger and rage that can accompany the loss of a loved one, especially if that person is one's self. Envy is an emotional equivalent of a death and burial. The corpse in the coffin is one's originality, one's unique character, one's exceptional perspective, one's sense of a joyful wholeness that can benefit others in its idiosyncratic beauty. The corpse in the coffin is also an individual's fidelity to one's own gifts, as professor of formative spirituality Adrian van Kaam has written (*Envy and Originality* 2). But our deepest originality can suffer permanent fatigue when it continues to be resisted by envy.

Envy's Corrosive Impulses

We can, as van Kaam writes later, envy our own unlived creative self that may be turned inward as self-loathing and self-denigration; it can also be turned outward and projected on any and all creative and authentic persons who dare to defy the mediocrity of mass thought and behavior in order to honor the best in themselves. We remember Sapia earlier, for instance, who delighted in the misfortunes of others, for then they became no better and no different from her. Such a stance allowed her to hide or ignore the self-betrayal that rested with a demonic grin behind her gloating over the suffering of others. Further, she was no longer able to see the gifts that surrounded her own good fortune. Envy promotes, then, a double-blindness.

Nor does envy ask the most fundamental questions of one's self: what am I called to? What am I willing to risk? What do I trust in my life that allows me to grow more fully into myself? What am I inclined to do? Am I on the right path (mine) or a wrong path (another's)? In this sense, then, envy is the expressed absence of courage, or *cour*—heart; a generous spirit free of envy has "the courage to live close to one's heart *(Envy* 7) as well as close to one's hearth. A heart free of the acids of envy lives in that Hestian space of the hearth-fire, where creativity and not the corrosive chaos of envy, fosters and nurtures the whole-hearted spirit of authenticity. Asking one's self not once but often: "What does the mystery of me want from me?" *(Envy* 4). It cannot be asked from within an envious heart.

As an example: when students apply to the Mythological Studies program at Pacifica Graduate Institute, either they or their friends will ask: "What will you *do* with a degree in mythology?" Of course, the question from one angle is the wrong one. It grows from a mechanical sense fostered by the myth of utility. It also completely bypasses the mystery of a life that may need just this degree to move into one's vocation that is not clearly delineated by cultural forces and economic impulses. It also ignores the deep calling of a life to relevance, purpose, passion as well as a platform from which to deliver it. "What will you do?" misses the deep concern: "Who will you be?" as a consequence of such a study. Perhaps the world needs more of us to BE something before we move to DO something.

Finally, envy often wraps itself in the garments of "for your own good," or "you are not measuring up," or "you are not good for business." Moralisms often disguise the insidious presence of envy. Van Kaam writes that "envious dispositions express themselves in habits of leveling all that is unique about a person's life. What envy despises is not one's pursuit of excellence but one's uniqueness" (*Envy* 36). The distinction is one I leave you to ponder for its keen insight. Moreover, we must all keep in mind that what we envy in the other is often the very programs and patterns that have been unlived in us that can roil enormous anger from within us.

In continuing to muse over Dante's insights into envy, I found myself comparing it to jealousy. I offer these distinctions for you to consider:

- Jealousy is one's desire to *have* what you have—fame, recognition, good fortune, possessions, or positions.
- Envy is one's desire to *be* what you are; as such, it is deeper and closer to the heart of one's being.
- Envy carries within its fabric a destructive element: I wish you bad fortune.
- Jealousy is more physical, literal and matter-focused.
- Envy is more metaphysical, more existential. It taps one's ontological sense of being.
- Jealousy is more emotional: "I want . . . ."
- Envy involves the intellect more than does jealousy; it is a distorted emotional intellect expressing itself as "I want to be . . . ."
- Jealousy is a more adolescent emotion towards the other.
- Envy is a more adult emotion; its emphasis is more on what has not been lived, less on what one has not acquired.
- Jealousy expresses something defective in the heart.

- Envy expresses something defective in the soul; it is a deeper expression of self-torture and self-molestation turned outward.
- Envy expresses a deeper form of hate than does jealousy.
- Envy is closer to an all-engulfing despair than is jealousy.
- Envy is a far greater threat to home-land serenity.
- Envy is a greater disposition toward self-resentment than jealousy.
- Envy is the impotent voice within telling me I am not in control.
- Envy is the impotent voice within telling me I am wounded and vulnerable but am unable to change.
- Envy is a defiant, though impotent, expression of willfulness.
- Envy is the voice of my unforgiving inner critic projected outward.
- Envy caters to and promotes a growing and pervasive dictator who specializes in self-disappointment.
- Envy slowly corrodes the beauty in life and soon spreads to create an entire worldview through negative energy.
- Envy is a dramatic form of self-shaming.
- Envy is not a part-time employee; it is full-time, all-pervasive and omni-corrosive.
- Envy fixates on another, is self-flagellating and self-crucifying on the cross of one's own inner yearnings.
- Envy is a hateful form of loving in a distorted way, as Dante illustrates. It grows out of both self-absorption and self-loathing towards one's perceived inadequacies.
- Learning to love one's limitations and imperfections, as well as one uniqueness, is the first step to being liberated from envy's corrosive clutches.

Works Cited

Alighieri, Dante. *The Divine Comedy.* Translated and edited by Allen Mandelbaum. Knopf, 1984.

---. *The Comedy of Dante Alighieri, The Florentine. Cantica II: Purgatory.* Translated and edited by Dorothy L. Sayers. Penguin, 1955.

---. *Dante's Vita Nuova.* Translated by Mark Musa. Indiana UP, 1973.

Bohm, David. *On Creativity.* Edited by Lee Nichol. Routledge, 2004.

Donohue, Timothy, Donald Carlson and Dennis Patrick Slattery. *Road, Frame, Window: A Poetics of Seeing. Selected Poems.* Mandorla Books, 2015.

Hofstatdter, Douglas and Emmanuel Sander. *Surfaces and Essences: Analogy as the Fuel and Fire of Thinking.* Basic Books, 2013.

Johnson, Robert. *We: Understanding the Psychology of Romantic Love.* HarperSanFrancisco, 1983.

Jung, C. G. *Aion: Researches into the Phenomenology of the Self.* Vol. 9, ii. *The Collected Works of C. G. Jung.* Translated by R. F. C. Hull, Princeton UP, 1970.

---. *Psychological Types,* Vol. 6. *The Collected Works of C. G. Jung.* Translated by R. F. C. Hull. Princeton UP, 1990.

---. *The Red Book: Liber Novus. A Reader's Edition.* Edited and Introduction by Sonu Shamdasani. Translated by Mary Kyburz, John Peck and Sonu Shamdasani. Philemon Series. Norton, 2009.

Lakoff, George. *Don't Think of an Elephant: Know Your Values and Frame the Debate.* Chelsea Green Publishers, 2004.

Slattery, Dennis Patrick. *Day-to-Day Dante: Exploring Personal Myth Through The Divine Comedy.* iUniverse, 2011.

Van Kaam, Adrian. *Envy and Originality.* Revised and edited by Susan Muto. Epiphany Books, 2004.

von Franz, Marie-Louise. *The Way of the Dream: Conversations on Jungian Dream Interpretation With Marie-Louise von Franz.* Shambhala, 1994.

9

◆▸●◂◆

DIONYSUS, APOLLO AND ASKLEPIOS: THE ROAD FROM DIS-EASE TO RECOVERY: A BIO-MYTHIC NARRATIVE*

The gods have become diseases; Zeus no longer rules Olympus but rather the solar plexus and produces curious specimens for the doctor's consulting room, . . .

~ C. G. Jung, *CW* 13, par. 54.

Like so many occasions when a god or goddess appears to someone, physical illness came to me as a total surprise, both as an intervention and an invasion. What surprised me most was its absolute suddenness. Let me recount the story. It was a revelatory situation, one in which I became aware of the power of the presence of several gods in a way that reading about them could never approach. If, as James Hillman reminds us, "pathologizing is a way of mythologizing" (*Revisioning Psychology* 99), then disease is double-edged in the imagination, both as illness and as dis-ease.

On April 2nd of 2017, I presented a lecture on "Reading James Hillman" to the Joseph Campbell Roundtable at Pacifica Graduate Institute. Afterward, I invited a few students and friends to my suite in the dormitory to

* Originally published as "Dionysus, Apollo, and Asklepios: The Road from Dis-ease to Recovery. A Bio-Mythic Narrative." *Jung Journal: Culture and Psyche*. Vol. 12, Number 3. Summer 2018. 34-42.

have a glass of wine and conversation about my talk on Hillman's work. I sat comfortably in one of the chairs and enjoyed the company and the wide-ranging topics of discussion. After a couple of hours, my guests stood up to leave; I rose to bid them goodnight, but as I did, I noticed immediately that my left leg would no longer support me. I leaned against my chair, said nothing to the group, and bade goodnight to all of them. I wondered, though, if I had strained my prosthetic hip standing for over an hour on the classroom's hardwood floor. I set the experience aside and went to bed.

About 4 a.m. I woke with shivers and a fever and instinctively knew that I needed help. My condition did not feel like a sudden cold or flu. It felt like something deeper. I called security and Guillermo, a friend on night duty, came to assist me. He helped me to his car and drove me to Cottage Hospital in Santa Barbara. I was admitted through the Emergency Room and examined an hour later. The orthopedic surgeon on call told me I had no infection, gave me a prescription for pain and released me six hours after my admittance. I thought I was fine, but I also realized that my teaching schedule beginning later that week was going to be a challenge.

Two nights later, I woke at 1 a.m. with chills and shaking that I could not control; it was much more severe and alarming than the first incident earlier in the week. I knew that my condition had worsened and that my life was in danger. Something had been missed or misconstrued by the initial medical team. Because of my extreme shaking, which was the beginning of sepsis, I returned to the emergency room at the hospital where I was once again admitted. I remember that my mouth was so dry and sticky that I could not adequately speak. My helper, Guillermo once again, explained my condition to the admitting nurse. Another nurse drew blood as soon as I was wheeled to my room.

Not long after this event, a young orthopedic surgeon introduced himself and informed me with some urgency that not only had the blood work they examined revealed a serious bacterial infection, but that I was in the intermediate stages of sepsis, an immune response to an infection. Sepsis can kill an individual if it leads to septic shock, so it must be treated quickly. The infection was systemic, having infiltrated my entire body, and it was gaining strength. Within twenty minutes I was prepped and in surgery for a "pelvic flush" to save my twenty-three-year-old prosthetic left hip. The bacterial invasion had attacked the appliance and would damage it further if immediate action was not taken.

The Body's Wounded Wisdom

The successful surgery lasted ninety minutes; I began rehab almost immediately in the hospital to gain enough strength to return home to Texas. I also had a pic line inserted into my left arm with a small tube that ran just above my heart, so the antibiotics could be injected frequently. Teaching, I quickly realized, was now out of the question. Our younger son Steve flew from San Antonio to be with me; he slept all that next week on the couch in my room and helped me in recovery. He also stayed with me in the suite on Pacifica's campus until I was ready to fly home.

After several days on campus, I was well enough to travel home with my son and a container of antibiotics in a cooler. But after less than a week at home, I began to feel achy and exhausted. The infection had survived the earlier flush and was now roaring back. My wife, Sandy, drove me to Christus Santa Rosa Hospital in New Braunfels, Texas, where I was admitted. I saw both an orthopedic surgeon and an infectious disease doctor later that morning; the latter informed me that they had isolated the streptococcus and were beginning antibiotics to combat its destructive effects on my body, especially the prosthetic left hip and potentially the right artificial hip that had also been replaced years earlier.

The surgeon told me he needed to open the left hip up again so he could examine the condition of the prosthesis and repair and/or replace it if warranted, as well as perform a second pelvic flush on it. I knew that once more I was to begin a journey into the underworld of the operating theater and anesthetics, after which I was to begin a slow journey back, but to what was still uncertain.

During the surgery, which lasted more than five hours and required blood transfusions, Sandy sat by herself in a plastic chair in the waiting room. The surgeon reported later that he had salvaged part of the hip and other parts he had replaced. It would be a lengthy recovery. I spent eight days in the hospital learning to walk, beginning with slow short shuffling steps using a walker in the hallways, and always accompanied by hospital orderlies who stabilized me. When I asked both doctors the origin of such an invasion, they admitted that locating the source in most cases was almost impossible. It simply occurs, and most often without warning and absent many symptoms. The best response was to get to a hospital quickly so the infection's spread could be halted with antibiotics.

I began physical therapy for one month in our home, and a second month at a physical therapy rehab center. So much had happened in such a short amount of time that I had not thought through what had occurred to me beyond the physical infection and surgeries to correct it. I felt, in retrospect, that I had put myself on a shelf and ignored it for far too long. In that interim I sensed that I had grown distant from who I imagined I was. One morning, weeks later, when I had begun walking on my own with the help of a cane, I had an appointment with the infectious disease doctor who was monitoring my blood. At one point in his treatment, he asked me how I was feeling. I realized that I did not know, truly, how I was doing. But his word "feeling" opened a sluice in me that had been blocked, stifled and arrested, and with it a sense of who I was. I found myself spontaneously saying to him and my wife: "I want to reclaim parts of myself so I can feel like who I was again," followed instantly by a burst of uncontrolled weeping.

I did not know what was happening in that moment but felt shattered and strange to myself. I also felt displaced, "beside myself looking in on a stranger." The Spanish mystic, St. John of the Cross's powerful image of being self-estranged, from his text of the same name, *The Dark Night of the Soul*, felt more familiar to me as I recalled his description from the book read years ago. But with one change: I called it the dark night of the dis-ease, the unsettling feeling that I was journeying now between worlds: the familiar images and memories of who I was, and a strange unseen desert landscape, austere and not without its own grace, of who I was becoming. But missing was a clear pattern or end in sight of what might evolve. I felt that this loss, this molting of a former sense of a competent and competitive self, created some strange new iteration of me that implicated my body's ordeal.

An accompanying spiritual awakening evoked a ferocious desire to reclaim the simply beauty and sacredness of the ordinary. I sought nothing but a quotidian, quiet, comforting, and, yes, a degree of control over a life that had moved out from under my feet in an instant. St. John speaks eloquently early in his mystical text of how his soul, "she, set forth from herself and all things, dying with unfeigned mortification to herself and them, to attain at last a sweet and pleasant life of love in God." His soul tells him that "this going forth from herself and all things, was 'In a dark night,' whereby she means purgative contemplation" (*Dark Night* 543). The language of "purgative contemplation" struck home because it captured for me something to let go of, even abandoned; as the body began its slow recovery, there arose a corresponding discovery: God is not *in* the ordinary; God *is* the ordinary. I sensed in a quite palpable way that psyche-soma-spirit enjoy a unified whole and that if any one of them is wounded or afflicted, all three in this trinity of human selfhood suffer dis-ease.

Gods as Wounding and Healing Presences

And something more: another revelation came to me with intense clarity. The ancient Greeks understood on a deep and existential level the god Dionysus and his capacity to dismember one in certain circumstances. My sense of a loss of self that I knew revealed that some of his qualities included being the great disrupter, the infiltrator and invader who could easily throw one off one's normal life trajectory, disabling, if not disconnecting, one's self from one's identity, from who and what one remembers one is. I realized that I had to somehow recollect who I believed I was; that was first task in a series of steps to reclaiming a dismembered self. I remember the strangeness of speaking of myself because I had lost a sense of that person, less through the physical invasion and more through the psychic trauma of the dis-ease.

As the god of trauma, of pain and suffering, Dionysus conveyed what I felt—that my own mythic sense of self, my "personal myth," had been invaded by an archetypal presence that threw me into a new terrain I could not identify and at least initially had no strategy to cope with. Had something of who I was died in this experience in a Dionysian dark dis-ese and was I sensing this loss now that I was physically out of danger?

I remembered that years before, in my book, *The Wounded Body: Remembering the Markings of Flesh*, I wrote about being afflicted: "To be wounded is to be opened to the world; it is to be pushed off the straight, fixed, and predictable path of certainty and thrown into ambiguity, or onto the circuitous path, and into the unseen and unforeseen" (13). Wounding creates both a wobbling as well as a wandering; some mainstay of my life had been detached, kicked out from under me, so that feelings of being shattered and dislocated become normative.

Psychologist and literary theorist Susan Rowland's study, *Remembering Dionysus*, focuses in large measure on exploring James Hillman's *Revisioning Psychology*. She paraphrases his work at one point in writing: "Touched by zoe, Dionysian dismemberment in pathologizing is a loosening from which a re-membered new life emerges" (152). Hillman furthers his own thought when he states: "Our falling apart is an imaginal process, like the collapse of cities and the fall of heroes in mythical tales, like the dismemberment of Dionysian loosening . . ." (109). In *Facing the Gods,* he reminds us that "Dionysos was called *Lysios,* the loosener. The word is cognate with *lysis,* the last syllables of *analysis. Lysis* meaning loosening, setting free, . . ." (*Facing the Gods* 162). I had my own yearning to splice together parts of myself, with no clue about what to do or how to begin, but with the thought that it was necessary for me to yield to this reclamation. I had not realized experientially before this experience how much the body is both physical and metaphorical in its ability to be a vehicle for psychic development.

I returned to Hillman's edited volume, *Facing the Gods* for a profounder understanding of what I had uttered from a deep place in my affliction. There he writes in the Preface: "the soul is entangled in myths. . . . We are learning what other cultures always knew: to know ourselves we must know the Gods and Goddesses of myth. We must face the gods" (iv). I had read this and his leading essay, "The Necessity of Abnormal Psychology," more than once, but only intellectually. Now I felt his words deeply in my bones, prosthesis and blood, as expressions of blood-knowledge. My sense of self was bloody, sometimes brutal, but not without a presence of beauty if, indeed, an illness can be called beautiful and even bountiful in its effects.

Wounded Memories

The constant ache in my left side was a persistent reminder of what had occurred; its memory was in my walk and in my inability to perform simple normal functions like showering or putting on my socks and shoes.

My self was subtracted by what I could not do, with new limits and boundaries defining me; recovery was reclamation and perhaps, I began to hope, renewal. I thought of how "to renew" is "to reknew," to know again and in that recognition or insight, to be transformed by the violence of illness. It was another rare moment in my life when I became fully conscious of limits, liabilities and vulnerabilities. It was a shift in consciousness itself, a profound form of "reknewal." And, yes, a feeling of liberation within all of these new restrictions.

As I thought about this invasion mythically and biologically, I came to understand that Dionysus is the force of psychic infections that may originate from a physical ailment, a wound or an affliction; the god imaginally infects as he affects; he transforms, shifts consciousness, and disassembles a personal identity—in my case, a dramatic analogy of my own hip needing to be disassembled before the surgeon could reassemble it with old parts that had escaped the infection and new replacements that had not. But the entire appliance had to be almost entirely disassembled because the bacteria tended to hide on the side of the prosthesis that cannot be seen, essentially guaranteeing its reoccurrence. Is that itself a strategy of Dionysus' hiddenness? What the god initiates is not so much physical illness but rather dis-ease with one's self as well as a dislocation of the ordinary, comfortable routine of each day that we "loosely" label "our life."

The cure can be as unnerving and dismembering as the disease: sleep deprivation, constant hospital staff coming in and out of the room day and night, a food diet that was often inedible, confinement to the room except when I took short walks through the halls, restriction to the inside of the hospital with minimal contacts, a steady barrage of medications that kept me in an altered state of consciousness, and the inability to shower or groom myself. All was turned topsy-turvy—dictated by others and best yielded to in order to avoid more dismembering. The disease pointed out a new direction in my life. Dionysus demanded that I give up, yield and surrender to a process that was imposed from without, driving self-determination into limbo and parking it there for an indefinite period. Fighting this powerful god's presence and direction risks further dismemberment, which would inevitably insist on a longer recovery.

This Dionysian divine presence slips into our lives in a whisper or a wham, reordering our values as well as our identity. Such a shift in what one values comprises in large measure how one is transformed by both the illness and the rehabilitation that follows the invasion. Dionysus' influence pulls all energies toward him. A sense of wholeness is sacrificed, held hostage. I yearned for a feeling of coherence and order within a self that I could identity, like meeting an old lost friend. Dionysus disordered not only my life but also affected all those who knew me. For instance, my wife placed her own full schedule on hold for two months to care for me and to help me with the most mundane activities, like showering and dressing. My son dropped his work to stay with me in the hospital. My other son and family members and friends visited me and helped when they could.

The war that takes place every minute between the infection and the antibodies that try to ward it off, along with pain medications to ease the war inside, also disrupt body/mind functions. I tried to read while in the hospital, but it was a lost cause; I remembered nothing of the media-driven world. I lost twenty-two pounds during my stay and misplaced food's enjoyment. A gulf grew wider between who I thought I was and who I was becoming. In between was a "no-Dennis land" described above which felt more like a Dionysus land, a landscape both horrific yet consoling. A Greek friend of mine informed me years ago that the name "Dennis" in Greek is Dionysus. The god whose name I share came into me resonating dominance. Enduring dismemberment is one of the most painful chapters of the dark night of the soul's journey. The intimacy was frightening but had to be endured.

I found it immensely helpful to read Hillman's essay, "Dionysos in Jung's Writings," using the Dionysian for an archetypal structure of consciousness (151). It seemed less true that the god *was* the disease than that the god *was in* the illness, a presence as a psychological and mythical reality not split from the body, as Hillman goes on to reveal. In the same essay he exposes C. G. Jung's own sense of this god, who "was called the divided one (*CW* 14, par. 350, fn. 6). His dismemberment was evidence of his divisibility into parts. In each part he lived as the pneuma dispersed in matter. He suggested that pneuma as soul spirit, as breath, pervades and animates matter. Bits of the Dionysian spirit are like "'white sparks' shining in the *terra foetida*" (*CW* 14, par. 64) or rotten stench of the decaying body as it dissociates into pieces ("Dionysos in Jung's Writings" 160). Hillman's observation helped me grasp that illness is often a way of matter disintegrating, of decomposing and of dying off, so to make room for what renews.

These "sparks" of the Dionysian spirit also close any gap between physis and psyche, both of which are subject to decay, dismembering and disintegration. Here was my revelation stated so clearly and comprehensively: that the flesh was part of the fantasy of brokenness into parts, a form that my "no-Dennis land" assumed; it also assumed that the mythic was intertwined with matter and that decay, decomposition and corruption were both psychic and physical aspects of loosening. The wisdom of myths rests partly in how they reveal a unity between matter, psyche, and spirit and develop rich analogies to reveal these correspondences. So, hanging loose can be an asset to healing.

Gods of Healing

And then briefly but no less importantly, to the other side of the equation: rememberment as part of the aftermath of the initial traumatic bacterial invasion. Slowly, in the last days of my hospital stay, I began to feel another force entering; I want to call it an energy promoting rearrangement and completion, even a force of renewal. I had thought it was another attribute of Dionysos but came to realize it as the presence of his antibody, Apollo and his son Asklepios. Walter Otto writes of Apollo, "[he] who cares for purifications and expiations" (1954/1979, 67). He continues: "Apollo purifies the guilty person of the pollution that adheres to and menaces him" (68). His functioning as a psychological presence "does not sever the corporeal from what we call spiritual or psychic, but always sees the one in the other" (68). C. G. Jung points out that Apollo and Dionysus represent a polarity (*CW* 9, ii, par. 134). In illness, both have their share in the entire process of *decomposition* and *recomposition*. In both words is the root—compost—an apt image for dis-ease.

Apollo's son Asklepios furthers his father's work as purifier. Jung tells us that the Greek god of healing, on being hatched from the egg, seems to have taken the form of a snake (*CW* 14, par. 483). In another context Jung observes that the serpent was "not only an animal that aroused fear and represented danger, but also signified healing. Therefore Asklepios, the god of physicians, is connected with the serpent; you all know his emblem which is still in use" (*CW* 18, par. 237).

Within my own illness and recovery, in which Dionysos, Apollo and Asklepios had active roles, I found myself saying: "I am beginning to feel more myself today than I did yesterday" or "I felt normal for part of yesterday." The familiar sense of myself drifted in and out at will like a dream that lingers in the daylight hours, nudging some awareness in my direction. I began to wait expectantly for those instances of a familiar self and grateful when they occurred on their own. I had no part in their arrival and withdrawal. I also began to be aware of the suffering of others, beginning with other patients whose open-door rooms I passed by when I walked in the early morning hours during my hospitalization. Some could not get out of bed; others chose not to. Their recovery was slow, their stay long, extended in large measure by their inability to achieve independence. I could not help but wonder if some had lost the will to live. I prayed for them as I walked the halls in my own recovery.

When I shambled behind my walker, I felt like I was taking small steps toward my former self somewhere in the foggy distance. Physical therapy at home continued this reclamation as strength began to flow within me, very possibly the energy of Apollo and his son through their ability to purify. I started to feel small impulses to return to tasks I had put on hold for two or more months but had shelved in the closet for the time being. I yearned and prayed for my former energy level to return. I thought of Dionysus in these instances as the force of energy itself, first drained out of me and now restored in slow beakers of strength.

Rituals' Healing Energies

Jung speaks of libido: "It really connotes *subjective intensity*. Anything potent, any content highly charged with energy, therefore has a wide range of symbolic meanings" (*CW* 5, par. 238). Perhaps the blood transfusion that became necessary during the surgery is another way that Apollo/Asklepios assisted in energizing the body once more. I sensed, developing slowly, a new relation to past-present-future that had been held at bay for months in the timeless fuzzy eternal present of a hospital stay and then at home. I felt at one point that I was waking from a coma—a state or condition of wearing a strange and vulnerable hospital wardrobe to make the body accessible around the clock to probes and tests. Reports of the blood migrating toward normalcy, free of contaminants, became more frequent with each visit to the infectious disease doctor.

I developed a regimen in the form of a ritual to assist my healing: daily leg exercises that were painful; remaining faithful to taking all drug prescriptions; not despairing when progress seemed to stall; accepting and reveling over tiny achievements, like finally being able to put on my left sock and shoe by myself; paying close attention to the body's functions coming back on-line; gaining confidence when I could take a shower and dry myself even partially; keeping the wound from the hip replacement clean—and so many more disciplined behaviors that slowly helped put my sense of self back into a story I could believe in with a familiar character in its starring role. I welcomed and relished each instance of normalcy. Ritualizing this process of reclamation made me conscious of each act rather than allowing them to be mechanical motions.

I credit Apollo the purifier for allowing me to put the pieces of my life into alignment. He was not alone in doing this, however. My memory returned partially and then more completely; it had been taken from me through the surgeries and the drugs, all in the service of allowing me to live. Normalcy, the mundane, the sustaining—these are treasures I had lost the ability to appreciate. Apollo helped restore them. I must also acknowledge in gratitude, however, the presence in Dionysos' nature, in his ability to re-member me as I grew more adept at re-membering my earlier sense of who I was.

Being dismembered by the god Dionysus can also, in the long run, be a form of healing where one did not even know one was wounded. My affliction and its accompanying surgeries, as well as the welcome road to recovery, made one idea existentially clear: each god and goddess has a place in our narrative, propelling them forward, warping their plot line, dismantling our sense of certainty and order, twisting the narrative to fit a design well beyond our own making. I like Edward Whitmont's way of understanding illness: "We could consider it instead of a disturbing calamity as meaningful dramatic crisis in an individual's life, as his or her way of being in the world and reciprocally interacting with the world." Such an attitude asks that healing "would then require discovering the inherent 'intent' of the crisis" (*The Alchemy of Healing* 35).

When the infectious disease doctor declared that he was going to remove the pic line from my left arm, I dreaded this procedure because of the length of the pic leading to my heart and the pain I assumed would attend its removal. The reality was that he slipped it out in a second, without pain or complication. At that moment I felt that Dionysus was liberating (loosening) me from his line of action. The experience has been a constant reminder of gifts we are each surrounded by, but that dismemberment is only an infection or an affliction away, always proximal as a symptom of our belief in control, separate from the invisible presences that haunt the phenomenal world. Such is the power and the beauty of the gods and goddesses who are always near and who always participate in shaping our ends, forget them however we dare.

I have recovered, some ten months after the original surgeries, but part of me has not returned and may never. I feel its absence. I think of it now as perhaps a price exacted by Dionysus for his visitation and Apollo and Asklepios for their curative presence. Perhaps when the gods visit us, they extract a fee, some coinage of ourselves for their active influence in our lives. I find that idea very comforting: having been charged something for divinities' visit and awakening. Perhaps I had to sacrifice that part of myself in order to make space for the memory of the gods—a re-membering of them as they graciously re-membered me.

Works Cited

Hillman, James. "On the Necessity of Abnormal Psychology: Athene and Ananke." *Facing the Gods*. Edited by James Hillman. Spring Publications, Inc., 1994. 1-38.

---"Dionysos in Jung's Writings." *Facing the Gods*. Edited by James Hillman. Spring Publications, Inc, 1994. 151-64.

---. Re*visioning Psychology*. New York: HarperCollins, 1992.

John of the Cross. *The Dark Night of the Soul. Wellsprings of Faith*. Barnes and Noble, 2005. 525-670.

Jung, C. G. "The Tavistock Lectures." *The Symbolic Life: Miscellaneous Writings. The Collected Works of C. G. Jung, CW* 18. Translated by R. F. C. Hull. Princeton UP, 1976.

---. "Commentary on the Secret of the Golden Flower." *Alchemical Studies, Vol. 13. The Collected Works of C. G. Jung*. Translated by R. F. C. Hull, and edited by Sir Herbert Read, Michael Fordham, et. al. Princeton UP, 1983. 1-56.

---. *Aion: Researches into the Phenomenology of the Self, Vol. 9, ii. The Collected Works of C. G. Jung*, edited by Sir Herbert Read, Michael Fordham, et. al. Princeton UP, 1968.

---. *Symbols of Transformation: An Analysis of the Prelude to a Case of Schizophrenia, Vol. 5. The Collected Works of C. G. Jung*, Second edition. Translated by R. F. C. Hull. Princeton UP, 1967.

---. *Mysterium Coniunctionis, CW* 14. *The Collected Works of C. G. Jung*. Second Edition. Translated by R. F. C. Hull, edited by Sir Herbert Read, Michael Fordham, et. al. Princeton UP, 1970.

Otto, Walter. *The Homeric Gods: The Spiritual Significance of Greek Religion*. Translated by Moses Hadas. Random House, 1979.

Rowland, Susan. *Remembering Dionysus: Revisioning Psychology and Literature in C. G. Jung and James Hillman*. Routledge, 2017.

Slattery, Dennis Patrick. *The Wounded Body: Remembering the Markings of Flesh*. State U New York P, 2000.

Whitmont, Edward C. *The Alchemy of Healing: Psyche and Soma*. North Atlantic Books, 1993.

10

◆●◆

MOSES:
THE MYTH AND THE FICTION

Moses, the inner light of revelation/lit up the top of Sinai, but the mountain/could not hold that light.

~ Rumi, *Delicious Laughter*, 44.

We might begin with a recollection: recall that moment, perhaps one of many, in which you strayed from your path because of curiosity over a burning bush that refused to consume itself and, like a force-field, drew you to it. This image carried such potency that you were willing to yield to where you were headed in order to sense its presence as some event that might just change all the terms of your heretofore well-planned life journey.

Psychologist James Hillman links this event to alchemy and to this first principle of a bush that burns but refuses to consume itself; moreover, he links Moses as founder of alchemy (*Mythic Figures* 285). Chapter 13, "Moses, Alchemy, Authority" became my burning bush as I journeyed through the essays of *Mythic Figures*. It stopped me in my tracks for reasons I am still sorting out, which is why I am writing about it—to give it a more comprehensible form.

In reading this volume, I paused to contemplate this figure of Moses, in large measure because James' imagination pushed me to think of this famous fierce personage beyond a biblical setting. Moses and other figures of the Bible often carry a moralistic veneer, but James sees in them figures with more than one psychological property, propensity and potency that opened something of my own history up for further scrutiny and reflection that was itself revelatory.

Second, and I cannot point to the exact line of print, this chapter brought forth a simple notion that perhaps you will not find surprising. Neither Moses nor any of the figures in this volume cannot exist without the fiction that shapes them, often developing more than one single capacity or psychological truth about their presence. Their identities assume mythic stature through the narrative that both forms and in-forms them.

Freeing the Forms

So, we are always being prodded to see and think in a double sense: in the same way as Michelangelo's famous observation that when he chisels into a block of stone, he is an archetypal liberator, intent on freeing the figure in the marble, the Moses in the myth, by chipping away at the extraneous stone that holds the figure captive. As aesthetic excavator, Michelangelo frees the figures(s) so they may draw their first breaths in the world; so too is the creation of chipping away a form of fiction that unleashes the figure, the myth deeply imbedded in the stone. It is a creativity by subtraction, a myth of removal to let the figure's presence shine.

Yes, I realize that mythic figures like Moses cannot be talked about, or perhaps should not be, without the stories that shape them, and then open themselves to be interpreted by its audience. I sense that James' own magnificent style of chipping away at the figure, excavating and liberating it from the stony confines of biblical exegesis—here of Moses—is in service of releasing the star of Exodus from the moralisms that have gathered like mortar around him, incarcerating him at times in marbleized familiarity. James, as if a Michelangelo of the psyche, sees imbedded in the rock of dogma, clichéd readings and unquestioned interpretations, more of the figure than the rest of us have been able to grasp on our own. His sculpting task is one of exposure, of letting into the light of day what has been encrusted in rock. By doing so, he discloses the link or connective tissue between the figure and the fictions that give rise to them and further, to the interpretations, angles of understanding and hunches which grow from the figure in the fiction.

One more notion here of what is taking place in the marbleized figure seeking both air and light. James writes in *Revisioning Psychology* that archetypal psychology follows "the method he [Plotinus] also initiated called 'reversion,' (*epistrophe*)—the idea that all things desire to return to the archetypal originals of which they are copies and from which they proceed" (99). It brings me to wonder if the desire underlying Michelangelo's artistic intent may be in part to return the sculpted figure of Moses from the stone and onto a path back to its prototype?

So, I wonder: where does the myth of Moses reside? Is it in the fictions and historical renderings of him, wherein in the "early Arab alchemist Jabir or Geber refers to Moses as alchemy's founder" (*Mythic Figures* 286), that begins a tradition "through the Medieval period . . . so that 'by the seventeenth century, the belief that Moses was a great alchemist was so widespread'" according to Raphael Patai, that writers "found it necessary to combat it" (286).

Yet another place of confluence and/or confusion regarding the meaning of Moses occurs in Michelangelo's statue of Moses, a figure "with the horns of an animal-man. Another alchemical transformation: the bull, not destroyed but restored and emblematic in Moses himself" (*Mythic Figures* 286). Now we are in the story of the story, the angle of vision or the facts or events; we are in, to use James' language, "mythical history, in the civilization of the psyche and in the monotheistic theology of nature . . . " (286).

Here is the burning bush's arena or field of mythic formulation because the quest is to find meaning in the figure through the fictions that enwomb him and, reverting back to the carving itself, the stone that had entombed him before Michelangelo's genius and skill safely removed him. He is birthed by subtraction.

Are, then, the figure and the fiction not unrelated but not synonymous? Is the power of myth to show or reveal how the figure is greater (or less than?) the fictions that shape it and give it the formative heft to instruct our psychic curiosity? Finally, what of the parts of the fiction, say of Moses, that we leave out or have not yet discovered? Do they not reconfigure the fictional image that is Moses to provide yet other stones or layers to this mythic architecture? Can a work of art, then, ever be exhausted, especially if its mythic dimensions are as deep in the historical psyche as is the figure of Moses?

Moses and Mimesis

After reviewing a series of legends, all of which contribute to a portrait of Moses, or, better said, to the mosaic of Moses (for James' methodology is to create mosaics into which we are invited to craft our own meanings), he returns to the literal events in the Biblical account: "Moses goes up the mountain, returns with tablets, finds the people worshipping the bull, falls into a rage, destroys the tablets, slaughters the back-sliders, again goes up the mountain, and returns with new tablets, which we know as the Ten Commandments" (*Mythic Figures* 288).

In the plot is the myth, writes James in *Healing Fiction*. Whenever we see plot, read mythos, after Aristotle, he suggests (11). May the mythic figure in all of his plot-lined presence offer an occasion or an opportunity for us to see into the patterns in its plot that defines the figure and, at the same time, invite us to analogize ourselves into these same patterns?

Can we then discern when it is we invent qualities or capacities of Moses, or any mythic figure, that transports us out of bounds of that figure to create something or someone new, including ourselves? Is this itself not a form of mythologizing? It also appears to be analogous to what occurs when "a person crosses the threshold into therapy, a whole new story begins—or rather, the former story has an entirely new slant as the original tale is re-visioned into the therapeutic genre" (*Healing Fiction* 16). We have entered at this moment the terrain of art therapy, of a rich healing plot.

I am more aware now of recognizing James' genius as it expresses itself in his ability to create a psycho-poetic field around this mythic figure. Moses resonates for me at a certain frequency that his figure did not contain before these pages. James' task so often is to shift our awareness to these presences that are mimetic of our own and others' conditions, stories and situations. His genius, furthermore, is his capacity to shape our imaginations in order that their dispositions allow us to see from an angle that is unique to mythic consciousness.

He offers several examples of the above, one of which appears toward the end of the chapter. For James, the crafting of the golden calf is the highlight of all the alchemical moments in the Moses narrative; the Israelites' great sin is one of "'having made a god of gold,' the golden calf— not the sin of killing his son and his brother . . . " (*Mythic Figures* 289). I want to consider in a moment that the burning bush and its transformative power might also be selected at the most alchemical moment of his journey into leadership. But first an observation on mimesis.

James conjectures that this moment of Moses berating his people for their idolatry "replicates the great divide presented in many mythologies where the animal is severed from the divine. Theology is born, and religion as we know it, its piety, its spiritual abstractions, credos and laws, . . ." (*Mythic Figures* 289). In the particulars arise the pattern, to be discerned throughout mythic history and in the exigencies of our own plot. In this field of deeper awareness, Moses assumes for me:

- A new way of seeing
- A form of understanding more deeply
- A form of me in disguise
- A guide that can lead me closer to the *anima mundi*, whose terrain may be the harsh desert of austerity before any sightings of the rich nourishments—most archetypally, both milk and honey
- An upending, in sections, of my own personal mythos
- A tilting of the abnormal towards a normative stance
- A place, a setting and a disposition in which myth and history meet and mingle to create a *tertium quid*: the third thing is meaning itself

James's insights and his way of reading the myth of Moses through history, legend, conjecture and archetypal interpretation now lead me back (reversion) to the story he does not entertain: the burning bush, there to perhaps discover something of the Moses journey that structures all of his subsequent actions. That is only a hunch, but it is my way of enacting his engagement with the same figure; my hope is that some coherence will accrue from this exploration.

If *poiesis* is a crafting of ourselves into a coherent form, then that form embodies a felt sense of co-herence: we listen closely in silence and hear something, some messing with the familiar and expected. As we move through the world, one day we come to a burning bush that does not consume itself; out from its benevolent flames emerges first the voice of an angel. I want to entertain the idea that it may be a voice of co-herance.

Destiny's Craftiness

The second book of the Old Testament, Exodus, records Israel's birth as a nation (Ex. 1:1-22). But as we read it closely, we see that such a birth requires an antecedent; that antecedent is the birth of Moses, and it arrives in the form of a voice first in the appearance of an angel of the Lord, who appears to him in a flame of fire in the midst of a bush (Ex. 3:2). Now one may call it a miraculous flame, or a flame of paradox, because it does not consume what it has engulfed, contrary to the laws of nature. C. G. Jung uses the term *opus contra naturam* to distinguish this dual reality in one as well as the reversal of nature's laws (*CW* 13, par. 414).

I can go with that, but want to add that it is a mythic flame, perhaps even the presence of the flame of myth itself. It is the flame of awareness, of presentness, of the impulse to create, and it appears along the path that Moses trods. The flame is no longer following the dictates of nature's law but of another world's format. It is the flame that arouses curiosity, that stops one in one's tracks to ponder mystery itself; that is why I think it is the flame of myth. Persevering with a myth may eventually point us towards mystery, the ineffable, even; for Joseph Campbell, the transcendent (*Thou Art That* 18).

Moses tries to look at the bush burning; God's voice calls to him from the midst of it: "Moses, Moses," and he answered, "here I am" (Ex. 3:3). We can puzzle over why God calls his name twice; are there at this instance two Moses, the one who is about to perish and the other who is about to begin a new life, more consciously unfolding his own myth? God tells him He has come to deliver his people out of Egypt, to a land flowing with those archetypal nutrients, milk and honey, products of nature rather than culture.

Then he calls on Moses to be the instrument of this Divine plan. Moses' response is as rich as the earlier nutrients promised. "Who am I that I should go to Pharaoh, that I should bring the children of Israel, out of Egypt?" (Ex. 3:11). "Who am I?" is crucial, for he does not know; being called is a moment of instrumental import, when one is willing to be an instrument of something one is called to do but not really understanding the terms motivating this action.   Such a yielding, myths reveal, often leads to a fuller sense of one's self-identity. Campbell reminds us that when the hero heeds the call, s/he makes an act of the will to give oneself over to something beyond the self in that vocation: "A blunder—apparently the merest chance—reveals an unsuspected world, and the individual is drawn into a relationship with forces that are not rightly understood" (*Hero* 42). It is a vocative moment; being willing to be instrumental, but not incidental, is the crucial instance of yielding that originates the formation of a coherent life. In Exodus resides the shards of Genesis.

Coherence is the by-product of a destiny; destiny is the occasion of a willing response to something outside oneself and at the same time is the noblest impulse within oneself. As James develops Michelangelo's Moses status as an example of the alchemical dictate, *solve et coagula*, where fluid solidifies and "where what is solidified must be dissolved" (*Mythic Figures* 290), so with the instance of the burning bush. Moses solidifies in his fear and liquifies in his assent to God's plan. As out there, so in here, to paraphrase Heraclitus.

Initially, Moses asks: "Who am I?" which brings into question his entire complex identity, to which God tells him *what to do,* not *how to be.* "Gather the elders of Israel together; tell them you will bring them out of the affliction of Egypt to a land of Canaanites and others" (Ex. 4:1). To be called, the story intimates, may be to heal a wound, an affliction, an injustice; one's orbit expands out of oneself to embrace others; in that act alone is a profound liberation from self-absorption, including personal needs and desires.

Deficits Point to The Middle Way

God continues by telling Moses that they will heed his voice; but Moses' doubts end-stop his acceptance of the calling. He waffles: "But suppose they will not believe me or listen to my voice; suppose they say 'the Lord has not appeared to you?'" (Ex. 4:1). The Lord then offers Moses a sign: He tells him to drop the rod he carries on the ground. It immediately morphs into a serpent. Moses picks it up by the tail, at which it suddenly transforms back into a rod. Sufficiently unimpressed because his fear is so great, he then scurries to another excuse to avoid the call: "But I am not eloquent neither before or since you have spoken to your servant. I am slow of speech and slow of tongue'" (Ex. 4:10).

Something new opens here in this vocation; precisely where Moses believes he is deficient is the very soft spot in himself he must enter to create a coherent life by yielding to this task of freeing his people. Any journey into the world is simultaneously a pilgrimage into one's own interior self and here, into one's own inferior self, the desert where one's fears can gnaw a hole in one's soul.

I would italicize here that vocation is a form of vacation: one is called to vacate one's own plans or one's self-absorption or fear-based hesitation, in order to enter into the spirit of another, to expand one more plausibly into his/her full nature, which occurs when one has enough heart (courage) to relinquish it. Now we are deeply enmeshed in the terrain of myth. Where one's soft spot is, where one feels most deficient, inferior and vulnerable frequently marks the territory s/he must step into.

Anyone of us could easily recite a story about this paradoxical moment in our formation. It may be our most sacred ground in the geography of our destiny. Destiny does not often play to our strengths but to our vulnerabilities; part of the reason that a true calling is so transformative is its insistence in pushing us to confront the less vital, more imperfect aspects of our being. Moses' fear rears up in him at this moment: "Lord, please send someone by the hand of whoever else you may send" (Ex. 4:13). The Lord grows impatient with Moses' deflection of his destiny and presses him. He calls up Moses' brother Aaron. "'I know he can speak well. He comes to meet you. Now you shall speak to him and put the words in his mouth. And I will be with your mouth and with his mouth, and I will teach you what you shall do'" (Ex. 4:15).

From mouth to mouth is a mythic move. I realize I am jumping from the Hebraic to the Greek world in what follows. In Greek, *muthos* means mouth and is the origin of the word *mythos*. So, when we open our mouth to speak, we are exhaling our *muthos*. If we allow this jump to the Greek etymology of the word *myth*, then what we speak to another is co-heard; in the process one's own *muthos* coheres in the hearing. No matter what we say or how we say it, our lexical landscape is brought into performance. James offers this insight: "But a mythos is more than a theory and more than a plot. It is the tale of the interaction of humans and the divine. To be in a mythos is to be inescapably linked with divine powers, and moreover, to be in mimesis with them" (*Healing Fiction* 11).

We note that Moses' brother Aaron is to be Moses' mouthpiece, his spokesman; so, the following dynamic cooperative equation emerges:

God---Moses
Becomes
Moses---Aaron

As Moses is God's instrument, so Aaron is Moses' instrument; the divine-human coherence is now replicated or mimed in the human-human conjoining. As the Lord observes, "So he shall be your spokesman to the people. And he himself shall be as a mouth for you, and you shall be to him as God" (Ex. 4:16). What an extraordinary compromise between human and divine figures intent on saving an entire people by assisting them in their epic escape!

What are we to discern here? To be called is not an act of isolation, even while it may take place in solitude. It is more one of communion, of *communitas* in the word of Victor Turner (*The Ritual Process* 111). We are beckoned or summoned into elevating ourselves beyond our self-imposed limits. I believe that to be called is not only vocational but fundamentally an act of faith, to which each of us is invited, not compelled, to make a leap. "And Aaron spoke all the words that which the Lord had spoken to Moses" (Ex. 4:30). Aaron echoes the words of God that Moses heard and then relates to his brother. Perhaps Aaron himself is being called as mediator between God's commands and his brother's compromise. So, any of our callings may implicate others who are called to vocate another's calling. Calling may be, more often than not, a call of one or more to a community with a common vision. Our calling is not only to a content of *doing* but to a context of *being* and then, further, of being-in-relation with others.

The exchange above reveals that we are con-textual beings; the texture of our lives in and out of callings will frequently engage us in a social context with others: communal—collegial—and connatural. As with the case of God, Moses and his brother, this trinity forms what C. G. Jung calls an archetypal situation; it is, in addition, one of transformation (*CW* 9, i par. 80), for to be called is often an invitation to enter the wilderness, the desert, the forest or the unknown landscape—the terrain of fairy tales, myths, legends and classic works of literature film and painting. But it is most often an analogy to one's inner landscape or terrain. One may be called within a solitary space, but the calling is social and, more largely contextual.

Moses' alchemical transformation begins with his curiosity that draws him towards the burning bush. The call we receive is not the road of comforts, clear street signs and well-lit affirming arrows pointing us to the right route or in any specific direction. Quite the contrary: Campbell reminds us that "one may be only casually strolling, when some passing phenomenon catches the wandering eye and lures one away from the frequented paths of man" (*Hero* 48). The implication here is that to stay on the frequented path is to follow the paths of others while abandoning one's true destiny. Moses finds a middle road between the two and successfully stewards his people toward a new mythic landscape and a new beginning in freedom. We are cautioned through the story of Moses not to give much oxygen to a path that deflects us from our authentic pilgrimage.

Works Cited

Campbell, Joseph. *The Hero with a Thousand Faces.* New World Library, 2008.

---. *Thou Art That: Transforming Religious Metaphor.* Edited by Eugene Kennedy. New World Library, 2001.

Hillman, James. *Mythic Figures. Uniform Edition of the Writings of James Hillman.* Volume 6. 1. Introduction by Joanne H. Stroud. Spring Publications, Inc, 2007.

---. *Revisioning Psychology.* New York: HarperPerennial Publishers, 1992.

---. *Healing Fiction.* Spring Publications, 1983.

Holy Bible (1982). *Containing the Old and New Testaments. New King James Version.* Nelson Bibles, 1982.

Jung, C. G. *The Archetypes and the Collective Unconscious, Vol. 9, i. The Collected Works of C. G. Jung.* Edited and translated by R. F. C. Hull and Gerhard Adler, Second edition. Princeton UP, 1971.

---. *Alchemical Studies, CW* 13. *The Collected Works of C. G. Jung.* Translated by R. F. C. Hull, edited by Sir Herbert Read, Michael Fordham, et. al., Princeton UP, 1977.

Rumi. *Delicious Laughter: Rambunctious Teaching Stories from the Mathnawi of Jelladin Rumi.* Translated by Coleman Barks, with John Moyne, A. J. Arberry and Reynold Nicholson. Maypop Books, 1990.

Turner, V. (2008). *The Ritual Process: Structure and Anti-Structure.* Transaction Publishers, 2008.

11

──────◆●◆──────

THE HEROIC AND HEALTH: EXPLORING PARKINSON'S DISEASE*

One has to remain pretty critical and independent about all ideas. Come to one's own conclusions on a basis of one's own frank experience.

~ Thomas Merton, *The Intimate Merton,* 114.

Years ago, I was invited by a colleague at another university in Santa Barbara to contribute a paper to a journal entitled *Literature and Medicine: Writers with Chronic Illness.* I accepted her offer and wrote an essay exploring the Russian writer Fyodor Dostoevsky's epilepsy to see if the disease affected his fiction. His dates are 1821-1881. I remember reading long ago as I worked on a dissertation on his novel, *The Idiot* (1870) that he contracted the disease and had his first seizure in Siberia where he was sentenced for several years for being present at a meeting of dissidents during the Russian Regime's crackdown on protestors challenging its oppressive mandates.

I wondered, as I began to write, if epilepsy, as an illness had its own autonomy and whether it was completely accurate to ask: Did Dostoevsky *have* epilepsy or was it more effective to pose: Did epilepsy *have*

───────────────

* Originally presented as "The Heroic and Health" to a group of Parkinson clients in a program directed by Robert Cochran of The University of Las Vegas. March 2020.

Dostoevsky? And the bigger question for this discussion: what can he do with it and about it? What he decided to do was create in the novel mentioned above a character, Prince Lyov Myshkin, who embodies epilepsy and who has in the course of the action several epileptic seizures. In fact, in many cases, the disease sets the beat of the narrative pulse and takes on a voice of its own in the narrative. The disease, I came to realize, had its own story to tell.

Ronald Frankenberg, a sociologist who has studied chronic illness, explores what he calls "sickness as a cultural performance"; he suggests that "chronic illness, whether continual or . . . spasmodic, leads clearly to a different and perhaps more complicated way of being sick. It requires a different and longer-lasting and more demanding cultural performance" (qtd. in "Seized by the Muse" 80). Each disease, he writes, has its own behavior and is acted out by the patient through its own metaphorical language and style. I would add that it may not be understood through biography and biology, but that it also contains a mythopoetic dimension, i.e., a formed expression of some values, beliefs and destinies living within a person or an entire people. It has and is, in short, a bio-mythic entity.

Disease as Destiny

But to return to Dostoevsky's own illness. Disease is part of that myth to which Dostoevsky gives form through his own illness, one that includes both the imaginative power of the artist and the autonomy of the illness. Both of these forces, it must be noted, begin in the body, in the relation of the flesh to the world. The body may be understood as the first and original metaphor that incites the creative act and is the origin of myth itself.

Mythologist Joseph Campbell ends his rich discussion of myth, ritual and culture with the observation that the body is the originary locus for mythology. There exists a deep correlation between biology and mythology. He writes that "from society as a whole the individual can only be an organ" (*Hero* 383). The individual can only be a part, but is indeed a composite of the culture/society that formed him: "through the past of that society descended the genes that built his body" (*Hero* 383). From his observations we can surmise that the myth embedded in the ill body may therefore be a greater influence on Dostoevsky (or any of us with such a condition) and his writing than the more intentional aspects of his craft.

Within the body, healthy or ill, myths germinate and seek expression. This disease is a response, or a symptom in its dual expression, to something Dostoevsky diagnosed as ill in the Petersburg community. In the novel, *The Idiot,* the disease enters in the figures of both Prince Myshkin and his dark, shadowy double, a young man by the name of Parfyon Rogozhin, to break open what has become fixed and deadened. It is a world that is petty, obsessed with economics and social success, full of self-interest as it promotes a total disregard for the sacred qualities of Mother Russia herself.

Personally, Dostoevsky constantly scrutinized his disease and was alternately fascinated and repulsed by it. He was attracted to it for its "ecstatic aura," that instant just before the convulsions and the unconsciousness that attended the seizure. He could also feel the onset of the attack, which would be proceeded by "an indescribable sense of well-being that might be present for a few moments." After the attack, the writer would experience intense depression and guilt, "which might last for several days" (qtd. in "Dostoevsky's Convulsive Poetics" 64). As he presents it in *The Idiot,* epilepsy is a disease of verticality, of extremes of high and low, conjuring images of lofty Swiss mountains and plunging waterfalls, and of depressingly deep falls into underworld darkness. That it is referred to as "the falling sickness" tells us its direction, the movement of the body as it pulls the individual having the seizure to the ground in an uncontrollable release of energy. It is a disease of verticality, of excessive highs and lows.

Writing *The Idiot* may have enacted a ritual of healing for the writer. As one of the most profound psychological novelists, he shares with the psychologist Russell Lockhart the belief that there is a close relationship between the psyche, myth and illness and that the power of disease finds its way into psyche's images, often in the form of wounds, dreams and fantasies, and certainly in the active disease (qtd. in "Seized" 65).

Somatic Sapience

I will share my own narratives of illness, surgeries and slow returns to some sense of normalcy in a moment. For now, let's think about both human embodiment and the image of the heroic as rich metaphors that can guide us, even reveal the inklings of a path forward. Every illness is itself a journey and a destination that we have some say-so about, even at times when we think that we are nothing more than a victim of circumstance, of inheritance, of bad luck or a random set of conditions. So, before we move into this arena, let me share with you a few ideas and convictions that Joseph Campbell came to in working with the body therapist Stanley Keleman in a set of dialogues gathered in a book, *Myth and the Body*.

Both men agree that each of us is on a somatic journey. Myths often center on just such a pilgrimage. They also agree that that the body is also a spiritual locus, a place of the sacred that needs tending, whether one is healthy or ill or migrating between both of these poles. I have discovered over the years that a disruption in my normal body functioning brings front and center my "internal somatic reality" (*Myth* xiv). It moves from being normally on the horizon of consciousness to blasting into front-and-center of my consciousness. For a time, nothing else matters than the journey towards diagnosis. Campbell writes in this regard that "the hero's journey is a way—a via—of grasping our own somatic destiny. The value of experience is a somatic, mythic reality" (*Myth* xiv).

Myths, he suggests later, "describes the experience of the body; they are in fact metaphors for internal bodily states, experiences and development. Myths help the body to organize and incorporate experience" (*Myth* xv). Now this word *in-corporation* suggests a knowing-by-being embodied. This includes a mythic consciousness, a mythic awareness. He writes, "Mythology is a function of biology, a product of the soma's imagination. What do our bodies say, what do they tell us?" (*Myth* 3). We can extend his thinking and question: Does my illness have a voice? Does it want us to know about its reality in other than a medical way? Further, does an illness like Parkinson's or the bacterial infections I contracted years ago have a knowledge that affects the very beingness that we are? These are questions that invite deep responses from us. And one more:

What narratives and what dreams arise out of our illnesses? Are there particular kinds of narratives as useful analogies of the illness we must learn ways to live with, even to befriend?

Does an illness also have the capacity to define or redefine our core identities? Do we have control over this redefinition and/or can we become free agents to further cultivate our own self-definition? I think that right here may be the locus for the heroic as a way of being and of knowing. I find extremely useful what Campbell suggests a few pages later: "Myth is structured in the cells. Each sperm cell, each egg, contains a story that is recreated in the full growth of each cell. This is part of our history as well as our destiny. Myth is about the body's journey, recreating endlessly in a particular way, to form an individual personal structure called the Self" (*Myth* 6).

I do not believe illness, chronic or otherwise, forbids us from being a part of that formation so that we are not simply passengers on the journey of our life, but full crew members. We must not surrender our presence in the wheel house of our own ship. The heroic may be just the best metaphor to adapt, perhaps in one of its formats, the warrior—a warrior for health, a warrior for improvising and thus improving our place within the landscape of our illness.

Ask yourself right now: who or what was your childhood hero or heroes? What did they offer you? In what ways did they give you hope? Or give you models of behavior and thought to emulate? One of mine was not the Lone Ranger but his milder alter-ego, Tonto. I liked his quiet assurance. He was like a therapist or minister to the flashier Lone Ranger: "Kemosabe," meaning friend. He was a counter-weight to the smart but often a bit compulsive white guy dressed in white, riding a white horse, Silver, with the dramatic aura of the mask to deflect his full identity. But Tonto was more akin to a Zen-presence, soft-spoken, carrying the wisdom of his people, imparting his myth to the white one. That too is an authentic form of the heroic.

In *The Hero's Journey* Campbell reveals that the hero "can give what the human spirit needs, perhaps less than what the human spirit wants." The hero's fundamental quest is not to attack or to show force. "And one part of the mythological motif of the hero's journey is acquiescence" (12). The heroic, as a fundamental archetypal image in the human psyche is shared by cultures across time and space from the beginning: "a kind of bliss consciousness or high energy form seems to come through people" (23). This is the terrain of a calm resoluteness, where one can thoughtfully plan and then honor a life that allows so much more in than a defect, an illness, a disability—all of which can define us completely if we permit it.

I believe a heroic journey is predicated in large measure on what choices we can see as possible, and if not immediately, then eventually. It also includes a sober assessment of what is perhaps out of range right now. What, then, one might ask, will you spend the greatest share of your energy on? Campbell reminds us that "one part of the hero's quest as a mythological motif is acquiescence—to yield to the dynamic of life but to always be reevaluating what this dynamic is comprised of both in force and intensity.

One of the choices that becomes present in your hero's journey is: what are you willing to be satisfied with and what limits do you impose on yourself? Then, what limitations does the illness impose on you and do you yield to them completely, or can you shift their terms in any way? These decisions themselves implicate the heroic code because they are not just biological but psychological and mythological matters as well. Let's use Campbell's language here: "Mythology relates psychological structures to the circumstances of objective life in the world today" (*Hero's* 43). We don't want to miss how myth is a relational element in our lives, a mediator as well as a guide. To assess this fairly, Campbell suggests, "you have to learn to recognize your own depths" (*Hero's* 49).

My Story

It was early morning like so many others, June of 2020. I had gotten up to use the bathroom. When I urinated, it stung harshly. I had no idea what was going on. I felt fine, but I instinctively knew that something was wrong. I went back to bed and tried to sleep. After about an hour I used the bathroom again and noted that the pain had increased.

In the morning I called my doctor; she told me she would meet me outside her office and evaluate me without my leaving my vehicle, a precaution because of the Covid-19 virus. I agreed. But later in the morning I began to shake with fever and chills. I knew I was in trouble because I had experienced something similar three years ago while teaching at Pacifica Graduate Institute in Carpinteria, California. That chill and fever was akin to this recent one: sepsis. Left untreated, it can kill one in a short time. My wife drove me to the ER at our local hospital. They kept me for six hours, found nothing, drew a blood sample, and released me with a prescription for a urinary tract infection. I began the prescription right away.

The next morning the hospital called to tell me that the blood cultures they took the previous day showed *e coli* in my blood and to report to the hospital immediately to begin a 24/7 round of high-octane antibiotics. I was there within an hour and admitted. I spent three days with round-the-clock antibiotics to rid my blood of *e coli* that had seeped in from my gut to my bloodstream.

After three days I was released; the next week I saw my urologist. He put me on a medication that I had stopped taking in order to help with urinating all of what was in my bladder. After almost a week, I felt like I was out of the woods. I did not know, nor could know, that I was about to enter another forest where there is no clear path—the paradox of the pathless path. Be careful about the desire to say "I am out of the woods"! From a mythological perspective, one may be just beginning the ordeal.

That Saturday I felt fine until my wife and I had dinner. Almost immediately after it, I felt a strong compression on my chest. I thought for sure I was having a heart attack. My wife drove me for the third time to the ER where the nurse gave me nitroglycerin, which helped ease the chest pain. They then admitted me once again.

For two days the hospital staff ran blood cultures until they found the culprit. It was an angry and exhausted gall bladder, full of gall stones and was adversely affecting the liver—dangerous stuff. I was scheduled for surgery in two days. They allowed me to return home until that Wednesday morning, when I would report for the fourth time to the hospital for a surgery to remove the gall bladder at noon. I was deeply into the journey of illness, with health the desired goal but with no guarantees. The surgery was successful and I went home that evening, exhausted but overjoyed to be sleeping in my own bed again. Then came the new journey of reclaiming as much of my former level of stamina as I could.

I want to bring up exercise at this juncture. During each of these stays when I was admitted as a patient, and except for the day when I had the surgery, I walked the Surgery Floor of the hospital with my IV pole dripping fluids into me. I set up a regimen: three times a day for fifteen minutes, or as close as I could get to it. I believed that this action was under my control; as long as my balance was good and I wore a mask, the nurses permitted me to circle the perimeters of their station. I always felt better after these walks and believe they helped me sleep better at night, even with constant interruptions by a nurse to draw more blood.

During the Covid-19 virus's initial invasion and then acceleration, I was advised by my doctor not to frequent our community recreation center to swim laps, a favorite form of exercise. So, I began to walk about an hour and 15 minutes each afternoon until the Texas heat forced me to shift to the early mornings before the scorching heat of the day. I believe fidelity to that regimen helped me navigate all these trials.

Now, in this healing stage and some 20 pounds lighter, I began each day walking for 15 minutes before exhaustion set in. I paced myself and over weeks I worked back up to one hour, walking every day. I know this has helped me in countless ways, not the least of which was an attitude towards my own health as well as recovered feelings of well-being. I sensed that my recovery was largely my body's own healing, but it needed my own active engagement in the process. The hero's journey is always a tension between outside forces and interior acts of the will and imagination. Walking in slowly-increasing increments was an act of imagination as well as a desire to regain my earlier sense of self.

Every illness is a form of a journey within; every recovery, as much as is possible and realistic, is also a journey. Both can be labelled heroic, heroic in wisdom in making realistic choices, heroic in staying with a plan that you had a voice in designing, and heroic in achieving outcomes that you set for yourself, and heroic in not descending into victimhood. What it also offers and includes in your life is a ritual. Rituals link biology to mythology; rituals are embodied forms of giving both space and boundaries to values held deeply. Rituals help us reclaim something we believe is crucial to our well-being. Campbell reminds us that "ritual is the way mythology is integrated into a life" (*Hero's* 205). We need rituals to further embody the myths we are living and to help us negotiate those myths as they age. Periodically, our myths need to be rejuvenated to reflect our development.

So may the forces and energies of myth be with you to aid your continuing journey as you both question and confirm what is essential to lead a life rich in meaning and purpose.

Works Cited

Campbell, Joseph. *The Hero with a Thousand Faces.* Bollingen Series XVII. Princeton UP, 1973.

Cousineau, Phil, editor. *The Hero's Journey: Joseph Campbell on His Life and Work.* New World Library, 1990

Dostoevsky, Fyodor. *The Idiot.* Translated by Constance Garnett, revised by Avrahm Yarmolinsky. Heritage Edition, 1966.

Keleman, Stanley. *Myth and the Body: A Colloquy with Joseph Campbell.* Center Press, 1999.

Hart, Patrick and Jonathan Montaldo, editors. *The Intimate Merton: His Life from His Journals.* HarperSanFrancisco, 1999.

Slattery, Dennis Patrick. *The Idiot: Dostoevsky's Fantastic Prince. A Phenomenological Approach.* Peter Lang, 1983.

---. "Seized by the Muse: Dostoevsky's Convulsive Poetics." *Literature and Medicine,* edited by Marilyn Chandler McEntyre. Vol. 18, Number One, Spring 1999. Johns Hopkins UP, 1999. 60-81.

12

---◆●◆---

JOSEPH CAMPBELL AND THE QUESTING SELF: PART I CREATIVITY, COHERENCE AND TRANSFORMATIONS OF THE SELF*

Myth comes in the same zone as dream, and this is the zone of what I would call the Wisdom Body. When you go to sleep, it's the body that's talking.

~ Joseph Campbell, *Transformations of Myth Through Time*, 94.

Welcome to this Questing Conference on the mythological thinking of the most famous mythologist of the last century: Joseph Campbell. I am grateful to each and every one of you for making the investment, on many levels, to be here. Without you, quite obviously, there would be no gathering.

I want to state my intentions up front. I am going to present to you, from Campbell's vast storehouse of material, what has interested me over the years in teaching a course on him and his work in the Mythological Studies Program at Pacifica Graduate Institute. His range is vast and deep, so I have chosen to present those arenas of myth that have sparked my desire to take them further, to see what the implications of his insights

---

* The first of two chapters to be presented to a retreat, "Questing for Our Personal Myth: Writing, Remembering and Renewing Our Story Through the Teachings of Joseph Campbell." Hotel Santa Fe, New Mexico, May 12-15, 2022.

contain, and to make whatever attracts you a vital, organic part of your own mythic path.

I don't plan to spend time rehearsing his history, his path in the world. If you are interested, there is the fine authorized biography by Stephen and Robin Larsen entitled *A Fire in the Mind,* originally published in 1991 and reprinted a number of times. My main interest, however, is in Campbell's own words as he explores, for the better part of a lifetime, the lineaments of both cultural and personal myths as well as how history affects and is affected by mythic developments and migrations.

But it is important to think about several of the major influences on Campbell's thinking, including C. G. Jung, Oswald Spengler, James Joyce, Thomas Mann and Heinrich Zimmer. There was, as well "a new luminary" to be added to the list, as the Larsens write *(Fire* 224); he too would play an important part in Campbell's subsequent life and thought: Leo Frobenius (1873-1938). He was an ethnographer and prolific author whom Campbell met when he arrived in America in 1973.

One of Frobenius' most enduring ideas, the Larsens inform us, one that had inspired Jung and others, "was the intriguing worldwide distribution of the 'night sea journey' of the solar hero. As does the sun, the human hero must fall cyclically into the watery abyss, meet his antithesis in effect, and arise once again, transformed through the encounter with the power of the underworld. Here are hints of the symbolic identity of womb and tomb, the chthonic enclosure of origins and destinies repeated continually; it is a theme that not only pervades mythologies all over the earth, but makes it seem as if everybody—not only the world of nature, but the human world and the world of the gods and goddesses—recycles" *(Fire* 226).

Now Campbell caught fire; he read all 15 volumes, the Larsens write, and the whole idea fell into place. Campbell writes in his "War Journal": I learned that the essential form of the myth is a cycle, and that this cycle is a symbolic representation of the form of the soul, and that in the dreams and fancies of modern individuals (who have been brought up along the lines of a rational, practical education) these myth-symbols actually reappear—giving testimony of a persistence, even into modern times, of the myth power" (qtd. in *Fire* 226).

The Larsens go on to observe that in the above quote "we have the first formulation of that informing energy which would later make its way to the cover of Campbell's best-selling book, *The Power of Myth*" (1988). I remember reading it in 1990 following the multi-part series on PBS with Bill Moyers, another cultural gift to us. Something changed in me in reading it and listening to the series more than once. Here, I thought in some unconscious way, is the bridge material that links to areas of interests of mine that I have carried for several decades: Myth is the lynchpin between psyche and poetics, between Jungian depth psychology, followed by James Hillman's magnificent work in archetypal psychology, and the classics of poetry that I have enjoyed rereading and teaching for 30 years. Myth as mucilage, as cement, as glue, that unites the creative spirit to psycho-poetic structures.

Campbell is very clear about myth's terrain: "Myth is not the same as history. Myth is the transcendent in relationship to the present. . . . The myth provides a field in which you can locate yourself . . . the sense of the mandala" (*Pathways to Bliss* xvi). Campbell uses the word "power" and C. G. Jung uses the words "energy" and "energic." But both are interested in the centering force of an organic, vital myth. You might ask yourself: "Where is the most vital energy in my life, my body, right now, and what is it in service of?" Meditating on that will open up where your myth is and what it is serving to give your life both purpose and coherence. Coherence is a guiding light in our lives, propelled by the myth one is living.

One citation from Jung may help us here. "What Campbell and Jung share and what mimesis adumbrates, is a relation of movement, or perhaps better said, a relational motion, whose nature and structure is captured and embellished in metaphor" (*Creases in Culture* 11). Jung relates early in his discussion of psychic energy, that in "the energic point of view . . ., some kind of energy underlies the changes in phenomena, that it maintains itself as a constant throughout these changes, and leads finally to entropy, a condition of general equilibrium" (qtd. in *Creases* 11). Let's swing back to Campbell at this juncture.

The Larsens comment on Campbell's grasp of myths: "The whole notion is that myths—transformations of deep structures into living images—are indeed possessed of power, and such tenacity that despite their acceptance or rejection by the dominant culture, they are still found in people's lives—their dreams and visions, their compulsions, their ecstasy and their madness" (*Fire* 226). To have a certain madness inform your life signals the presence of a mythic awareness.

As Campbell discovered these deep archetypal patterns in the psyche and throughout history, he experienced a sea change in his life's work, writing, "The emphasis of my studies shifted from the historical to the mythological. I began to read, with fresh understanding, the novels of Thomas Mann and the *Ulysses* of James Joyce. The role of the artist I now understood as that of revealing through the world-surfaces the implicit forms of the soul, and the great agent to assist the artist in this work was the myth" (*Fire* 226). Campbell's *augenblick*, his pregnant moment, was in discovering the wisdom within the image.

Perhaps, then, we take a few central ideas from *The Power of Myth*, since we are engaging it right here. I will stay located in the second chapter, "The Journey Inward" (37-60) because that is one of our central themes for this conference: All of the mythic images from one culture to another are most often telling the same story, but inflected in different ways by that people's cultural mythology as well as their placement in history. Campbell finds most fascinating "that they are speaking about the deep mystery of yourself and everything else. It is a mysterium . . . tremendous, horrific, because it smashes all of your fixed notions of things, and at the same time utterly fascinating, because it's of your own nature and being . . ." (*Power* 39).

Characteristics of Myth and Poetics

I like this chapter for a number of reasons. One is that Campbell goes back and scoops up so much of what animated him in the study of my-thologies. Let me list a few:

1. He explores the relation of mythology to biology—which of course implicates the historical ground of all of us. Our bodies' continual morphing and changing ushers in various new facets of our personal myth. Limitations, illnesses, surgeries, incapacities—all of these can be strengths as we gain in our knowledge base, our widening and

deepening perspectives, and our understanding of others' plights, their losses in our lives, and our own eventual expiration date.

2. He joins the thinking that surrounds archetypes and refers to the psyche as the inward experience of the human body. I am reminded of Jung's analogy that the archetypes are to the psyche as the instincts are to the body. Archetypes are embodied and the instincts are psychological, for it is finally, all of a piece. So, for Campbell, "the archetypes are biologically grounded. . . . The Jungian archetypes are of the unconscious, are biological. The biographical is secondary to that" (*Power* 51). They point each of us to the realm of the timeless and eternal structures that shape the world. It seems to me that it is of our nature to be grounded and transcendent at the same time.

3. He reveals the interconnection between temporality and eternity: "The source of temporal life is eternity. Eternity pours itself into the world. It is a basic mythic idea of the god who becomes man in us" (*Power* 49).

4. From the above notions Bill Moyers offers that "the one great story is our search to find our place in the drama" of unity—the original story, to which Campbell enjoins, to be in accord with the grand symphony that this world is, to put the harmony of our own body in accord with that harmony. It is as if our life were a poem and each of us is part of the verse "and yourself participating in a poem is what a myth does for you" (*Power* 55).

5. And, if we are to spiral back for a moment and think of power/energy as forces that myths coagulate, we note some important, even dramatic observations, by Campbell in *The Power of Myth*: "Dreams are manifestations in image form of the energies of the body in conflict with each other. That is what a myth is. Myth is a manifestation of the energies of the organs of the body in conflict with each other. This organ wants this, that organ wants that. The brain is one of these organs" (*Power* 39).

6. Mythic accord: every myth, both universal and personal, "integrates the individual into his society and the society into the field of nature. Myths unite the field of nature with my own nature—it's a harmonizing force.

7. He draws support from the German poet, Novalis: "The seat of the soul is there where the inner and outer worlds meet" (*Power* 57). The power of metaphor is perhaps the mucilage that unites these worlds, gives them a center. Myths are one generous and gratifying form that brings into some deep harmonious correspondence the worlds of nature, body, spirit and psyche to create *a life of coherence.*

8. Let's think for a moment of 12-step recovery programs for many afflictions; they are based in large measure on what Campbell offers here.

9. We could call them rituals of discovery, rituals of recovery. When one makes these steps like stations of re-covering a self lost in the forest of an addiction, one needs rituals to revive and renew oneself. Campbell writes of myth and ritual: "Repeating the myths and enacting the rituals center you. Ritual is simply myth enacted; by participating in a rite, you are participating directly in the myth" (*Bliss* xix).

10. But the sense of eternity, mentioned above, is worth noting. Campbell insists that "eternity isn't some later time. Eternity isn't even a long time. Eternity is that dimension of here and now that all thinking in temporal terms cuts off. And if you don't get it here, you won't get it anywhere . . . the experience of eternity right here and now, in all things, whether thought of as good or as evil, is the function of life" (*Power* 67).

11. Why art and artists are so crucial to cultural health and civilizational survival: The following is one of Campbell's constant refrains in much of his writing—"Myth must be kept alive. The people who can keep it alive are artists of one kind or another." They function in the mythologizing of the environment and the world. They speak the mythic dimension of the human experience; they continually offer us images to penetrate that world (*Power* 85). The gifts of the artists include their ability to penetrate to the invisible plane that supports the visible one; they engage it and shape it into a coherent form to be shared with the rest of us who cultivate the open attitude of listening and contemplating. This idea, for Campbell, is the basic theme of all mythology. In this respect, the artists enliven us by giving us a vision that we need them to discover and create for our meditative practice.

12. But we also have a responsibility: to study the particulars of our own myth, to discern its power to shape our stories that give us direction and purpose.

13. Phil Cousineau, who worked closely with Campbell on several projects, including editing the book, *The Hero's Journey* and creating a film of the same title, wrote a fine book entitled *The Oldest Story in the World*. In his gifted storytelling capacity, Phil writes of the hungers we all have that cannot be satisfied by any literal food; we feel a hunger of the spirit for stories (50). "These hungers reflect the longing for another world, the one beyond or beside this one, the one deep story to transport us toward" (50). We have, I would add, a hunger of curiosity about others, to see ourselves refracted through stories of others.

14. What is the richest element between us are the stories that both connect us and that reveal the insights of how we are different in our diverse narratives, those that enclose the myths that guide us, shape us and reveal our destinies.

15. Perhaps one of the most valuable achievements in his writing is that Campbell showed us how to read narratives not as literal facts but as imaginative forms. Pay attention to the metaphors, he encourages, for "Metaphors are the native tongue of myth" (*Thou Art That* 8)

Pathways to Bliss: Mythology and Personal Transformation

This volume, published in 2004, is one of my favorites for the theme of this conference. Let's explore some of these passages together. We can pause and discuss some of them on our journey as well as engage in a few writing meditations to invite in our personal myth.

We are interested in Joseph Campbell's thoughts, but for the purposes of his thinking, we can use his guidance as a way to warm to our own imaginations in the cauldron that we might call the self. The creative imagination, to my mind, is always the theme of Campbell's work, regardless of the subject matter or mythic image he is entertaining. His Introduction has several tasty morsels that we might take in and savor as we approach the main body of this text.

He relates a time when he was giving a talk at Esalen in Big Sur. The question posed to him then was whether the role models of contemporary society also existed in classical myth, and were there any for women who wished to serve in the military or as executives (there weren't, acceding to Campbell). But then he goes on to give a working definition of the gods, which seems important for our purposes: "The gods represent the patron powers that support you in your field of action. And by contemplating the deities, you're given a kind of steadying force that puts you in the role, as it were, that is represented by that particular deity—the deities of agriculture, war, domestic life" (*Bliss* xv). Perhaps in your own life you pay homage to a saint who serves you as a presence when in crisis or in need of assistance with a life circumstance. Many people pray to St. Anthony when they have lost or misplaced something, or to the Blessed Virgin when they are in need of guidance and support. Or to the Hindu god Ganesh who is often invoked at the beginning of a new enterprise, a new adventure; Ganesh is often invoked to remove obstacles that block one's life at various moments.

But what Campbell emphasizes is that myth is not the same as history: myths are not inspiring stories of people who lived notable lives. No, myth is the transcendent in relationship to the present. Of course, as he does often, he pivots to the poet's role in all this mythmaking: "The function of the poet is to see the life value of the facts roundabout, and to deify them, as it were, to provide images that relate the everyday to the eternal" (*Bliss* xvi). This function is imaginative bridgework, a linking, a finding correlatives within our temporal life with something more eternal. And then he offers a key word that may aid us here: "But in my experience it has always been *the model* that gives you the idea of the direction in which to go, and the problems and opportunities that come up" *(Bliss* xvi).

If we step back and reflect for a moment, it may occur to us that the problem *is* the opportunity, not a block to one; it shares a relationship with how being wounded is the opportunity for healing, for overcoming or integrating a trauma that has shaped your image of yourself as well as the way you move in the world. What follows is one of those staples of Campbell's world: "A mythic figure is like the compass that you used to draw circles and arcs in school, with one leg in the field of time and the other in the eternal. . ... Now, when you have a deity as your model, your life become transparent to the transcendent, so far as you realize the inspiration of that god" (*Bliss* xvii). Let's turn to one of the richest images of this compass, found in John Donne's famous poem, "A Valediction: Forbidding Mourning."

He learned from the German psychiatrist Emile Durkheim; "There lives in each of us, says Durkheim, a life wisdom. We are all manifestations of a mystic power: the power of life, which has shaped all life, and which has shaped us all in our mother's womb. The wisdom in us represents the force of this power, this energy, pouring into the field of time and space. But it's a transcendent energy. It's an energy that comes from a realm beyond our powers of knowledge—and that energy becomes bound in each of us—in this body—to a certain commitment" (*Bliss* xvii).

I would call this our destiny, our fate, our purpose in life.

- When the energy becomes blocked, we may fall out of our purpose, our path, which is ours alone.
- We can become ill at this juncture, when no energy is flowing through us (*Bliss* xvii).
- The image of a god may look like a human or animal form, but its reference is transcendent of that" (*Bliss* xvii).
- "When you translate the moving, metaphoric foot of the compass into a concrete reference—into a fact—what you have is merely an allegory and not a myth" (*Bliss* xvii).
- "Where a myth points past itself to something indescribable, an allegory is merely a story or image that teaches a practical lesson" (*Bliss* xvii). I ask you: does his approach here seem too narrow? It does for me.
- The end result here is that "when you have a deity as your model, your life becomes transparent to the transcendent, so far as you realize the inspiration of that god" (*Bliss* xvii).

Riting Myth Meditation

- On what God or deity do you call up for assistance? Or, what God or deity has aided you in the past?
- Handout, Rilke's poem "Sometimes A Man Stands Up During Supper."

Riting Myth Meditation

- What altar have you erected to your life's purpose? What is on your altar? How often do you dust it off, clean it up, change the flowers on it?
- I want to cite for a second time the attunement of myth with ritual; one is attuned "to a living mythology, one that is actually organically relevant to the life of the people of the time, repeating the myths and enacting the rituals center you. Ritual is simply myth enacted; by participating in a rite, you are participating directly in the myth" (*Bliss* xix).

Riting Myth Meditation

- Where in your life do you need a ritual to help you in remembering? Or what ritual could aid you in anticipating something on the horizon? What ritual might be created to serve you on your quest? (Share my ritual as I prepared for skin cancer removal on my face.) How did it serve you?
- What ritual do you already follow that aids you frequently, perhaps even on a daily basis?

Thoughts on Bliss

- Myths are always referring in part to a participation in the transcendent.
- We can, Campbell asserts, live according to a model, perhaps from our personal life, perhaps from someone we have learned about.

- Or—we can live for bliss (*Bliss* xxiii). Your bliss becomes your life. Campbell outlines the five sheaths that comprise energy flows in the individual: 1. the food sheath; 2. the sheath of breath; 3. the mental sheath; 4. the wisdom sheath, wherein one detects "the transcendent pouring in" (*Bliss* xx); "5. the sheath of bliss, . . . which is a kernel of that transcendence in and of itself. Life is a manifestation of bliss" (*Bliss* xxi). One can learn much more about the atman, the soul, the self, God, from *The Bhagavad Gita*, a Hindu text which has been translated *The Song of the Lord*. It influenced Campbell's thinking in perduring ways.

- At *The Gita*'s beginning, the young warrior, Arjuna, on the eve before an epic battle that he hopes will install him as rightful heir to the throne, listens to his charioteer, who is the god Krishna in disguise.

- At one point in his teaching, Krishna enjoins his charge: "Remember, Arjuna, true knowledge is knowing the Atman, the True Self Within. When you clarify your intellect through either contemplation or selfless action you get to realize the Atman. Both paths lead to realization of Self" (*Gita* 28).

- Campbell confesses that he has become more uncertain of what being means, or consciousness means, but not bliss.

- "Bliss is that deep sense of being present, of doing what you absolutely must do to be yourself. If you can hang on to that you are on the edge of the transcendent already" (*Bliss* xxii).

- Bliss, he continues, "can guide you to that transcendent mystery, because bliss is the welling up of the energy of the transcendent wisdom within you" (*Bliss* xxi).

- When it dries up, keep searching for it; maybe that is the ultimate or the foundational quest—to discover, rediscover and enact one's bliss, for it is the welling up of the energy of the transcendent wisdom within you. You feel cut off without it.

- Feeling homeless, disconnected, alienated, orphaned are the emotional responses to be severed from your bliss.

- By continuing to search for it and to enact it, that is the way you work out your myth in a concrete way.

Riting Myth Meditation

- How do we recognize, then organize the events of our lives into a coherent narrative?
- What is the logic of our plot, our mythos, our *muthos* as plot?
- What fantasies gather around the plot of our lives?
- What new sprigs are forming in the rich cultivated garden of our lives right now?
- What is in process of dying off, atrophying so that these new buds may find room to flower?
- What is budding forth?
- Anytime we are between myths or between parts of ourselves dying off and new elements gaining life and traction, who or what do we turn to for support, where the way seems almost completely invisible: No path, no direction, and after a time, perhaps no will?
- However you respond to this, consider that what we choose or have descend on us to support us, is a major presence in our personal myth.
- What, if anything, do we ask of our own narratives? They too have energy, vitality and an organic life.

Bliss and the Five Sheaths

- Campbell offers that the "way" or the via of our life provides us with a field, a field of influence or energy, by which we can be guided, as a beacon can guide ships safely to a harbor. That harbor may house the grail, the goal of our life and its achievements.
- The atman is the spiritual ground or germ of the individual
- First: the food sheath, concentrating on the body.
- Second, the sheath of breath; the breath oxidizes the food; the breath turns it into life.
- Third is the mental sheath: here resides body consciousness, which coordinates the senses with what makes up your identity.

- Fourth is the Wisdom Sheath, the sheath of the transcendent pouring in. The wisdom sheath has knowledge of how to heal us when we are wounded or ill.
- Fifth is the inward sheath of wisdom, the sheath of bliss.
- In the fifth sheath resides the kernel of the transcendent.
- Life itself, Campbell acknowledges, is the manifestation of bliss.
- The Bliss sheath contains all opposites as well—we rise above the opposites in the sheath of bliss.

And while we are at numbering things, it might be good to continue with the four functions of myth as Campbell understands them.

- The first function of a myth is to reconcile consciousness to the preconditions of its own existence, but the reconciliation must be done in a spirit of gratitude, with love, and with the recognition of Life's sweetness (*Bliss* 4). So, this first function of a myth is to evoke in us a sense of gratitude before the monstrous mystery that is existence, its awe-inspiring function.
- The second function of mythology is to present an image of the cosmos, an image of the universal round about, that will maintain us and elicit this experience of awe. This is myth's cosmological function (*Bliss* 7).
- The third function of mythology is to validate and maintain a certain social system, a shared set of rights and wrongs, what is proper, what is fitting for us, on which our particular unit depends for its existence. It has a sociological function (*Bliss* 8).
- A fourth function is psychological. Whatever myth we choose to develop "must carry us through the stages of life, from birth through maturity, through senility to death." It includes "the cosmos as understood by this group and the monstrous mystery" (*Bliss* 9).
- Campbell, ever the bard, the story-teller, relates one of a man who worked all his life, then retires and goes back to fishing, which he loved when he was 12; but that's not working anymore. He needs something else to sustain him.

- We all can recognize that the myth we continue to cultivate does not have to be rational, nor reasonable, nor true but always we ask: according to whom? It does not even have to be comfortable. But it should offer some sense of coherence.

- Campbell likes to use the metaphor of the kangaroo's marsupial pouch for the young kangaroo after birth. From out of the mother, it enters her pouch, a second womb, where it will continue to develop until it is ready to move about on its own.

- Myth is the equivalent organ for humankind to finish gestating and growing up to where it can function somewhat on its own (*Bliss* 18).

Riting Myth Meditation

- When you come up against a brick wall or feel that you have lost direction, what do you fall back on for support? What or who do you turn to assist you on your mythological journey?

- Do you turn outward or inward for guidance?

- Have you had a situation where what you counted on to support you failed, or was otherwise inadequate to the task of supporting you? What was your response?

Let's Get Personal: Mythology of the Individual

Before we move on to a slim volume, *Myth and the Body,* where Campbell engages with body worker Stanley Keleman on the relation of biology to mythology, let's end our gambit through *Pathways to Bliss* by exploring the possibilities in one's personal myth.

In Chapter V, "Personal Myth," Campbell cites the very famous observation of his mentor, C. G. Jung, who, upon finishing *Symbols of Transformation,* posed to himself one of life's basic questions. "'Hardly had I finished the manuscript . . . when it struck me what it means to live with a myth and what it means to live without one.' It occurred to him to ask himself by what myth he himself was living, and he realized he did not know" (qtd. in *Bliss* 86). It was a turning point for Jung and I sense that it had a revelatory impact on Campbell as well.

The latter continues citing Jung: "'So, in the most natural way, I took it upon myself to get to know my myth, and this I regarded as my task of tasks'" (qtd. in *Bliss* 86). We can think about this realization by Jung and its impact on Campbell. But more importantly, how would each of us answer this question?

Here is one possibility, one that I carried out recently. I asked myself: What is your guiding narrative, the one that you have lived by from the beginning and that you continue to cling to for support even when parts of this narrative need to be let loose in the cosmos? Then I wrote out one page that captured the large contours of my overarching myth. I believe that our personal myths are always in transition, always shape-changing and yet wants to maintain some particular motifs in our development. Asked another way, what images have been prominent in your life's journey—in dreams, in fantasies, in daydreams and thoughts as well as behaviors? Can you list three of these motifs that seem to be constant presences?

In a few moments I am going to ask you to take this question of Jung's on and see what arises. Not too much thought, but rather what is the feeling element of your story that wants expression? Campbell is helpful here as well. He asks us: what seizes you, or what has seized you? He cites the explorer of African cultures, Leo Frobenius, who uses the word "*Ergriffenheit*, being seized by something so that you are pulled out" (*Bliss* 89). Campbell connects this seizure with a sense of awe. What is awe-ful in your life now or in the past? One can sense in this word both a terror and fascination, which is what awe can trip-wire in us, and we grasp or intuit in the process some of the contours of our personal myth.

Such a deep personal experience includes "the awakening, of fascination, of the experience of mystery—the awareness of your bliss" (*Bliss* 89). An awakening is at the heart of this existential pronouncement. Such a moment is at the heart of Buddhist thought as I understand it; it can elicit in each of us a deep sense of connection with all other life forms. And, just as importantly, this moment is a gift, one that we receive and then give. It is at the center of our creative selves, which we could devote an entire retreat to.

But for now, I want to spiral back for a moment to Phil Cousineau's fine reflections in *The Oldest Story in the World* on Lewis Hyde's now classic work, *The Gift.* Hyde suggests that one of the earmarks of a gift is "that it must keep moving." It has its own power as "an agent of change, and has its own spirit" (qtd. in *Story* 52). I would extend this discussion to include that our personal myth is a gift to each of us; it is the vehicle by which we can create change in the world that improves the lives of others. They are also located in the body, as we will explore later when we present some of Campbell's thinking on story and embodiment.

But to return: paradoxically, as Cousineau informs us, the word *gift* has roots that "reach down into the Indo-European word *ghebh*, meaning both 'to give' and 'to receive,' as well as duty or obligation, and *provender*, a noble old word for simple food" (*Story* 52). Is it too much to suggest that for many of us, our stories can be like pillars in our temple to life, that they support us when we face crises; they help us to remember what our identity is and must remain when disasters strike? At moments when our cultural surroundings, instead of supporting, fail us, we must turn inward to where our values sustain us in a wasteland of a failed culture cohesion.

I want to include, in this field I am developing here, one of the best books I have read in a while, Amy Tan's *Where the Past Begins: Memory and Imagination.* After my wife and I watched a Netflix documentary on her life, I ordered the book immediately. Early on, as she rummages through boxes of photos and other family memorabilia, one discovery after another of her earlier life rose up to be remembered. Listen to how she writes of them: "The discoveries arranged themselves into patterns, magnetically drawn, it seemed, to what was related. They include artifacts of expectations and ambition, flaws and failings, catastrophes and the ruins of hope, perseverance and the raw tenderness of love. This was the emotional pulse that ran through my life and made me the particular writer that I am. . . . I am a writer compelled by a subconscious *neediness* to know, which is different from *a need to know*" (*Past* 6).

I think she offers us another grand way to think about our personal myth, with all its moments of bliss and the ever-present reality of the blisters that also comprise our mythic selves, "the emotional pulse" of our lives.

Each of us carries within our imaginations an image of greatness about ourselves; it can spin out of control and turn into a titanic version of ourselves, but when it is in place and in play, it can be a gift from ourselves to ourselves. Campbell suggests as well that religious symbols can act as life preservers in our lives when they feel dissociated from a culture that no longer feeds us. "Choose the images you want to meditate upon. Our world now is what could be called a terminal moraine of broken mythological traditions" (*Bliss* 100).

He applauds those individuals who in their quest for understanding their own mythologies "take an image from Egyptian or the Aztec or almost any culture and use that as a base for a kind of support for their own psyche. What do you think would be better than that?" (*Bliss* 100). Only you can decide the efficacy of integrating an image from another culture into your world; perhaps Campbell is right and we have all these images within us that pay no attention to boundaries of time and culture.

Creativity encompasses a large part of this assembling of images. Whether we create our own imagistic world, or meditate on those of other artists, such an act can be healing. "The work of the artist," Campbell writes, "is to present objects to you in such a way that they will shine. Through the rhythm of the artist's formation, the object that you have looked at with indifference will be radiant, and you will be filled with esthetic arrest" (*Bliss* 105). We might pause here and say something about esthetic and organic form.

There is also the stance of the artist herself that is worth noting here. I want to return to Amy Tan and note what she says as she develops her own history through this memoir: "In my writing, I recognize myself" (*Past* 20). Her insight helped me to understand my own passion for journaling every morning at 4:30 as I recollect the day before. This act of remembering what wants to be acknowledged, as Tan revealed when she rummaged through the boxes of family lore, is a way to see myself in sentences that most often write themselves, without censorship. Writing is a mythic pathway to self-identity.

Campbell ends this chapter with some final observations on finding one's own myth: "So, I say the way to find your myth is to find your zeal, to find your support, and to know what stage of life you're in. . . . Don't try to live your life too soon. . . . This thing, wisdom, has to come gradually" *(Bliss* 108). I love his use of a word that has been left on the sidelines: Zeal. Zeal is enthusiasm, passion, a passionate love of something and I believe it drives a life of purpose and pattern. And zeal is central to any deep and lasting quest. Zeal may also be another way one's "emotional pulse" as a thread in life finds its most vibrant expression.

Campbell's final observation is worth repeating: "What is it we are questing for? it is the fulfillment of that which is potential in each of us. Questing for it is not an easy trip; it is an adventure to bring into fulfillment your gift to the world, which is yourself" *(Bliss* 108). Nothing, he asserts, is more important than this feeling of fulfillment: "You become a signal, transparent to transcendence; in this way, you will find, live, and become a realization of your own personal myth" *(Bliss* 108). I could not create a better way of saying to you what I hope we accomplish in our time together musing on Campbell's brilliant insights.

Works Cited

Campbell, Joseph. *Pathways To Bliss: Mythology and Personal Transformation.* Edited and Foreword by David Kuder. New World Library, 2004.

---. *The Power of Myth, With Bill Moyers.* Edited by Betty Sue Flowers. Doubleday, 1988.

---. *Transformations of Myths Through Time.* Harper & Row Publishers, 1990.

---. *Thou Art That: Transforming Religious Metaphor.* Edited by Eugene Kennedy. New World Library, 2001.

Cousineau, Phil. *The Oldest Story in the World.* Sisyphus Press, 2010.

Hawley, Jack. *The Bhagavad Gita: A Walkthrough for Westerners.* New World Library, 2001.

Larsen, Stephen and Robin. *Joseph Campbell: A Fire in the Mind. The Authorized Biography.* Inner Traditions, 2002.

Slattery, Dennis Patrick. *Creases in Culture: Essays Toward a Poetics of Depth.* Fisher King Press, 2014.

Tan, Amy. *Where the Past Begins: Memory and Imagination.* HarperCollins Publishers, 2017.

13

◆◆●◆◆

JOSEPH CAMPBELL AND THE QUESTING SELF: PART II SOMATICS, STORIES, AND MYTHS*

While Campbell did not write extensively about the body and myth, he had a series of conversations with Stanley Keleman over decades that were gathered in a book, *Myth and the Body: A Colloquy with Joseph Campbell.* Another source is in Chapter II, "Bios and Mythos" in *Flight of the Wild Gander: Explorations in the Mythological Dimension.* Sometimes I have the feeling that in discussing myth that the body is lost or backgrounded to some extent. So, this section wishes to recover and bring embodiment back into the conversation.

I have been interested in embodiment for many decades, especially in how embodiment is depicted as a grand metaphor in literary works stretching from Homer's *Odyssey* to Toni Morrison's *Beloved.* The results of that research were gathered in a book, *The Wounded Body: Remembering the Markings of Flesh.* I began the study by relating the experience of having a hip replaced that had lost all cartilage because of osteoarthritis. There I wrote: "The wounded body is sacred in some deep level of its existence; it is a body specialized and formed by experience. In its new way of being

---

* The second of two chapters to be presented at a retreat, "Questing for Our Personal Myth: Writing, Remembering and Renewing Our Story Through the Teachings of Joseph Campbell." Hotel Santa Fe, New Mexico, May 12-15, 2022.

present to the world, the wounded body gains something not possessed before" (*Wounded* 7).

I suggested further that "The wound becomes the distortion through which we revision its phenomenology as a lived experience. Wounding is one way the body shows its hyperbole, drawing our attention to it in unexpected ways" (*Wounded* 11). At that time, I had not been reading Campbell's work and so failed to realize how important embodiment was to his larger exploration of the mythic and poetic senses of being embodied. So let's turn to his insights now.

This second work, *Flight of the Wild Gander,* which I will touch on for only a moment, is worth considering for the metaphor Campbell uses to reveal the connection between the infant and society: "Society, as a fostering organ, is thus a kind of exterior 'second womb,' wherein the postnatal stages of man's long gestation—much longer than that of any other placental—are supported and defended" (*Flight* 36). His connecting this process to myth is worth noting:

> Myth is everywhere the womb of man's specifically human birth: the long-tried, the tested matrix within which the unfinished being is brought to maturity. . . . Mythology fosters a balanced intuitive and instinctive, as well as rational, ontogenesis, and throughout the domain of the species the morphology of this peculiar spiritual organ of *Homo sapiens* is no less constant that that of the well-known, readily recognizable human physique itself. (*Flight* 40-41)

Now that last observation is loaded. It seems to me to form a tripod—embodiment, spirit and myth—and their working in some unison to create a sense of unity within the diversity of being human; myth, it becomes clear, is not an add-on to life but central to its development and well-being. But there is no guarantee that either the physiological or mythological womb will always offer perfect births: "Misbirth is possible from the mythological womb as well from the physiological: there can be adhesions, malformations, arrestations, etc. We call them neuroses and psychoses" (*Flight* 41); these malformations are the consequences "after some five hundred years of systematic dismemberment and rejection of the mythological organ of our species" (41). We can, of course, speak of this continued abandonment of the mythological in our world today.

The Somatics of Myth

My hope is that you will find the pieces of the conversation between Campbell and Keleman I cite of personal value in widening the scope of myth and of the mystery of being enfleshed. Early on, Campbell offers, "For me, mythology is a function of biology . . . a product of the soma's imagination. What do our bodies say? And what are our bodies telling us? The human imagination is grounded in the energies of the body" (*Myth* 3). Our callings in life, which often implicate the deep interior urgings of what we should do, and the world's body in which to perform these callings, has as its medium our own flesh. Being called is largely incarnational.

What I like about this confluence of bios and mythos is that our embodied being is itself mythological—our bodies contain our stories and the psyche is always an embodied psyche, enfleshed and ensconced in the flesh of the world's body out of which it expresses itself, most often in narrative form. How we feel physically can, we all know, affect our attitude, our energy level and our capacity to engage life as fully as possible or to hide from it, a hermit in our own dwelling. The felt sense of how we feel and who we are cannot be separated, but it is possible to live in such a split register.

Riting Myth Meditation

Let's pause and engage our own embodied being in a short writing meditation: Stanley Keleman observes in the Introduction that "myths help the body to organize and incorporate experience" (*Myth* xiv). They are ordering principles or even impulses, I would add. Given this notion:

- Where have you experienced this ordering or re-ordering force of myth in a somatic way?

- When has an illness, an accident, an injury to the body shifted, magnified, or even erased your somatic sense of yourself?
- What are you noticing about being embodied as you age? What wisdom is the body informing you of?
- Where are new limits and boundaries posting themselves in your life presently?

Think for a moment of words like *organic, organs, organization* as all part of a biological and mythological energy field in which we move daily. Often this network is translated via language, into the stories that guide us. I have called this creation a *somatic semantics*; our language comes from our embodied presence. Campbell even calls them "scripts of my genetic shape in social language" (*Myth* 4).

The above leads me to ask: are our bodies in shape and structure mirrors of nature's conscious structure? Is there a form of *biomimicry* present, a term I take from the title of Janine M. Benyus' book, *Biomimicry: Innovation Inspired by Nature*? I suggest this because of Campbell's insight that "Myth is structured in the cells. Each sperm, each egg, contains a story that is recreated in the full growth of each cell. This is part of our history" (*Myth* 6). I carry my sons, my wife, my granddaughters, my daughter-in-law in my body; they are not ideas or concepts but visceral memorial presences that contour my history daily. My stories shape me with the same intensity that my body shapes who I am; in telling a story by way of my embodiment I enter the long historical legacy of storytellers by tapping into the ancestral past of wisdom and insights. I enter the archetypal field of storytelling.

Speaking Myth Meditation

- Pair up with someone you do not know. Think of a story that will inform the other of something you wish them to know about yourself, your history, your embodiment. The intention here is to have you each enter the archetypal field of storytelling as a rich, magical experience of and with the other.

Campbell senses that myths evoke our deepest, inmost somatic self. "When we lose our somatic reality, we inhabit a Wasteland: the myth of the abandoned body. To be filled again is the grail" (*Myth* 19). To have a *gut* feeling about someone is to know that person from a visceral sense of place. I know that person viscerally or somatically. Further, there develops a group embodiment in the classroom with all the energy fields gathered there. For example, after teaching a seven-hour class, I could not drive directly home; the field would not let me. I would drive to a restaurant on Coast Village Road, sit outside, have a glass of wine and watch the traffic as I sat quietly.

Living Organic Wholeness

While occupying this liminal space between classroom and living room, I would check in with how *I felt* about the day's experience. My visceral response never lied to me. I might have a sinking feeling or a feeling of elation or some excitement about what I had learned. I called these moments of reflection a *somatic sapience*. It comprised an imaginal-mythic space in which I remembered not just the events of the teaching day but the experience as it lived in acute embodied ways. I sensed at these moments a symbolic sense of the day, beyond the literal, when something connected that fled quickly but could not be disremembered. Its remnants in my body were too acute, too insistent. I realize now that I was feeling the day's meaning somatically revealed.

I don't think it is a stretch to call our embodied selves symbolic selves, both soma and psyche. It seems to me that symbols orient a double experience: first is the outer world of events, and second is the interior geography of experience; the two coalesce to create a coherent matrix involving both worlds. We are each a living process; we continually organize and embody what we encounter. I pursue the Grail as an internalized image of a personal inherited somatic self.

I further speculate: our organs are innate, but do they come with stories as part of their own organic lives? And do we help to create stories of our inner somatic experience? Keleman suggests that "from our experience comes an inner somatic image. This image may conflict with the life-structuring somatic images that society imposes" (*Myth* 26). Our organs are innate; but do they come with stories as part of their own processes? Further: do we assist in creating stories of our inner somatic world? Do we, in addition, help to create stories of our inner somatic experience?

It seems from both Campbell and Keleman that the function of mythology is to put experience into stories because stories have the capacity to organize bodily experience that form us as individuals. Stories both form and in-form me; I am a gestalt of storied formations, a composite of narrative gnosis. Myths reveal themselves in the immediacy of experience. They transcend social reality, the immediacy of hunger, or waves of worries. We dramatize our inner experiences as somatic images. Keleman suggests that "an image is the same as a pattern. It is a cellular organization, a complex, specific somatic shape. Our body shape is an image of our animal and personal body" (*Myth* 28). Campbell became aware of this phenomenon as both a musician and a runner; these gifts congealed in his scholarship, in running into the woods in search of the Grail and in his devotion to his writing, which often carries a poetic and mellifluous flow to it.

The Fabricated Self

I would add to these observations how we wear things to memorialize them, to give a part of our story, a chapter or a verse, a tangible memory, through the body. So, a rich trinity is forming here: memory, myth and matter, the matter of our embodiment. The language we use when we say "I have a body" is inaccurate, for it splits my consciousness from my flesh. Perhaps more accurate to say "I am my body" or "I am embodied" so that they are of a piece phenomenologically. Think of our manner or fashion of clothing as metaphors for our embodied attitude towards ourselves, the way our worn fabrics fabricate ourselves to be witnessed.

We create the fiction that is us. Myth is not static; it is in motion, like psyche is always in motion. Both correspond to the body's movements. When we say "I was moved by" a painting, a story, a film, a musical performance, we are implicating an embodied affective response to something in the world that touches our souls. To be touched affirms our embodiment.

I also do not want to lose what Campbell observes early on in their colloquy: "We can think of ourselves as a living process, continually organizing and embodying what we encounter. This is why journeys and paths are so prominent in myth" (*Myth* 5). It seems then that we are always in motion, in process and in progression. Embodiment is a verb and a noun; we require it in our becoming.

We might here address how the way we structure any given day of our lives is an embodied, creative action. It defines purpose and pattern, both of which are embodied gestures. Further, do we have one body? Hardly. Think for a moment of the following list of embodied states, far from complete:

- The efficient body
- The wounded body
- The pleasured body
- The absent body
- The sleeping body
- The remembered and remembering body
- The anxious body
- The overabundant body
- The body in pain
- The conscious, meditative body
- The dreaming body
- The excessive body
- The Grail=My given life
- The referenced body, the way we self-reference matter that is our bodies.

Campbell writes that "The long body is the chain of bodies we are part of. The human is an amalgamation of the parade of somatic images. . . . Myths also present us with the body images of various ages and eons" (*Myth* 29). Said another way, our being and becoming as bodies is predicated on our embodiment being always in transition, never static.

Keleman pushes this idea a bit further: "Images that are grounded in the soma are authentic. When we live concepts and images that are not grounded in our body, we do not believe who we are." We can become in this pocket of disbelief "alienated from the sacred" (*Myth* 33). We all have felt moments—days or years—when we felt dissociated from our embodied reality. A way back on this journey of alienation can be aided by self-compassion, of becoming more tender-hearted towards ourselves, then allowing this generosity to ripple out to others.

A myth is a story that grows out of the history of bodily processes to orient life along a particular corridor of values, I suggest. Campbell offers, "Our mind makes myth not from its own rational programs, but in response to suggestions from the body as to what is needed" (*Myth* 36). We are wise when we listen to the body's wisdom, *our* embodied wisdom. *Rituals* are embodied gestures, words, incantations to help us remember what we value, both on individual and collective or national planes of awareness. Look to any country's annual celebration days that recall something of value to be reinvested in and you sense what their myth is.

If a ritual we perform has lost its anchor to an event that carries a deep meaning for us, we are engaging not in a ritual but in an empty gesture, a bad habit of sorts, and perhaps inviting in gratuitous violence, as the American writer, Shirley Jackson magnificently reveals in her short story, "The Lottery," which you can read online.

To lose our somatic reality is to be snatched by the myth of the abandoned body. Keleman believes that "The life of the body is the source of our myths. . . . Myth has to do with the movement of our universal and personal body. . . . Biology is a mythology. . ." (*Myth* 37). As biology cannot be separated from mythology, so too our memories, carried in the body, cannot be separated from either.

Riting Myth Meditation

- Let's meditate on what ritual one practices to reclaim or recall something of value in one's life, or as preparation for a particular task. What body gestures could be used to bring such an experience forward?

Inhabiting a Storied Moment

A felt sense of the body in motion is captured in this example from my life. I was in our yard one morning sawing broken limbs from two trees, a Live Oak and a Mountain Laurel. I thought it would be a task to rush through, then to move on to what was next on my agenda for the day. But then there was an inexplicable pause and something took over, a felt sense of what I was doing. I stopped thinking and began feeling into the saw, my gloved hands moving it, the smell of the dried woods' aromas as I dismembered them from the lower part of the tree. I then felt the strain of muscles in my back and down my arms in the rhythm of my repeated motions. I felt the perspiration form under my hat and begin to drip onto my glasses.

My breathing increased but was still tolerable. I sensed my lungs expanding and contracting, the slight pressure in my chest from my heart stepping up a notch or two. Overall, I settled into a feeling of well-being, of satisfaction, and of joy. The simple joy of being alive and feeling its conditions. What had begun as a mechanical task transformed into a moment of intense pleasure in the feeling of being alive and of being healthy enough to perform this simple, rewarding task. I felt the tree's pleasure in shedding these dead limbs from its torso, lightening its load. I felt a quality of healing in these moments, accented by the tree's appreciation of my efforts. Projection? Maybe, but then maybe for an instant I felt the tree's soul responding to my soul, both of us through our embodied presence in a communal effort to improve each of our lives. It was a mythic moment laced with joy. Trimming the dead branches became a rich moment of soul work.

"Embryogenesis is cosmogenesis: the birth of the body is the birth of the inner emotional cosmos," suggests Keleman. He continues this correspondence between the matter that we are and the myth that forms within: "The parent of somatic images is the body's process to make form and expression" (*Myth* 29). I glean from his insight how much of a piece, of a wholeness of a formed expression each of us is. Further, my world view depends on how I am somatically and emotionally formed. We can ask at this juncture: What is it about our embodiment that is ethnically or racially critical to our sense of identity? Let me offer another story here.

When my wife Sandy and I visited areas in Ireland that the Slattery clan gathered so many years ago, back in the Irish mist, I was astonished to see and to hear not just in this region but in others, to a lesser extent, speech patterns, gestures, and a particular liveliness of spirit, a generous open heart ready to help us. In other words, I saw my grandparents, my uncles, aunts, and cousins echoed in their patterns of behavior in the world. I saw my family's lineage extended throughout the Irish people; the consequence was that I felt so at-home in this region among strangers who were actually further relatives of our clan. What an astonishing breakthrough this was, and all through the embodied gestures of generosity and humor. Sandy felt the same resonances because she knew so many of my relatives; but she also saw many of these gestures in our two sons.

The Mattered Earth

Campbell asks some penetrating questions at this juncture: "When does myth become effective as the body, and when does it not? When does the earth become an operating image, the structures of a life process? This is really what we're talking about here. . . . But what myth are you living? What are the images of your structuring process?" (*Myth* 40). These questions comprise, for me, the heartbeat of the book. We can become "mythically dissociated," Campbell's term, from our own embodiment and live like an orphan or even an exile within our own flesh; we can extend such dramatic alienation to the Earth herself. The Earth is then transformed into a commodity to be pillaged, raped and left on her own to recover. But are these not indicators of our own relation to our enfleshed being that we have displaced on to the Earth's rich, yet increasingly brutalized matter?

So, the divorce is not just from our own matter and transferred to the Earth so she too does not matter, but we also alienate ourselves from the energies that inhabit all matter as part of their soul-life. When, however, we become more attuned to these energies that I believe are akin to psychic energies that C. G. Jung develops in his insights into matter, we move closer to one of myths' main purposes: to help us harmonize our lives with that of society and the Earth more generally.

Rituals—to return to them for a moment, rituals that are both personal and collective, can help us along the way. Marching on Martin Luther King, Jr. Day for example, or celebrating Memorial Day or Labor Day. These are celebrations of embodiment in some of their iterations. Rituals like these, when well-constructed with an engaged imagination, move us from a center beyond the personal to the collective and even to the transcendent. Rituals aid us in activating our imaginative life, which springs from inside, though not exclusively in response to outside information. Myths are activated through corporeal remembrances that revitalize the individual with the collective in order to create a society of coherence, beyond all of its conflicts.

Mythopoetics

No surprise then, that Campbell returns in the latter part of this book to the epics of Gilgamesh and Parsifal. Give him enough time and leeway and Campbell will inevitably return to the poet and the artist to glean a deeper wisdom, as he does here. Epics often reveal their central characters to be in service to something beyond themselves; likewise, through our embodiment we can serve the world through aiding others. To do so for Campbell, "means putting yourself in play. It's that compassion which is the essence of the Grail experience" (*Myth* 60). The Grail is the goal and the instigator for the quest to reach it. "But the divine power is really within. When we open to it, we open to compassion. . . . The quest for the Grail is the quest for that level within yourself which is beyond the little boundary of your ego thoughts. You break through to the human" (*Myth 60*).

The paradox gains sharper focus: what we seek in the outer world is most often already within us. The journey outward is duplicated in a corresponding journey inward. I think this truth helps us understand more deeply that embodiment is a condition by which we can mobilize ourselves in the outer world as we quest within for the truths that already inhabit us, an "inner emotional cosmos," as he called it earlier. "In the pursuit of learning how to be a warrior so that you can ward off the invaders, you also learn of your own somatic unconscious" (*Myth* 61), Campbell observes.

Myths have a potent capacity to suggest, to symbolize, to seek out correspondences—yes, they are that organically active!—and may be very familiar with synchronicity, when two worlds meet a-causally, not through the more traditional and limited paradigm of cause/effect. Myths align us intimately with our somatic imagination "not to resolve the tension of opposites, but the ability of opposites to organize a somatic form. Opposites are the tensions that are part of the formative process. When we embody these tensions, we form our individuality" (*Myth* 64). We live, in short, within our own unique myth. So, let's rethink this pathway of resolving the tension and consider Campbell's call to live in this tension that appears to characterize life itself. Resolution may not be *the solution.*

Writing Myth Meditation

- Identify in your life currently where you feel somatically a tension of opposites, a place where you sense a push-pull between contending or contrary forces. Imagine if this tension carries an underlying form of agreement but expressed in two different formats.

Mythology opens the world so that it becomes transparent to something that is beyond speech, beyond words—in short, what we call transcendence (*Myth* 80). When a society lives organically within a myth, then their rituals are organized in such a way that they help us experience ourselves, the world, and the social order we are part of, in this mystical way, as Campbell understands its perennial dramatic structure.

I take from his insight the sense that we are then a composite or a constellation of energy fields most often in tension with one another. Can we say that they intend one another, that they serve as one another's in-tensions? The two forces hold, as it were, the earth of the self in orbit—a place of orbituary—the tracings of the orbit in our autobiography. The Self as an orbiting constellation of energy opposites that keep us in a trajectory, perhaps less circular, more spiralic.

Campbell finishes this rich discussion towards the end of *Myth and the Body* by affirming that "Myth and biology are a source of reference" (*Myth*

65). We could add that what we reverence in our lives we reference repeatedly; they are like gravitational fields we spiral back to often, perhaps daily, for they refer us back to our life of meaning and propel us forward to a life of purpose. "In this sense," he concludes, "embryology is cosmology and the somatic process is an evolutionary drama, our personal cosmology" (65).

Let's conclude with a few observations on the nature of stories themselves, and most particularly the story that shapes and defines our myth. It will give us opportunities to reflect back on our narrative from our current roost. We seem to be telling our stories in what we think about, value, gesture, believe, aspire to and reject, among other responses. Campbell believes "Storytelling is a form of integration and a script for bodying. It might be called the somatic imagination. . . . and all myth and all stories seek the origin and the end of our somatic structure. Myth as story is the life of our body in one or another of its forms" (*Myth* 68).

I wonder how you feel about equating myth with story? Are they simply synonyms, or do they suggest some nuanced differences? I do agree with him in what he says a bit earlier, namely, "When we pay attention to our stories, we know something about how we body our life. That is one of the functions of mythology" (*Myth* 68). It reminds me of Theseus, Duke of Athens' ruminations at the end of Shakespeare's world of wonder, *A Midsummer Night's Dream,* as he recollects the action of this enchanted and enchanting story that reads like a fairy tale.

Theseus, Duke of Athens, has changed in his thinking in the course of the play's plot, migrating from reason to imagination as a way of knowing. Here is part of his insightful speech in Act V, Scene i to those assembled:

> The lunatic, the lover, and the poet
> Are of imagination all compact: . . .
> The poet's eye, in a fine frenzy rolling,
> Doth glance from heaven to earth, from earth to heaven;
> And as imagination bodies forth
> the forms of things unknown, the poet's pen
> Turns them to shapes, and give to airy nothing
> A local habitation and a name.

such tricks hath strong imagination. (V. i)

I want to single out the line "And as imagination bodies forth/the forms of things unknown" because it closes in on some of Campbell and Keleman's observations: The imagination is a somatic organ of understanding and creativity; we each are poets of our own story, and when we speak or write them, we create ourselves anew; our stories bring us home to ourselves and to others. We leave the orphanage of our own self-absorption and become members of a wider community of narrative bodies. Keleman proposes that "Storytelling synthesizes somatic experience. It organizes the elements of experience into a body form that gives us a personal shape, a direction and even a felt sense of meaning. That's why I insist on looking for the body in a story, rather than looking for symbols and their meanings" (*Myth* 75).

In other words, storytelling is a shaping act of the soul to give it form in the world so that it matters more. We become more a "matter of fact" in relating our stories. The poet's pen, Theseus remarks, shapes the experiences of imagination into coherent forms to be shared communally. We in turn give our own existence a formative reality through the stories we choose to utter and in a particular style. Each of our personal myths includes a style of being present in the world, a style of gesturing, posturing and purposing ourselves.

I believe what Campbell expresses immediately after Keleman's fine insights is important as we conclude this series of explorations: "When we know that the transmission of experience is somatic, we can see how to find our way back to a somatic reference" (*Myth* 78). Such a fine sentiment: storytelling as a form of homecoming. Storytelling as an expression of community-constructing. How can I truly know another except through the stories they choose to relate that expose their mythic selves? To share our narratives is to join the larger human municipality by shedding like a snake's skin the image of the orphan.

We can then say to ourselves and to others who care to listen to the narratives that have shaped us: "My house is composed of many stories."

Works Cited

Benyus, Janine M. *Biomimicry: Innovation Inspired by Nature*. William Morrow and Co, 1997.

Campbell, Joseph. *The Flight of the Wild Gander: Explorations in the Mythological Dimension*. New World Library, 2002.

Keleman, Stanley. *Myth and the Body: A Colloquy with Joseph Campbell*. Center Press, 1999.

Shakespeare, William. *A Midsummer Night's Dream*. The Illustrated Library Shakespeare. Robert Frederick, editor. Illustrated by Sir John Gilbert, George Cruikshank, and R. Dudley. Robert Frederick, Ltd., 2004. Vol. 1, 241-66.

Slattery, Dennis Patrick. *The Wounded Body: Remembering the Markings of Flesh*. State U of New York P., 2000.

14

LIFE AS A CANVAS: PAINTING OUR STORIES, TRANSCRIBING OUR WISDOM*

In many ways, stories are uncannily similar to living organisms. They seem to have their own interests. They compel us to share them . . .

~ Ferris Jabr, "The Story of Storytelling." *Harper's Magazine,* March 2019. 35-41.

Deep Creativity makes itself known in as many ways as individuals are prone to tell their stories. One form of creativity shared by Deborah, Jennifer and me is the impulse to relate ourselves through our narratives. Perhaps above all else, we are story-making mammals, narrative bi-peds who live and breathe stories. To paraphrase Deborah's breathing in/breathing out meditations at the beginning and end of each of the seven sections of our book, *Deep Creativity*, we breathe in (hear) stories and we breathe out (relate or tell) stories. They may be ones that we created from within and/or heard from without that we felt were valuable enough to share with others.

---

* Originally presented at the conference "Deep Creativity: Invoking and Inspiring Your Creative Soul." With Deborah Anne Quibell and Jennifer Leigh Selig online, March 5-7, 2021. Hosted by Pacifica Graduate Institute.

One of my favorite authors of the last 40 years is the Trappist monk, Thomas Merton, a creative soul whose writings in prose and poetry persistently call for social justice. His insights have influenced millions of people over decades. In the first book of his I read many years ago, *Conjectures of a Guilty Bystander*, he writes: "To live well myself means for me to know and appreciate something of the secret, the mystery in myself, what can't be communicated, what is at once myself and not myself, at once me and above me" (81). I am led to think that when we write or tell our stories, we invite the other that is us into the narrative and to befriend this stranger. Stories have this miraculous capacity, to befriend the stranger within, as well as those we meet in our travels.

While I generally agree with his observation, I do think that on some meaningful level we can and do communicate the deep mystery moving within us through our narratives; perhaps it is the most basic form creativity assumes. Deeply creative acts allow even a spark of that mysterious self to emerge, to be seen and heard. Creativity involves both my self that I know and my self that remains unknown, perhaps unconscious, but sensed, and often given shape through the power of analogy. Our stories then, may indeed be analogies of ourselves given a plot-line, which is a form of a necessary and blessed life-line. I believe that the three of us filled this canvas that is *Deep Creativity* in order to talk to ourselves and be overheard by the other two writers on the pilgrimage. A sense of what anthropologist Victor Turner calls *communitas* is formed most deeply by means of the stories that weave us together.

Exploring my topic of "Life as a Canvas" on which we place our storied parts into a coherent whole, I gravitate back to the book of Genesis. Here is where the Bible begins: "In the beginning God created the heaven and the earth. And the earth was without form, and void; and darkness was upon the face of the deep. And the spirit of God moved upon the face of the waters" (Genesis: I:1-2.). Here we are offered the beginning of the creative process in storied form. Here God comes into His own being in the act of creation. Might the angels in his world be the extension of the original forms of the muses that assist Him in his masterpiece? Perhaps they include feminine presences that also participate in the origin of the world.

What connects our work with your work as creatives, is in giving whatever we explore, meditate on, contemplate in the stillness that Deborah reveals in her "Sea Turtles" exploration, for example, is the miracle of giving form to the formless, the not-yet-shaped into matter that hibernates meaning.

Mythically, God wishes to give form to Himself in and through his creation. As the first depth poet, He grasps in mythic time the need to give the void a volume of matter so it matters to us, who are soon to be created in His image. In His image our own divinity matters. So *Deep Creativity* is an impulse in the soul to make of our life canvas a flawed but fierce masterpiece that bestows on our existence meaning and texture. In fact, behind everything that happens from the origin of creation to last Thursday is a story shaping it and being shaped by it. And one more observation: our stories are small cargo ships that carry in their hold what we believe, value, remember and aspire to as well as darker shades of existence that left unchecked, can debilitate us.

Our *Deep Creativity* is an invitation and an imitation, a rich series of analogies to this originary act of God—to create the world; we in our own storied ways with each of our essays imitate this first act, one of creating something, as a way to further form both our being and our becoming. As divinity begin to paint the world out of the void on a canvas that had been void, yearning for impressions and expressions, so did we in creating this book yearn towards expression with you in our divine minds. As I reread it a year after it was published, I saw it so much more clearly: *Deep Creativity* is ontological, mythological and analogical because in creating it we recreated ourselves in each storyboard of our lives. So much to say about each, but not now. Only this: musing on each of your creative impulses, canvas your own life for images that have extended and deepened your creative genius.

Given the rich image of a life canvas, I want to share a poem I wrote some time ago that incarnates this image by a master painter. The poem is entitled "Painted Perceptions" and dedicated to Paul Cezanne, one of my favorite artists, who told us, as Deborah does in her "Sea Turtles" essay in "The Way of Nature," to cultivate silence and solitude in order to go deep. Sitting quietly in my study at 5 a.m., I had my journal open and was remembering some paintings of Cezanne I had enjoyed studying recently; then the following began to unfurl through my blue-inked pen. Jennifer beautifully develops the idea of ekphrastic poetry in her essay on "The Way of Art." They are poems written about works of art: Here is mine.

Painted Perceptions

He went along the blue river
casting it in the summary of a
brush stroke
then stepped back, gazed with one eye
at the mountain
and knew that it existed only in
space given by the mind
where numerous dolphins
could swim just below its
summit, nuzzling the blue
of mountain air with their
hard snouts, then
diving deep into air swirling
in eddies without bottom.

Skeletons swam in swirls
and paints mixed, creamy
with impressions of where
mind and matter spent
themselves in arias
of noble smells that
retreated into one another
full of nakedness of form
with no gaps, no fissures
or fingered grooves.
No,
the world came to a
cunning conclusion
in paint the color

of perception.

Completed was its death
so he stepped back
for lunch and left it
to dry into itself
with a firm conviction
of its empty fullness.

The painting came to rest
in a gallery brimming with
galaxies of other palettes
that carried their own pastel fictions (*The Beauty Between Words* 26-27)

My first response to this poem, which I fussed with over the next days, was a fullness, a glow of satisfaction of making some replica, some shadowed reality of Cezanne's effect on me. Something achieved, some new form of expression to honor his genius. That is all I needed. Well, not quite; what I needed was a story, a narrative line to place on my canvas of his creations. It surveys something of my belief in Cezanne's genius. Like our own myths, our stories are metaphors that give us some philosophical, spiritual, sacred and psychological grounding. Stories carry some certification of what I believe. Throughout *Deep Creativity*, which on one important level is a story book, a book about the creation of narratives, which may be the oldest form of creativity in our species as humans, we continually tell stories.

How frequently, I noticed in rereading *Deep Creativity,* do Deborah and Jennifer pause for an instant, then say: "Let me tell you a story." Or, "Let's put another log on the fire out here under the dark night sky, and tell yet another story."

Another great painter, Leonardo da Vinci, believed that analogy was a way to appreciate the unity of nature, and among the analogous forms he explored was the branching pattern that could be found in trees, in the arteries of the human body, and in rivers and their tributaries (*Leonardo* 109). In a similar pattern each of us found both connections within our own histories that fed the fables of our own creativity as well as interconnections between our stories that textured the book with inter-textual narratives. We tried, in fact, to practice what we preached.

I believe what we cultivated in our essays are a series of stories that define us. Jennifer remembers at the beginning of "Love, Death, and a Loaded Gun," "The story of how I came to be shot is embarrassing. . . . Not as stupid as shooting someone point-blank in the middle of the fore-head, but that's his story to tell, not mine" (28). An important insight here on narratives: tell yours, not another's. Let your own story be painted on the canvas of your life, not another's. Sure, use others' stories as they cultivate depth in your own. But so often in life, we can short-change our own story because of feelings that trivialize it. And we trivialize our own identity in the process.

We can also deny our mytho-poetic presence in the world, our storied self shaped by the myth that lives within us. The stories we tell about ourselves mirror the myth that we are living out in the world. Story telling is myth revealing. If you desire to know the myth you are living, pay close attention to the stories of others that attract you and the stories within you yearning to be told and witnessed by others. Pay close attention to their plot-lines, for they are analogies of your myth-lines.

We might recall here Joseph Campbell's insight that "the function of a mythology is to integrate one's conscious life to one's unconscious life" ("Mythology and the Individual," tape); we see this beautifully demon-strated in Deborah's "Sea Turtle" story that balances surface and depth as necessary to contact in the act of creating. Dan McAdams furthers Campbell's observation when he suggests that "to revise one's narrative is a mythological action and a crucial one on our journey to wholeness, of recognizing the whole self" (*The Stories We Live by* 57).

And on the other side, our stories can point us to the holes in our-selves, the gaps, the fissures, the unlived story; we can spend our entire lives in constant story-revision, refining and ennobling our narratives as we continue to live forward in time. The other life we live is backward in time to re-collect ourselves in the stories we cultivate, imagine and per-haps learn to treasure (Deborah uses the word "revere") that may aid us in closing/healing the gaping wounds in ourselves through the sutures of our story lines. Our stories carry this mysterious suturing potential that can heal as it reveals where we have been afflicted, either by ourselves or others.

Writing Meditation

Let's pause here to offer a writing meditation for you to consider. At the end of her essay on "The Way of Practice," Jennifer poses this question: "What is your relationship with yes, when it comes to your creativity? When do you give yourself permission to say yes? Who supports you in saying yes? Who (besides yourself) challenges you and makes saying yes difficult? When you get in your own way of saying yes, what sorts of psychological justifications do you wrap yourself in?" (219). Allow 20 minutes for writing. You can see that there are many ways to approach her questions.

At a talk I gave on Joseph Campbell and narrative in Utah many years ago, and because I was not to give a workshop the next day, I posed to the audience an extended way to access and shape into expression their personal myth: "Recollect your life up to this moment. Write out ten sentences. Each one is to express a turning point, a crisis, a crossroads, a threshold crossed, that you recollect with detailed vividness. Put them in order of importance, not in sequential time. Then write ten pages on each one, aiming for a one-hundred-page memoir consisting of these nodal moments of transformation."

Take as long as you like, but stay with it, a little at a time. You might even want to record into your cell phone, or write in a small notebook or tiny spiral notepad what furthers this project. The process is going on all the time in the imagination: be ready to catch in a quick scribble the insights that descend or come up from below without a moment's notice; hang on to these as the psyche, when prepped, will work the material outside of time and space; it has its own musing and creative impulses beyond your control, which may be the best quality about it.

In keeping with the metaphor of the canvas, think of these ten nodal moments; they are the first pencil or brush strokes on your life canvas that, taken together and aligned with one another, will paint a rich sketch of who you are and what your destiny has revealed to you. These are moments of threshold crossings, which in the original Greek word "crisis" means "the turning point in a disease" or later, a decisive point—a time for decision-making. Crisis is a time of crossing over from one life or one of life's dimensions, to another; it is a rich opportunity to create something new.

The Power of Stories

Another tenet we three share: stories carry their own subtle wisdom that we may not come to expect in the moment of their expression. In her essay, "Amidst a Sultry City: The Muse is Not Only in the Meadow" (105), Deborah tells the story of her beloved city, Amsterdam, enriched, of course, by her own stories to relate to those passing through her habitation. City as muse, city as wisdom. Deborah writes: "We are here to notice and tell her true tale, to love her fully in that way. . . . I shall tell you another story" (*Deep Creativity* 111) and off we go on the hero's adventure as she ventures through the city, noticing its beauty and allure through the particular way she sees the city's beauty and expresses herself in unique poetic ways.

Deep creativity continues to lean against the truth that stories are the way in. Not exclusively, but largely. When Toni Morrison spoke of her award-winning novel, *Beloved*, (in "Profile of a Writer," video) which I taught for many years at Pacifica Graduate Institute, gaining new wisdom from each rereading, she said that writing the story of slavery in the format of a history text had no juice for her. But her muses told her, in her words, "If I wrote something narrow and deep, then I had a chance to say something about the experience of being enslaved." She knew as well that writing a history would not add anything new to the horrors and courage in being enslaved.

Almost all the voices that have created the slavery narrative have been white, so they create the narrative from their point of view. Morrison knew that would not do. She then turned to analogy: "I wanted to write a novel about all the ways we self-murder, how we self-incarcerate." Shame, guilt, the inability to speak it, accepting an image of oneself as an animal, not a human being---are some of the ways that we self-sabotage, she observes, often through experiences of woundedness and dismemberments that we can devote a lifetime piecing ourselves back together from this initial fragmentation. I believe that in writing *Beloved*, Morrison healed something in her people's history as well as in herself.

She did not want to fall into the trap of sociology in describing slavery; rather, as she observed in the same interview: "The heart of the story is in the minds of the slaves themselves." Stories do have a heart, a beating, vital center where the myth that propels them resides like an energy field that fuels the artistic engines of a new creation. And the ability to experience both suffering and survival is the ability to speak it, to tell it, to create it in some form of language: painting, embroidery, a patch-work quilt with codes threaded into it. As she writes, what is needed "is some fixing ceremony," some way to hold the story in place, to give it the dignity of permanence yet fluid enough to be added to.

Yes, the novel is based on a historical person, one Margaret Garner, a slave, who in the 19th. century did attempt to murder all of her children to save them from repeating her fated life as a slave. But history is not exactly myth and poetry is often, in the making of a story, some alliance of the two. One more note from her on the creative process regarding her own fiction and others: "The writer's job becomes how to rip that veil drawn over proceedings too terrible to relate, to find and expose a truth about the interior life of people who didn't write it—to fill in the blanks that the slave narratives left (*Toni Morrison: A Casebook*, 81). The author of this essay, Mae Henderson, adds: "For Morrison, only the act of imagination can provide such access" (83). We might pause on this fine insight on imagination as access to levels of reality that only it can bequeath entrance.

In "The Way of Suffering," I write in my essay "Suffering the Story into Being," about the 'placement' of suffering, how suffering can place us somewhere new if we can endure it. I posed the following question: "Have you experienced the kind of suffering that has moved or migrated you to a new place, a new locale or location, a new state of being, or a new attitude?" (181). I continue with this possibility by adding here: What you have not been able to write about, or even think about, from your past? Is it time to give it a narrative shape to help you understand it? Could it be possible that giving it expression in some form—not just writing, but painting, sculpting, drawing, dancing—free you from self-incarceration? Might laying out the plot line be a life-line back to yourself?

As a way to heal? To integrate, to add to your wisdom bundles from your life story? To bring it into a fuller consciousness by the assistance of the unconscious? To paint its image on the life canvas you are continually adding to, amending, revising through revisioning might deepen how your suffering is an essential chapter in your life story.

C. G. Jung offers that "the unconscious is best understood if we regard it as a natural organ with its own specific creative energy (*CW* 8, par. 720). I sense that Jennifer intuited this possibility after witnessing a mother cursing and abusing her two young children on a subway station platform in New York City. The mother's abuse was both physical and verbal, as she continued "yanking their fragile too thin arms when they couldn't keep up" ("To Create is To Re-Create: Repairing and Restorying Childhood Suffering" 161).

As she boarded her own train, she meditated on what she had witnessed: "And then, all of a sudden, in my mind's eye, I saw it in a vision" (11). I believe she sees the event recollected from a different register of reality—the imaginal and the mythical, the creative and the timeless. She sees a different ending, one that is creative and therapeutic; she realizes at that moment that creating a "screenplay and writing it would be the only way to know what happened next" (162).

This incident is so critical to the entire project of *Deep Creativity*: the space of unknowing in creativity, the gap between what has been witnessed and what its possibilities might be in the creation of a world through story, not unlike God's impulse to create in Genesis. Does it suggest that the creative impulse has a divine origin, a yearning to return to the source of the world itself through our own spark of divinity that propels us forward, into the ambiguous realm of unknowing? Such is the beginning of the artist-as-hero's quest: to question what we have experienced and to journey towards another possible outcome.

But this progress might begin in a feeling of "I don't know what to do with what I have just experienced," leaving a blank space that requires patience to nurture. I believe that often we are stopped, made to pause, so a space of time is allowed for "creative nurturing," creating the right vessel into which we place an event that has changed us by the power of that experience.

This moment of Jennifer's envisioning, when she saw in an instant what it was to be created, recalls for me a very important part of a book by physicist and president of The University of Dallas, Donald Cowan's *Unbinding Prometheus: Education for the Coming Age.* Though published in 1988, its relevance extends to today. So here goes with my own sense of analogy that creates a story.

Chapter Five of *Unbinding Prometheus* is entitled "The Three Moments of Learning." I want to allow some slippage here and say that they are also three moments of creativity, and this process is evident in many of our essays. For how can creating not be simultaneously a moment of learning? I will collapse his descriptions in the interest of space: "The first is the immediate apprehension of a thing; the second is the unfolding and structuring of it in the mind; the third is a truly creative action, transforming the initial thing into something new, which is then given to the shared world of knowledge" (*Unbinding* 85). While Cowan goes on to observe that "the bulk of education is devoted to the middle term, structuring and systematizing," the other two, apprehending and creating, "are far more important to the complete action of learning. These two are so internal, however, that they cannot be taught" (85).

He will later call the first moment "a kind of grasping," in which the reality of an experience is taken in whole and complete, "a love-at-first-sight experience." I call this the first creative moment when one is open, receptive and nonjudgmental. Cowan claims it occurs before any analysis, explanation or categorizing. It is a kind of "active receptivity" (*Unbinding* 85). What he states next is worthy of further meditation: "What comes to the mind through sight is *meaning*, but what comes in through sound is sensed as *form*" (85 my italics). Jennifer's envisioning moment is a grasping of form, perhaps as well as meaning. Some creative outlet must be introduced to lead a life event towards its fullest expression: what it ultimately means for us.

The second moment is present in Jennifer's essay, but again, this can be repeated in so many of our writings. Deborah's "The Rupture Within: Releasing the Soul Bird" (148), for instance, reveals a moment of grasping when she is with her dying client looking at his paintings, "'of making something out of the mess,' he said softly" (154). For she apprehends the deeper meaning of suffering and creating. She moves to mapping this experience, then making a poem: "I had to write that poem. It was my way of remembering that I am not alone when suffering" (157). This storied pattern is repeated throughout our volume. But to return to Jennifer's story: From apprehending or grasping, and perhaps even gasping, a word Deborah uses to great effect in an earlier essay, Jennifer moves to mapping: "I wrote about. . . ." "I wrote about. . . ." "The story took on themes eventually, as a good story will do" (162). All this in the service of mapping. Cowan asserts that "A mapping is a device for presenting experience to the mind in a manner the mind can handle. . . . If the map is simple everyone is seeing the same thing" (*Unbinding* 87).

He then offers the following on the third moment of learning: making. I am making the metaphor of creating a mirroring of Cowan's metaphor of learning: "Learning must cause a metamorphosis of the person, not merely elevating him—must make him into something different from what he was before" (*Unbinding* 88). So, after grasping and mapping, something must be made of the two experiences—a poetic response, or better said, a *mytho-poetic* reply, where one's deepest original nature comes forth as an analogy of what is made. In the process, we don't want to lose sight that in a moment of creative making, we too are remade in a reciprocal response. Creativity is, then, always dialogical—a dialogue between one's soul and the world's matter. Often a story then emerges to create a place of coalescence between imagination and matter, a congealing through a shared plot line.

The act of making a story, a narrative in infinite forms, includes a moment of waking, of becoming more and more deeply conscious. It is the most essential story of our lives. Its center, its heart beat, is our in-formation, a form earned in the creative experience. Phil Cousineau helps us here when he writes, "Storytelling has been my way of redeeming myself, strange as that sounds. . . . I've needed a way of proving myself to some unseen titanic force, my father, my coach, my God" (*The Oldest Story* 23). Creating is a journey towards redemption. The implications of his insight are profound.

I pose a series of questions at this juncture in the pilgrimage:

- Does what you create, which includes creating each day you have the privilege to live, have a specific recurring theme or set of themes such that you paint them anew with a parade of colors on the canvas of your life?

- If so, what do these narratives support in you?
- Another way to ask the above questions would be to consider what patterns or forms of life do you enjoy creating and recreating to give your life sustenance?
- What do the narratives, the stories you live by, awaken you to?
- Do the stories that feed you and the stories you create, add to what Dan McAdams calls "an integrative life story"? (*The Stories We Live by* 21).
- Do the stories that you are drawn to create contribute to your sense of coherence?
- Do they address places in your story that breed incoherence, fragmentation or division in yourself?
- Where in your life story calls to you in need of change or even complete deletion?
- Our personal mythic life is format-ive in creating an identity we seek. Do the stories you deploy add to this formation? Do they at times lead to a de-formation of who you believe you are and who you believe you wish to become?
- What might be done if you reached a place where you sensed your life story is beginning to buckle and collapse under the weight of circumstances, crises, losses and disruptive changes? Or simply of old age?
- Are there any stories you relate to yourself or that are told to you that have the effect of shredding your identity, sapping your life energy and leaving you feeling anonymous, even orphaned from your true self?

As I reread all the essays in *Deep Creativity*, I found that one structure, pattern or mode of expression pervades our individual essays—an analogical imagination—which seems essential to creativity in whatever form that assumes. Such a way of perceiving recalls mythologist Joseph Campbell's insight in *An Open Life*: "You see, myths do not come from a *concept* system; they come from a *life* system; they come out of a deeper center.

We must not confuse mythology with ideology. Myths come from where the heart is . . ." (23). When each of us marks our life canvas with a story or stories, we gain some connection to this realm of the mysterious timeless nature of our species. Creativity is a form as well of envisioning these life systems that power all of our narrative beings.

Creativity may always include what Dan McAdams suggests about story's power: "At some point in our lives we become aware of the task to create an integrative life story. Through it, as perhaps a prism, we come to understand who we are and how we fit into the adult world" (*The Stories We Live By* 21). Let's add that the form our stories assume is the medium, the vehicle, through which life becomes manifest in its grand complexity. Our stories also tie us, sometimes imprison us, within the conditions of society that may complement or put us at odds with its mythic values and ideals.

Our creative life allows us to rewrite our story in order to liberate us from such tetherings. We might want to keep in mind that our stories need not have happened literally in order to be true. It seems less important that our stories "really happened" than that they evoke wonder in the imagination because we recognize that a psychic reality exists that has its own force field.

And right below the surface of all our creative acts is the movement of energy transfer systems that ties us to perhaps all life forms—the stories in our souls are mimetic, namely, they re-present the plots that hold the created order together, as did God's original act of creation; one source, then all is part of a complex unity that allows such tremendous diversity. In his arresting autobiography, *Memories, Dreams, Reflections,* C. G. Jung orients us in his "Prologue" to how to read the stories that follow: "My life is a story of the self-realization of the unconscious. Everything in the unconscious seeks outward manifestation and the personality too desires to evolve out of its unconscious and to experience itself as a whole" (3).

When speaking of performing his songs, by himself or with others, Willie Nelson admitted that he liked to play to live audiences because the energy exchange between artist and audience has so much value. The energy-transfer, from creator to created, flows in two directions; it is never one-directional. Narratives as tinctures on the canvas of our lives is also another form that this energy field is constructed; they are the mainstay, the essential mucilage that binds us with others. These moments of narrative creating free us from bondage to ourselves, to self-absorption, and allow us to feel the prevailing largesse that is the heartbeat of originality.

Writing as Ritual: Creative Enactments of Imagination

In *Deep Creativity*, readers are invited into dozens of ritual enactments or ways of embodying meaning through rites of passage, including the passages Deborah, Jennifer and I wrote to share with you as well as to inspire you to enter your own creative energies. Rituals are acts of imagination in thought, behavior and even attitude to help us through life circumstances or to celebrate those already achieved. Rituals seem to increase mindfulness by encouraging us to be attentive to something remembered or anticipated and to embody them in gestures and words.

In this spirit and context, I want to share a ritual I created recently to prepare me, and to lighten the level of anxiety I was experiencing, as I prepared to drive one early morning to San Antonio for face surgery to remove a basal cell carcinoma. I had already had a number of face surgeries but this one had stirred up a beehive of emotions. So I decided to prepare for it by crafting a ritual. Here is what I created:

- The day before the surgery, I risked Covid-19 contagion and had my hair cut at a local hair salon. I needed to do this for both physical appearance as well as emotional stability.
- I swam a half mile at our local recreation center because I love this form of exercise and suspected that the facial wound would keep me out of the pool for several weeks to avoid infection.
- I awoke the morning of my appointment and followed my routine of lighting a candle in my study at 4:30 a.m. and making a cup of coffee.
- I chose to read the chapter in Karen Armstrong's calming book, *Twelve Steps to a Compassionate Life*, most specifically the chapter on

"Compassion," which included practicing self-compassion. I needed to reinforce that attitude.

- In reading the above, I brought to mind all those in surgery and recovery this same day. I also thought of all those who could not afford modern medical coverage in order to alleviate an ailment.
- I also prayed that those in power would shift their attitude to make universal health coverage a standard practice in the United States and globally rather than a political chip in their mindless games of winning political capital.
- I sat quietly back in my lounge chair and rehearsed the position I would be in when the surgery took place.
- I showered and dressed up a bit, as much for me as for the medical staff I would present myself to.
- I ate a very light breakfast.
- I drove 50 miles south in morning traffic to San Antonio.
- When I arrived early, I sat in my truck and meditated on the gratitude I felt at being able to receive treatment for the cancer that, if not removed, could threaten my life.
- I prayed again for universal health care for the entire planet so no one would be denied the basic dignity of good health, free from suffering.
- Then I meditated on the reality that healing often requires an unpleasant antecedent—being wounded—and considered that healing actually begins with the wounding by scalpels and other utensils.
- I meditated on remaining centered, and focused on the task of showing up on time, following directions and letting the surgeon and assistants work as efficiently as possible.
- I wrote out a Happy New Year card for my doctor who had operated on me several times over the years. I expressed my gratitude for him, his staff and his skills as a skin cancer surgeon.
- Then I thanked all the health care workers who are exhausted, some now with Covid-19, and who every day show up for work to save those who are Covid-19 infected.

- I entered the building and checked in early to let them know I was there.

- I consciously displayed a congenial attitude to lower my own anxiety and tried to create a relaxed atmosphere with each person involved in the procedure.

- The above helped me to shape an attitude of cooperation and relaxation that served me well, especially as it became apparent that scar tissue on the right side of my face, the consequence of inadequate skills from an earlier surgery in which assistants sutured the wound, would have to be re-addressed.

- The doctor was not pleased with how I had healed and suggested we open the scar tissue and remove the pulp of scarred flesh and close it so that it would heal smoothly. That turned out to be a much greater ordeal than any of us had planned, so my preparation aided me in having two surgeries instead of one. My ritual preparation helped ease the reality of two surgeries simultaneously.

- Both procedures were completed over two hours later; now bandaged on two sides of my face, I drove home with feelings of gratitude that it was a both a success and over.

The ritual was a way of imagining my way into the wounding in order to heal. It gave my experience a structure that it would have lacked without it; the ritual grounded me in my body and in my history of many skin cancer surgeries over the course of two decades. It gave my imagination something to hang on to so my fear did not unmoor me from myself.

I bring all of the above up here because of what a potent creative act crafting a ritual can produce. The ritual voiced my experience within a container that pacified my panic and fear. Said another way, I created a metaphor of my impending experience to allow me to enter it through imagination first, then literally second. I hung on to this simple ritual as I lay there in the chair, waiting for the lab results to tell me if the surgeon had removed all of the cancer on the first round. He had, so now the suturing could begin as the final station in the journey.

I hope that these series of reflections have put you in touch with your own creative ways in negotiating suffering. Sharing our deeper stories is one of the most human compassionate acts we can perform for one another.

Works Cited

Andrews, William L. and Nellie Y. McKay, editors. *Toni Morrison: A Casebook*. Oxford UP, 1999.

Campbell, Joseph. *Mythology and the Individual*. New Horizons, tape 4. The Joseph Campbell Foundation, 1996.

---. *An Open Life: Joseph Campbell in Conversation with Michael Toms*. Selected and edited by John M. Maher and Dennis Biggs. Larson Publications, 1988.

Cousineau, Phil. *The Oldest Story in the World*. Eleventh Printing. Sisyphus Press, 2010.

Cowan, Donald. *Unbinding Prometheus: Education for the Coming Age*. The Dallas Institute Publications, 1988.

Holy Bible (1982) *Containing the Old and New Testaments. New King James Version*. Nelson Bibles, 1982.

Isaacson, Walter. *Leonardo Da Vinci*. Simon & Schuster, 2017.

Jabr, Ferris. "The Story of Storytelling: What the Hidden Relationships of Ancient Folktales Reveal About their Evolution—and Our Own." *Harper's Magazine*, March 2019. 35-41.

Jung, C. G. *The Structure and Dynamics of the Psyche*. Vol. 8. *The Collected Works of C. G. Jung*. Translated by R. F. C. Hull. Princeton UP, 1960.

---. *Memories, Dreams, Reflections*. Recorded and edited by Aniela Jaffe. Random House, 1963.

McAdams, Dan P. *The Stories We Live By: Personal Myths and the Making of the Self*. The Guilford Press, 1993.

Merton, Thomas. *Conjectures of a Guilty Bystander*. Doubleday & Co., 1966.

Morrison, Toni. "Profile of a Writer." 1988.
   https://www.youtube.com/watch?v=7KxJ_Gx3Zio

Quibell, Deborah Anne, Jennifer Leigh Selig and Dennis Patrick Slattery. *Deep Creativity: Seven Ways to Spark Your Creative Spirit.*
   Shambhala, 2019.

Slattery, Dennis Patrick. "Painted Perceptions." In *The Beauty Between
   Words: Selected Poems by Dennis Patrick Slattery and Chris Paris.* Water
   Forest Press, 2010. 26-27.

15

◆▶●◀◆

CALLING AND PURPOSE*

*A key distinction between myth and modern logic is that mythical coherence
follows an existential form while conceptual logic follows an abstract form, but the
fact that there is form in myth . . . undermines the accusation of
irrationality often leveled against myth.*

~ Lawrence J. Hatab, *Myth and Philosophy* 29.

Being called to life through our birth is an invitation to join life's adventures, challenges, heartbreaks and joys. It is the most primal calling we can respond to. And then, once here, to ask what is our purpose, our reason for being on the planet, and what might we contribute through our creative selves, is another crucial moment in our lives. It may of course repeat itself every time our plot pivots anew.

Joseph Campbell assembled so much interest around our callings in *The Hero with a Thousand Faces.* There he began with a fairy tale and an occasion that highlights the power of the blunder to incite the journey. He tells us that "a blunder—apparently the merest chance—reveals an unsuspected world, and the individual is drawn into a relationship with forces that are not rightly understood" (42). A blunder can have a ripple effect, spooling out from the original error; even falling down and

---

* Originally part of a Zoom interview with Machiel Klerk, Director of the Jung Platform in Salt Lake City, Utah that was aired during a Summit entitled "Calling and Purpose," May 19-22, 2021.

blundering into another world "can be very deep—as deep as the soul itself" (42).

In another work he outlines the characteristic of a myth: "For since it has always been on myths that the moral orders of societies have been founded, . . . (*Myths to Live By* 11). Life's abiding and undergirding myth carries one's life's purpose at the heart of a sense of coherence. Our beliefs as contents and as patterns of interpreting the world have their origins in mythic foundations that support them.

Myths, classical works of literature, a piece of music, dreams, fantasies, chance, a fated moment—all can be occasions for being called out, called forth, called on the carpet, called to create, called to change and even recalled when at first we may have refused earlier beckonings or responded: "No, not now. I'm too busy. Call me back." No guarantee the muses may make a second house call.

I think of the ancient Sumerian story of Queen Inanna who is called to the underworld, a descent that strips her naked and finally, she experiences a death, eventually to be transformed and returned to the upper world.

Or Gilgamesh, who loses his beloved Enkidu, a trauma that kindles his journey to discover how death might be defeated. The inevitability of Death too can call us in many registers through a major shift in our plot line. Fairy tales, as Campbell illustrates, are filled with callings, sometimes in whispers, sometimes in shouts and sometimes through illness, woundedness or other forms of dismemberment. A dis-ease may be the foundation for a calling to another life. The Roman Warrior Saul is called when he is struck from his horse and loses his sight on his crusade to persecute the new members of the Christian myth; his blindness is a calling to a transformed way of seeing and understanding. We can be recalled by something that happened to us earlier in life; we are called back to reassess its wisdom and attraction later in life and may then decide to follow what that remembrance evokes in us.

To name a few other figures within this profound landscape of vocative moments which can alter our life: Achilles, Odysseus, Moses, The Blessed Virgin Mary, Veronica, who wipes the face of the suffering Redeemer on his path to Golgotha to be crucified, Simon of Cyrene, Ishmael, Dante, Hamlet, each of us—all reveal dramatic instances of being called forth. I do not believe that anyone escapes being called, nor just once but repeatedly, during one's life. Some do not hear it, some hear it but ignore or refuse it, while others both hear and assent to it; the entire briefcase of what their life was going to be is refashioned. Each of the figures mentioned above are attentive enough to be still, to hear a calling and to act on that moment of divine grace. All of the above, including each of us, enter a new dimension of the mythic landscape when we are called. Being called is a mythic event because it clarifies our destiny, and through it, our purpose in life.

Earlier I mentioned illness as a time of calling. Dis-ease can halt one in their ambitions and dreams, as is Leo Tolstoy's Ivan Ilych, when an illness calls him to his deepest self. One ladder he climbs as a magistrate in the courts of Russia, is a judicial one that leads to further promotions and more status. But at home, in his new, larger home, he climbs a ladder to hang new curtains and loses his footing, injuring himself when he falls against a knob of one of the windows. Slipping on that second climb inaugurates him to a disease; it also forces him into deep interior reflections on the value of his life up to those moments of being pulled down by illness into his true authenticity (*The Death of Ivan Ilych*).

Here he blunders into his true authenticity, of which he has had little consciousness while pursuing success and status. C. G. Jung comments on such a blunder when speaking of a case of a fifteen-year-old girl who was a somnambulist; when in that state, she acted as a medium in response to questions addressed to her. Jung writes, "She is an example of the general psychological law that in order to advance to a higher stage of development, we often have to commit some mistake, which apparently is so terrible as to threaten ruin in our lives" (*Notes of Dream Seminar in 1925* 6). The insight applies to Ivan Ilych; but his situation is also a calling into the void, into the vacuum of one's existence where one's eyes are opened through suffering, and where deep silence can make one want to scream.

Tolstoy uses the elegant image of a black sack as a metaphor for falling into darkness before a moment of illumination (*Ivan Ilych* 147). It may seem strange to speak of illness as an inner guide, but the forms of being called to a destiny can assume countless permutations and voices. Where one might at first see disability, one may ultimately enter a profound discovery of one's life's purpose and destiny. One senses in this condition how being disabled enables.

Moses as well is a figure from Exodus who fascinates me in his story of being called. I believe that we are each called to a purpose and to a coherent life. The calling is an invitation to coherence. Moses is called to a task that is epic: to aid in Israel's birth as a nation (Ex. 1:1-22). But for this to occur, it requires an antecedent—the birth, or rather rebirth, of Moses, and it arrives in the form of a voice speaking through the natural order. At first, he sees a bush burning that is not consumed by the flames engulfing it. Then he hears a calling by an angel of the Lord, who appears to him in that same flame of fire. The mystery in the moment deepens.

Now one might call it a miraculous flame, or a flame of paradox, because it does not consume what it has engulfed, contrary to the laws of nature. C. G. Jung uses the term *opus contra naturam* to designate: "In its psychological meaning, individuation is an *opus contra naturam*, which creates a *horror vacui* in the collective layer . . . "(*CW* 9, i par. 256). I want to call this flame's presence nature's *opus contra naturam* as a mythic illumination—the flame of myth itself. It is the flame of awareness, of presentness, and it appears just off the path that Moses travels as he tends his herd. The flame does not follow the dictates of nature's law but that of another world's format: the miraculous hidden in matter.

The flame both distracts him and arouses his curiosity; it is so strong that it stops him in his tracks to ponder the mystery, which is why I think it is the flame of myth. I also sense that it is the flame of calling and of creativity. Noticing it first, then deviating from one's familiar path, as Moses does when herding his flock, puts him face-to-face with mystery, the ineffable, even, for Joseph Campbell, the transcendent (*Thou Art That* 18).

Moses tries to look at the bush burning; God's voice calls to him from the midst of it: "Moses, Moses," and he answered, "here I am" (Ex. 3:3). We can puzzle over why God calls his name twice. My guess is in the form of a question: are there in this instant of being called, two Moses'—the one who is about to be burned off and the other who is to begin a new life through the aperture of this divine acknowledgment of his destiny? It may be a moment of purpose, of unfolding his own myth. On this last notion, I cite C. G. Jung's belief that "God always speaks mythologically" (*Letters*, vol.2, 9). God tells him He has come to deliver his people out of Egypt, to a land flowing with those archetypal nourishments: milk and honey.

Moses at first balks: "Who am I that I should go to Pharaoh, that I should bring the children of Israel, out of Egypt?" (Ex. 3:11). "Who am I?" is crucial, for he does not know; being called is a moment of instrumental import, when one is willing to be an instrument of something one is called to do but not really grasping the terms underlying this action. Such a yielding, myths repeatedly reveal, often leads to a fuller sense of one's self-identity. It unfolds from life's purpose that one is willing to submit to, even if they present themselves as a mistake or a blunder.

Campbell and others remind us that when the hero heeds the call, s/he makes an act of the will to give oneself over to something beyond the self in that vocation. "A blunder, the merest chance, expands out to reveal an unsuspected world, and the individual is drawn into a relationship with forces that are not rightly understood" (*Hero* 42). It is a vocative moment: being willing to be instrumental, but not incidental, is the crucial instance of yielding that originates the formation of a coherent life, which is to say, a life guided and held together by a myth of purpose. Biblically and historically for each of us, in Exodus resides the shards and memories of Genesis.

First annunciation, then initiation, then creation, followed by the road leading to transformation. The Blessed Virgin Mary is often depicted in paintings reading, which can be a deeply reflective and meditative state of being. "And the angel came in unto her and said, 'Hail, thou art that highly favored, the Lord is with thee: blessed art thou among women'" (Luke 1:28). Mary is a virgin who listens with virginal ears. To be virginal is to be pure, open, unobstructed, a woman unto herself. She is at first confused and disoriented, then accepts the voice with total acquiescence: "And Mary said, 'Behold the handmaid of the Lord; be it unto me according to thy word.' And the angel departed from her" (Luke 1:38)

In Matthew's gospel Joseph is also called to a purpose that transcends his ordinary, daily life. Although he and Mary are initially espoused to one another, she is already carrying a child. His thoughts are to "to put her away privily" (Matt. 1:20). Then in a dream he is called to his destiny by an angel: "'Joseph, thou son of David, fear not to take unto thee Mary thy wife: for that which is conceived in her is of the Holy Ghost.'"

And again, in their flight into Egypt, angels appear to Joseph in a dream: "'Arise, and take the young child and his mother and flee into Egypt, and be thou there until I bring thee word: for Herod will seek the young child to destroy him'" (Matt. 2:13). Likewise, after Herod's death, an angel appears to Joseph in a dream: "'Arise, and take the young child and his mother; and go into the land of Israel'" (Matt 2:20). So many callings; Joseph responds to each and thereby fulfills his purpose in life. We are each called to some destiny of service, of aiding others; that may be the most treasured act of freedom we engage in: our yielding to a call.

Simon of Cyrene, seemingly a minor figure in the gospels, is given a place in Luke's gospel. We learn that he came to Jerusalem for Passover and was standing with the crowd when Jesus was condemned to death by Pontius Pilate. Roman soldiers pull Simon from the crowd to carry Jesus' cross to Golgotha. "And on him they laid the cross, that he might bear it after Jesus" (Luke 23:26). The deepest call we receive, perhaps, is the call to service; such actions can liberate us from the cocoon of our own self-absorptions.

Herman Melville may have given us one of the most dramatic callings of a soul to one's purpose and destiny in the opening of his novel, *Moby-Dick:* "Call me Ishmael" (3), which begins the journey when we as readers address him by that name. But if we read it aloud, we hear more clearly that we too are Ishmael in that calling forth. As doubles, we are the other. Two points to entertain here: one, that this marginal figure in Genesis, son of a slave woman, Hagar and her master, Abraham, will become the father of nations. Two, that his name means "God shall hear." Exhausted in her exile, Hagar places the child under some bushes and sits far from him so she will not hear his cries of hunger as he perishes. "And God heard the voice of the lad; and the angel of God called to Hagar out of heaven, and said unto her, 'What aileth thee, Hagar? Fear not: for God hath heard the voice of the lad where he is. Arise, lift up the lad, and hold him in thine hand; for I will make him a great nation'" (Genesis 21:17-18).

My own calling, the one that forged my life's destiny, arrived in the form of a literal phone call. When I picked up the phone, I learned that the caller originated in the office of the Assistant Superintendent of the Ravenna School System in Ravenna, Ohio, approximately 15 miles east of Kent, Ohio, where I was working towards a Master's Degree in Comparative Literature while working part time at odd jobs.

The man who called me asked if I was the husband of Sandy Slattery, who had been hired weeks before to teach history and math to middle school students. Mr. Fedoravich then informed me that their Special Education teacher, who was to begin teaching at the beginning of the school year in five days, had abruptly resigned; would I be interested in that position? I immediately said yes, without having the slightest inkling of what "Special Education" meant. But my whole being assented to this phone call. I yielded to its mystery and did not question its arrival.

I began teaching less than a week later without any guidance about lesson plans, nor how to work with special needs students; but with the help of my wife and the kindness of a couple of the women who taught at Palmyra Elementary, I stumbled through one week after another, admitting along the way that I truly enjoyed helping my young students achieve whatever level of competence they were capable of.

So began what has become as of this writing fifty-three years of teaching: the wonderful students I taught at Palmyra for two years; then two years of high school teaching in Lorain, Ohio; adult learners in three separate junior colleges in the Dallas Community College system; two years teaching undergraduates at the University of Dallas, first in Rome Italy for two years in their semester abroad program for sophomores, as well as an additional year on the Irving, Texas campus; undergraduate writing courses at Texas Christian University for one year; seven years teaching the same subject at Southern Methodist University; five summers teaching teachers the classics at the Dallas Institute of Humanities and Culture; five years teaching in the Fairhope, Alabama Institute of Humanities and Culture under the direction of Dr. Larry Allums; ten years teaching at The University of the Incarnate Word in San Antonio, Texas; then for the past twenty-seven years teaching in various graduate programs but anchored in the Mythological Studies Program at Pacifica Graduate Institute in Carpinteria, California. I also began offering talks and orchestrating writing retreats to various Jungian-oriented groups in the United States, Canada, Italy, Switzerland, Ireland and the Philippines. In all of these venues, I was challenged, frustrated, overjoyed, nourished and pushed to the extremes of my abilities—in short, a life in the classroom driven by the energy of a life-long love of learning and wanting to share that enthusiasm with others.

I like what Michael Meade writes on fate and destiny, given the above itinerary. It rings true, like the phone ringing that September morning in 1968. It was the ring of destiny, so always be prepared for a call when you need it most. Meade writes, "What I am calling fate has to do with the way a person's soul is seeded and shaped from within, like a story trying to unfold and become known. What I am calling destiny has to do with the inner arc and arrow of one's life. For each soul is aimed at the world and inclined towards a destination that only becomes revealed in crucial moments and at turning points in life" (*Fate and Destiny* 18).

When we find our purpose, we discover our destiny as well as our ecstasy. It may appear as a force and a face coming up on us from behind, not advancing towards us from the future. In addition, our callings may arrive in the transport vehicle of dreams that can awaken us in the night, after which we take action on it in the morning. Destiny and fate are mythic beckonings, apertures to a future we had not planned for; but when they arrive, we may find ourselves exclaiming: "Finally! Something I can believe in and love!"

A friend who mentors me through his writings, Ashok Bedi, writes in *Crossing the Healing Zone* of the importance of archetypal presences in each of us that can energize or demoralize us: "The archetypes that guide you in the Healing Zone have a quality of bringing two states of consciousness into alignment so that a new state emerges that restores health and wholeness . . ." (*Crossing the Healing Zone* 42). I would add that each of us is a mythic figure in search of the Grail of our purpose in being. Then we must face the life we choose to live; failing that we may have it dictated by others if we relinquish this crucial responsibility.

The question Joseph Campbell poses is: "Are you going to go on the creative soul's quest? Are you going to pursue the life that only gives you security? Are you going to follow the star of the zeal of your own enthusiasm? Are you going to live the myth or is the myth going to live you?" (*The Hero's Journey* xvii). The responses to these questions, if authentic, may change your life overnight. Campbell often referred all his work to one journey: the soul seeking its own understanding and its own life of purpose and relevance. Choose, insists Campbell: the path of the Grail or the path of the Wasteland (xvii).

The editor of the above volume, Phil Cousineau, elaborates further in this early part of *The Hero's Journey*: "There was now the *clew,* the winding thread of Campbell's path through his own labyrinth, the relevance of the work to his own life, which made sense of his sometimes-arcane connections" (xx). At the bottom of the page is a gloss on clew: "The skein of Ariadne's thread that Theseus used to lead himself out of the labyrinth, the origin of the word clue" (xx). Might one conjecture that in one's life, to be clueless is to be mythless, directionless, without clear purpose, not in the pursuit of securing employment but in service of the right deployment on the path of one's purpose-inspired destiny. To be clueless is to be unconscious of the crucial plot that guides a myth-enhanced life.

That skein can also mean entangled, snarled, web and yarn. We think of how often a yarn is a story, so the entangled yarn is a snarled story, needing some untangling. I think my phone call from the Assistant Superintendent described earlier, was my skein leading me out of the central question—what am I to do with my life?—to a straightening out, a yarn I could believe in and use to weave a life of meaning. We all have moments of this awakening—to fabricate one's life into some meaningful whole, in which one is excited to get up in the morning, for she now has a lodestar to guide her into the uncertain, yet directed, future.

May we each continue to know and learn our life's purpose by recognizing the deep woven patterns that sling it together in a benevolent tension of opposites, confluences and influences that offer our story texture, purpose and meaning. Now *there* is a story worthy of relating to others.

Works Cited

Bedi, Ashok. *Crossing the Healing Zone: From Illness to Wellness.* Ibis Press, 2013.

Campbell, Joseph. *Thou Art That: Transforming Religious Metaphor.* New World Library, 2001.

---. *The Inner Reaches of Outer Space: Metaphor as Myth and as Religion*. New World Library, 2002.

---*Myths to Live By*. Penguin Group, 1972.

---. *The Hero with a Thousand Faces*. Bollingen Series XVII. Third Edition. Princeton UP, 2008.

Cousineau, Phil, editor. *The Hero's Journey: Joseph Campbell on His Life and Work*. Joseph Campbell Foundation. New World Library, 1990.

Hatab, Lawrence J. *Myth and Philosophy: A Contest of Truths*. Open Court P, 1990.

The Holy Bible. King James Version. Hendrickson Publishers, Inc., 2006.

Jung, C. G. *Mysterium Coniunctionis*. Vol. 14. R.F.C Hull and Gerhard Adler, translators. *The Collected Works of C. G. Jung*. Bollingen Series XX. Princeton UP, 1970.

---. *The Archetypes and the Collective Unconscious*, Vol. 9, i. R.F. C. Hull, translator. *The Collected Works of C. G. Jung*. Bollingen Series XX. Princeton UP, 1971.

---. *Analytical Psychology: Notes of the Seminar Given in 1925*. William McGuire, editor. Routledge, 1992.

---. *Letters of C. G. Jung: Volume 2:1951-61*. R. F. C. Hull, translator, Gerhard Adler and Aniela Jaffe, editors. Routledge, 1975.

Keen, Sam, and Anne Valley-Fox. *Your Mythic Journey: Finding Meaning in Your Life Through Writing and Storytelling*. Jeremy Tarcher/Putnam, 1989.

Meade, Michael. *Fate and Destiny: The Two Agreements of the Soul*. Newly Revised and Expanded Edition. Greenfire Press, 2002.

Melville, Herman. *Moby-Dick; or, The Whale*. Introduction by Clifton Fadiman. Illustrated by Boardman Robinson. Collector's Edition. The Easton Press, 1971.

Tolstoy, Leo. *The Death of Ivan Ilych and Other Stories*, translated by Aylmer Maude. Signet, 1960. 95-156.

16

◆•●•◆

BELIEVING IS A WAY OF SEEING*

*The things a man has heard and seen are threads of life, and if he pulls them care-
fully from the confused distaff of memory, any who will can weave them
into whatever garments of belief pleases them best. I too have woven
my garment like another, but I shall try to keep warm in it, and
shall be well content if it does not unbecome me.*

~ W.B. Yeats, *The Celtic Twilight: Faerie and Folklore.*

I owe a debt of gratitude to my former dissertation student, Dr. Emily
Asia Ruch, who cited Yeats' beautiful meditation in her masterful dissertation, *Wyrd Webs and Woven Words: Archetypal Expressions of Fate in Classical, Celtic and Norse Mythology* (117). I was attracted to the rich image, "garments of belief." It suggests that we wear our beliefs as a fashion statement of the psyche and our history; we have freedom, if we so choose,
to refashion it in a new woven pattern when we realize that old beliefs
are painfully out of fashion for the life we are now living. Makeovers
happen periodically with our personal myth as well as our personal dress.

My interests during the pandemic have largely been on the nature of
beliefs that each of us holds, where they originate, and what may make
us cling to beliefs long after they have been proven untrue or massively
exaggerated. I also want to explore the relation of belief to myth, both

---

* An earlier, shorter version was published as "Believing as Seeing" in the *Herald-Zeitung*
newspaper of New Braunfels, Texas, October 24, 2019.

personal and collective. Further, we cannot uncouple our beliefs from the story or stories we tell ourselves or have been told to us that relates intimately to our sense of identity and even purpose in life. Perhaps we can propose that our narratives serve us as the spine of our beliefs; our stories are made up of what we believe in narrative form. I hope together we can make sense of them.

Recently I read an op-ed piece in our local newspaper, the *Herald-Zeitung,* in which the writer suggested, "The foundation of those democratic institutions is the belief of the public that elections are free and fair . . ." (*Herald Zeitung,* December 12-13, 2020 4A). Belief as foundation, belief as base line. We have a natural impulse or instinct to believe in something. Why? is a fascinating question.

It seems, in the period we are slogging through today, that a belief rests less on its being true than on its level of emotional value and persuasion for an individual or a people. Whatever each of us accumulates in our storehouses of beliefs will in fact shape the story we live by. In other words, our personal narrative, regardless of how much or little we reflect on it, is an amalgam of what we believe, sense, intuit, assume, accept and reject about what we loosely call "reality." The efficacy of a belief is highlighted most often by how much affect or emotional response it elicits from its adherents. From this observation we begin to sense how what we term "reality" may be much more fluid in its boundaries than we thought.

When any of our beliefs calcify into an ideology that "this is *the* truth," rather than "this is *my* perception of what is true," then out of that stance often arises resentments, denials and even violent responses to what others have settled on what is true for *them.* Acceptance, or even tolerance of another's angle on "reality" transports us in a different direction, towards tolerance and perhaps even compassion. In such an attitude we bypass the beast—fundamentalism—that not only literalizes all we say and believe, but end-stops all conversation. One slips into a bumper-sticker outlook on the world and others.

The Myth of Fact

The situation becomes more complex when the phenomenon of *fact* is introduced into the argument over what is true. In his insightful book on revising education, *Unbinding Prometheus: Education for the Coming Age,* physicist and university president Donald Cowan writes of "the myth of fact," which he claims has been "the prevailing myth of the modern age" (4). Fair enough. But he then points out an historical move that I think may be responsible for the conspiracy theories enjoying such tight-fisted ascendency today.

He suggests that the myth of fact shifted in the early Renaissance [14th. century Italy] in a substantial way: "In it the observable objects of the world came to exist in their own right. Rather than taking their meaning from a context . . . in order to participate in a larger reality, facts began to be considered the unchallengeable substance of life . . ." (*Prometheus* 4-5).

What evolved has come down to us in the rhetorical bromide, "facts speak for themselves." They can be measured and verified and trusted as entities to believe in. But we have entered a different iteration of grasping our relationship to facts. "Fact-checking" has become necessary to counter the dizzy world of "alternative facts." Facts are then weakened in their ability for many to believe in. Often unmoored from a reality we generally share and make decisions based on, "fake news" is the term of choice to counter what counts as facts. The spiral of comprehension, much less conventional agreement about "the real" is distinctly downward.

When facts lose their *contexts,* their veracity diminishes; facts in large measure help us to construct our narratives that shape our identities. But if facts are relativized, so at its core is reality itself. If individuals and groups or nations are no longer certain what or who to believe or believe in, then their identity as a coherent and cohesive body with shared senses of purpose and ideals to pursue are orphaned. And with it, a shared cultural myth is deeply wounded, if not assassinated. Moral injuries begin to populate news cycles as the culture carries these afflictions in its individuals.

We have all heard and perhaps accept without question the adage, "Seeing is believing." But the title of this chapter, "Believing is a Way of

Seeing" is a bit more interesting. It suggests that unless we already believe something, we cannot see it. The battle over beliefs today seems to have passed a boiling point; news shows, opinion pieces and other public forms of communication are all intent on showing us one position or another so we might succumb to and defend, even violently, believing it. Our growing climate crisis is being mirrored in our "crisis of fact."

The Myth of Belief

Historically, battles, wars and ethnic cleansings are fought for primarily the same reason: a clash of beliefs. The thinking goes like this: "We don't agree with *your* beliefs so we will set out to silence what threatens *our* belief system." The underlying assumption, or belief, is that *we* are right and *you* are wrong. Because I believe this version/vision of what constitutes reality and yours does not, I may be compelled to silence you through threats in order to eliminate the gnawing discomfort of hearing ideas, attitudes, and beliefs that contradict mine.

No room or open space allows for, if not the possibility of a truth to your beliefs, then at least a toleration for what you accept as true. Violence against others often has its genesis in a contrary belief in what is *real.* Then, just as often, a huge push ensues to amass "evidence" that my way is true and yours must therefore be false, misguided and to be silenced. The evidence gathered may be a string of fantasies made up to appear as facts, however ungrounded in any reality that can be examined. Substantial evidence, not often forthcoming, is dismissed as irrelevant in the face of the promoted falsehood. In this progression or regression, something basic to human understanding is assassinated.

The trouble here originates in the squishy soil that often what I believe or what you believe cannot be proven as an air-tight and iron clad position or perspective. The fantasy, however, is that what I muster to "prove my point" or "point of view" can also be manipulated to fabricate the veracity of my perspective. We can hear even from here the resonant echoes of George Orwell's dystopic novel, *1984.*

Closer to our own moment is history are two studies that explore this slippage taking place today. Cultural historian Chris Hedges writes in *Empire of Illusion:* "Cultures that cannot distinguish between illusion and reality die. The dying gasps of all empires . . . have been characterized by a disconnect between the elites and reality. The elites were blinded by absurd fantasies of omnipotence and power . . ." (143). In addition, Canadian sociologist Henry A. Giroux's *The Violence of Organized Forgetting* is insightful. In a chapter, "America's Descent into Madness," he observes: "At the heart of neoliberal narratives is a disimagination machine that spews out stories inculcating a disdain for community, public values, public life, and democracy itself" (17). Both explorations are sober assessments backed by thorough research to support their claims.

Furthermore, I have noticed how on various talk shows or news panels, how quickly the "discussion" heats up to the point that two or more voices all begin talking at once so that nothing short of the Biblical image of the Tower of Babel descends on what could have been a legitimate conversation; in this moment, most or all participants lose both the desire or the ability to hear the others' interpretation of what we may loosely label "the truth." Then one side's "truth" becomes the others' scapegoat point of view, and little if anything but a simmering resentment is often the residue. This description is what rhetorical and psychological paralysis sounds like.

Of course, we all wish to have at least some solid ground under our feet most of the time; it gives our sense of self stability and our life something to rely on and trust. But how quickly such a desire, a yearning, as it gathers intensity, even as it may lose direction, can usher in violence—emotional, psychological, linguistic and physical.

The Truth is not, however, necessarily a relative, free-floating entity, but the lines we draw between what is true and what I believe (to be true) can float or even dissolve. And with it, all perspective is dulled, left by the side of the road; because "my truth" gives my life order and stability, I cannot afford to have it yanked out from under me. But is there another perspective possible?

The Buddhist nun, Pema Chodron, offers an image that she makes a part of her Buddhist practice: "To cultivate equanimity we practice catching ourselves when we feel attraction or aversion, before it hardens into grasping or negativity. We train in staying with the soft spot and use our biases as stepping-stones for connecting with the confusion of others" (*The Places That Scare You* 70). When you find yourself clinging to one description or understanding of the Buddha, or any idea or point of view, then it may be time to give it a closer look so as not to be hooked by its intensity or the absence of any energy. Beliefs fall into this category as well.

The Reality of Belief

Let's bring the discussion back to C. G. Jung for a moment here: In *Psychology and Religion West and East* he offers us this insight. After suggesting that "no science can consider its hypotheses to be the final truth" (*CW* 11, par. 377), he continues: "The very existence of a belief has in itself the reality of a psychic fact . . . since all perception is of a psychic nature and we have only indirect knowledge of what is non-psychic" (par. 377).

So, for example, I believe that X is true or false. Metaphors aid us in approaching what cannot be known through a knowable form. When I tell my myth, what am I questing to know? To affirm? To know the unknowable is one option. Or so I believe. Facts are not synonyms for truth. But a narrative couched in metaphor can gain closer access to what is true. And here we approach the rich terrain of myth, for as Joseph Campbell reminds us: "The life of a mythology springs from and depends on the metaphoric vigor of its symbols" (*Thou Art That* 6).

Shortly thereafter, he digs deeper into this finding: "There can be no real progress in understanding how myths function until we understand and allow metaphoric symbols to address, in their own unmodified way, the inner levels of our consciousness" (*Thou Art That* 8). His insights suggest that our beliefs may be metaphorical realities we have confused for literal truths. Learning to discern this difference reflects a developing deeper consciousness.

Jung's writing is additional fertile soil for this entanglement of truth, fact, belief, opinion, conjecture, myth and narrative. I don't want to wear him or you out, but bear with me in this next citation: "Scientific criticism must, of course, adhere to the view that when something is held as an opinion, thought to be true or believed, it does not posit the existence of any real fact other than a psychological one. But that does not mean that a *mere nothing* has been produced. Rather, expression has been given to the psychic reality underlying the statement of the belief or rite as its empirical basis" (*CW* 11, par. 376).

I wonder, in passing, if this juncture is where the confusion resides today: taking a psychic reality and transforming it in story to a literal truth, thereby bypassing the recognition that psychic reality may of course be true, but it does not make it a literal truth. The organic quality of the myth hardens into an ideology, effectively beheading any further discussion. One says, essentially: I have *the answer* and you don't.

Beliefs As "As-If" Fictions

I believe that Jung's insight carries us closer to the nature and function of myth and story here, or myth as story. Myths are narratives that behave as "transport vehicles," a term Campbell has used more than once. They take us to a land far away and yet so near, the interior of our individual soul. To read myths, to live a myth, is to connect to the attitude of the imaginal realm and to the autonomous psyche. Myths are psychological and spiritual teachers; they exist in themselves. Psychic realities underly the stories we tell ourselves as true, or stories others have convinced us we *should* believe. Myths believe us even as we accept and believe in them. Perhaps we can speculate that the story, the narrative is the rich metaphoric field that resonates the beliefs, opinions and even gaps that support and guide our stories.

The perceptive and often profound philosopher of the early 20th. century, and one quoted by both Jung and James Hillman, is Hans Vaihinger, a major scholar of Immanuel Kant. His foremost work is *The Philosophy of 'As-If': A System of the Theoretical, Practical and Religious Fictions of Mankind*. He figures into the major puzzle we are tracing when he suggests that "myths are formed by "as-if" fiction-building" and that these fictions can be useful practically in living one's life" (19) He noticed that in daily life people often challenge the idea, correctly in Vaihingen's view, that "because some constructs are devoid of reality that they are devoid of utility" (19). Hence the fictional nature of "as-if" constructions that most of us live in and out of daily.

A paradox, he suggests, may develop here, namely that "I can believe, assume, conjecture, fictionalize something that is theoretically wrong but from a practical standpoint be fruitful in results" (*The Philosophy* 15). But what then are they in the service of? In order to navigate our way through the world, Vaihinger observes, we may create any one of multiple varieties of these "as-if" fictions with the caveat that they "should be accompanied by the consciousness that they do not correspond to reality and that they *deliberately substitute a fraction of reality for the complete range of causes and facts"* (*The Philosophy* 20, italics in original). Hence, their sublime utility.

His observations reveal that our fictions can become or contain my method of understanding, my *mythodology*, if you will. I also sense that our fictions comprise and conjure the patterned bedrock of my personal myth. The metaphors we live by help us to construct "as-if" realities; they assist us by allowing us to metabolize what we comprehend. Metaphors metabolize. Our fictions allow us to sort life out according to certain patterns and fictions that comprise our personal myth. They offer us frames in order to "as-if" our life events into coherent experiences. I borrow from James Hillman's *Revisioning Psychology* here; he writes in the Introduction that soul is "that unknown component which makes meaning possible, turns events into experiences, is communicated in love, and has a religious concern" (xvi). Myths are formed in just this way—through an "as-if" system-building to promote coherence in our life narratives.

Creating "as-if" fictions is a psychological form of cherry-picking: we select from an array of complexities in our experience to create an artifice by ignoring or neglecting a series of other characteristics to shape and confirm in writing a form of reality that we can adhere to and believe in. Here one may assume a great deal about what is chosen to include and what to keep at arm's length. Vaihinger calls these "provisional assumptions." But some slippage enters here. These provisional assumptions mentioned above "should be accompanied by a consciousness that they do not correspond to reality and they are deliberately substituting a fraction of reality for the complete causes and facts" (*The Philosophy* 20). Useful rather than true is the criterion deployed here, along with an accompanying question that deserves its own chapter: at what point or under what conditions do these assumptions become harmful or instigate thoughts and behaviors that are destructive?

An example close to home would be our current cultural belief that myths are false, imaginary and not to be trusted. A recent case in point aired on CNN: "Debunking Myths Surrounding the Coronavirus." It is not surprising to add here that many people—I dare not say most because I don't know if that is true—do not believe their dreams are very important or are worth recording and thinking about. Not surprising, for most people do not know of or believe in the reality of an unconscious, either personal or collective. All of this forms and shapes their worldview, however little consciousness they bring to it. Beliefs are one of the most potent forces establishing our reality. Let me offer a personal example.

In June of 2020, my wife drove me to the Emergency Room of our local hospital because of pain in my chest and abdomen. After I finished many tests, a surgeon visited me in my room. He told me my gall bladder was inflamed, full of stones and needed to be removed very soon. I did not doubt him for an instant. I believed him unconditionally. He scheduled me for the next afternoon and I relaxed into *the belief* that this necessary surgery would fix the problem. I believed him because

- He was in a position of authority
- I *trusted* that he was indeed a surgeon
- I had *faith* that his staff was well-trained
- I *assumed* this removal of the gall bladder would put me on the road to a healthy recovery
- I *believed* I was not going to be the first person from whom he removed a gall bladder
- I had *heard and believed* the many good reports on this surgeon's skill; they were not falsehoods

I took all of the above as *facts;* they were true so I did not need to research to prove them. In addition, all of these bullet points together formed in me a composite and a coherent story—a viable myth—of belief. Perhaps this next idea from Joseph Campbell may help us here. In *Myths to Live By,* he writes of myth that "not only has it always been the way of multitudes to interpret their own symbols literally, but such literally-read symbolic forms have always been—and still are, in fact—the supports of their civilizations, the supports of their moral orders, their cohesion, vitality, and creative powers" *(*10). If these pillars of mythic certitude are dissolved or yanked from under the collective psyche of a people, then "there follows uncertainty, and with uncertainty, disequilibrium" (*Myths* 10). For example, the Constitution is a document that outlines and codifies the core values of our national mythic identity. Such contained and comforting beliefs it expresses goes to the heart of our ontology as a nation and is fiercely defended from attack and dilution. Well, up until recently, that is.

Would it make sense then, to suggest that when a person's beliefs begin to harden and calcify to such an extreme that they lean towards ideologies promoted by fantasies of what is true, that they may then no longer serve their original intention because they are no longer in touch with current conditions? I believe it takes immense courage to decide what of or in a myth is no longer operative, whose shelf life is well past expiration and should be modified, revised or cut loose, so to let the dead branches give way to promises of new growth. I sense that a life can begin to fade into incoherence from a healthier condition of coherence, by an outmoded myth: the former when it creates such friction in our lives that it best be deleted, the latter when it informs and supports our sense of purpose and meaning, especially for the common good.

The beliefs we adhere to, even cling to, should, as part of our mythic structure, enhance life, not desecrate it. The patterns of thoughts and feelings might best be examined periodically and questioned to rediscover what is still operative for the individual and what has frozen into paralysis, suffocating any further reflections as to one's life purpose. Myths do indeed call us; they call us to a work and a life as well as to a particular mode of experiencing them. One of the great misfortunes in life is to approach the end of it and realize that one perhaps lived out someone's else's myth, not one's own. Now their children, or even other family members or friends, may have to carry the burden to live the myth that one did not—that an individual relinquished, said no thanks, not now—so others may have to put their own mythic journey on hold. That burden we must all work to avoid placing on others we love; compassion dictates that we wish instead for their own mythic pilgrimage in life to be honored and cultivated.

Whose Reality Do I Believe, and Why?

Have you found that sometimes the books smallest in size carry the greatest wallop? Such a realization happened to me some months ago when I found Brooke Gladstone's *The Trouble with Reality: A Rumination on Moral Panic in Our Time*. I found it a wonderful place to pause and reflect on for my own thinking. We start by considering our beliefs as having some connection to a shared common sense of what reality is. But even this today has come under scrutiny, if not attack, with what looks to be dire consequences for uniting anything in the interests of shared common goals. From her perspective, "Reality is what forms after we filter, arrange, and prioritize those facts and marinate them in our values and traditions. Reality is personal" (2). Gladstone found a common spirit in the earlier philosopher, Arthur Schopenhauer in his book, *Studies in Pessimism*: "Every man takes the limits of his own field of vision for the limits of the world" (qtd. in *Reality* 8). Fine. But when those who attain power decide to make such a limited worldview public policy, often for personal and selfish ends, we all may suffer these constrictions to our own beliefs and behaviors.

Such a belief carries a mighty cargo of assumptions: where my understanding ends, the world ends too; my field of vision is the accurate one. I don't have limits; however, the other person does. The world is no bigger than my imagining it; stereotyping the world in this way allows me to believe I know it.

Now a stereotype has been created as a belief system, a way of seeing and knowing that has unacknowledged limitations. Gladstone believes that "our worldview is built on a bedrock of stereotypes, not just about people but also about the way things work" (*Reality* 9). She cites the classic work by the journalist and critic Walter Lippmann, whose 1921 classic, *Public Opinion: How People Decide; The Role of News, Propaganda and Manufactured Consent in Modern Democracy and Political Elections,* has been reissued. It reads with the freshness of having been published last week.

Stereotyped thinking has many specifics uses. For example, in Lippmann's understanding, "'they focus and feed on what is familiar and what is exotic, exaggerating each in the process': 'The slightly familiar is seen as very familiar and the somewhat strange as sharply alien'" (qtd. in *Reality* 9).

If so, then if one clings to stereotypes to frame their worldview, one's myth torques itself into an ideology—it forms their reality with the most minimum of discomforts. One then adjusts, distorts and twists themselves to fit its absolute requirements. Their purpose, as I grasp it, is to filter, to shrink our field of vision. They give rise to vast blind spots and lead to smash-ups when worlds collide. Lippman adds: "'No wonder, then, that any disturbance of the stereotypes seems like an attack upon the foundations of the universe. It is an attack upon the foundations of our universe . . . and we do not readily admit there is any distinction between *our* universe and *the* universe'" (qtd. in *Reality* 10, italics added).

The slippage becomes more evident: what one has set up as *their version* of what is real and therefore true, is now *the version* of what is real and therefore true. Such an act of imagination renders all conversation mute, at least in this terrain of truth. We can box ourselves into a life devoted most frequently to cleaning and brushing off the altar that enshrines our statue of reality. We could divert our attention right here to exploring the role and complicity that the media play in such a project. Our belief has become a mythology if it continues to draw adherents, converts to such a zeitgeist, bolstered by a dogma that insists on its own truth. We live today within a culture that has boldly put forth false notions as real truth and then begun passing laws founded on these squirrelly falsities. But to revert back to a voice of sanity.

I return to this most rewarding volume of Jung's collection, *Psychology and Religion, West and East,* for I think we have been talking about beliefs and faith as religious concerns and therefore red-hot as items for conversation. Stereotypes, dogmatic thinking, assumptions about good and evil are religious concerns as well. It is not infrequent for individuals to speak dogmatically and then offer as an "Amen" a quote from scripture or to ask God to set all this right, meaning to get others on board with this version of reality.

He ends Part II, "A Psychological Approach to the Dogma of the Trinity," with the following reflection, only part of which I will explore here. His interest in these last pages is with the symbolic nature of religious dogma, specifically Christianity. When he realizes that he is in the presence of a "universal archetypal background," he gains the courage "to treat 'that which is believed always, everywhere, by everybody' as a *psychological fact*, which extends far beyond the confines of Christianity, and to approach it as an object of scientific study, as a *phenomenon* pure and simple" (*CW* 11, par. 294) regardless of its "metaphysical" resonances. He then candidly admits that "this latter aspect has never contributed in the slightest to my belief or to my understanding. It told me absolutely nothing" (par 294).

But his thinking and point of view shift radically when he understands that the "'symbolum' possesses the highest degree of actuality" since "it was regarded by countless millions of people, for close onto two thousand years, as a valid statement concerning those things which one cannot see with the eyes or touch with the hands. It is this fact that needs to be understood." He sees in the clearest way that only "the unbiddable gift of faith lifts us beyond all dubiety and all uneasy investigation" (*CW* 11, par. 294).

Jung concludes by distinguishing an act of faith from one of belief: "It is dangerous if these matters are only objects of belief; for where there is belief there is doubt, and the fiercer and naiver the belief the more devastating the doubt once it begins to dawn" (*CW* 11, par. 294). One continues to pursue investigations that focus on their metaphysical significance "that may possibly underlie archetypal statements. There is nothing to stop their ultimate ramifications from penetrating to the very ground of the universe" (par. 295). At the same time, studying the objects of archetypal statements in order to pretend to explain them in order to expose their psychological aspects, is itself insufficient.

His conclusion is one of hope that he has "succeeded in stimulating discussion," for if the world were to "lose sight of these archetypal statements, [it] would be threatened with unspeakable impoverishment of mind and soul" (*CW* 11, par. 295). I grasp here that if the archetypal realities were subsumed by metaphysics, a loss of faith would result. So, Jung moves in these last paragraphs from belief to faith—the grasping of things unseen, as St. Paul describes faith: "Now faith is the substance of things hoped for, the evidence of things not seen" (Hebrews: 11: 1).

Today, as with other moments in history, we are confronted with a crisis of belief: what to believe, what to reject, what to be suspicious of, what beliefs to note that are driven by the engines of greed and power, what to cling to those supports a mythos that is benevolent, compassionate and bends towards benefitting the greatest number, not the least of which are those who continue to be marginalized and kept in a strait jacket of economic, social and cultural vulnerability.

Without keen powers of discernment with an eye to what is just and benefits the greater whole of a people, we find that the intensifying shaping of realities that are not in line with the facts the majority share will lead us headlong to our own destruction. We should all believe it!

Works Cited

Campbell, Joseph. *Myths to Live By*. Penguin Books, 1993.

---. *Thou Art That: Transforming Religious Metaphor*. New World Library, 2001.

Chodron, Pema. *The Places That Scare You: A Guide to Fearlessness in Difficult Times*. Shambhala Publications, 2002.

Cowan, Donald. *Unbinding Prometheus: Education for the Coming Age*. Dallas Institute Publications, 1988.

Giroux, Henry A. *The Violence of Organized Forgetting: Thinking Beyond America's Disimagination Machine*. City Light Books, 2014.

Gladstone, Brooke. *The Trouble with Reality: A Rumination on Moral Panic in Our Time*. Workman Publishing, 2017.

Hatab, Lawrence. J. *Myth and Philosophy: A Contest of Truths*. Open Court Press, 1992.

Hedges, Chris. *Empire of Illusion: The End of Literacy and the Triumph of Spectacle*. Nation Books, 2009.

Hillman, James. *Revisioning Psychology*. HarperCollins*Publishers*, 1975.

Holy Bible. King James Version. Hendrickson Bibles, 2006.

Jung, C. G. *Psychology and Religion: West and East*. Vol. 11. *The Collected Works of C. G. Jung*. Translated by R. F. C. Hull, edited by Sir Herbert Read, Michael Fordham, et. al., Princeton UP, 1977.

Ruch, Emily. *Wyrd Webs and Woven Words: Archetypal Expressions of Fate in Classical, Celtic and Norse Mythology*. Dissertation in the Mythological

Studies Program, Pacifica Graduate Institute. Defended 1 April 2021.

Sohan, Jim. "Voices" Section. *Herald-Zeitung,* December 12-13, 2020.

Vaihinger, Hans. *The Philosophy of 'As If': A System of the Theoretical, Practical and Religious Fictions of Mankind.* Translated by C.K. Ogden. Routledge, 1968.

PART II

THE SOCIAL FABRIC
OF STORIES

17

THE POETICS OF MYTH AND ITS EMBODIED EXPRESSION

In the last few years, a resurgence in the nature of narrative, of story, including personal and collective identity, has gained widespread attention. My interest in one's personal narrative is tied to the nature and structure of myths-- personal, national and global. So what is it to make a myth and to live by a myth?

First of all, myths are the most inclusive expressions of a people's beliefs, superstitions, values, aspirations and memories. They also contain illustrations of what is not valued and perhaps are no longer useful and might best be left behind as one develops one's purpose and understanding of what one is called to be. I would add that a mythic disposition is a poetic attitude. I use the term poetic in its earlier, more original form, *poiesis,* to mean a making, constructing and shaping something into a coherent form—often but not limited to a narrative, a functional fiction—that helps us navigate our way through each day. The prevailing attitudes one carries constantly has consequences on the way one understands and negotiates one's life journey.

Moreover, a myth is intimately tied to our identity, to the plot line or through-line of our being. So myth is also ontological because it addresses our being-ness, our reason for existing and for knowing who we are. I like to think of an individual or a collective's myth statements as comprising their mission statement; it addresses what one stands for and is willing to fight for to preserve its existence. If we do not know who we are, why we are here and what we are willing to defend as crucial shaping values, we travel along the lip of living a mythless life. A life without meaning is a life without a coherent mythos.

Going a bit deeper, a mythic imagination, what we turn to in the *poiesis* or making of our myth, captured in the term mythopoiesis, seeks to intuit the invisible presences that guide our existence, form our behavior, and structure our perceptions. That includes our prejudices. In recognizing them, we can deepen our own scope of vision and understanding. The analytical psychologist and mythologist, C. G. Jung, called this adventure the individuation process, by which we become the unique and whole person we were born to become (*CW* 9,₁ par. 490).

A mythic life also carries a paradox: it is at once in the vital act of becoming while simultaneously completely being the person we are. The poetics of myth, then, attends to how we shape our life into a meaningful purpose(s) that guides us towards wholeness and independence as well as being a contributing positive force in and for the collective. A maturing personal myth understands the truth that each of us is responsible for all of us, beginning with one's self.

Myths are also pattern-generating and pattern-following. Every life develops a series of patterns that helps one negotiate what is familiar and, one hopes, helps one discover new ways to apprehend and deal with the unforeseen, the unfamiliar, and finally, the unknown. What I don't know is part of my personal myth; what I have yet to live is part of my personal myth; the stories I tell myself and others is part of my personal myth. In the best sense of it, we are each narrative fictions functioning in a world with other narrative fictions. Our fictions encompass the essential fabric of our lives. We create, foster and live them out "as-if" they were true. So the myths we live by, as philosopher Hans Vaihinger suggests, may indeed be constructed of a blend of reality and fictions about that reality that help us make sense of what each day delivers, seeking expression (*The Philosophy of 'As-If'* 17).

We can sometimes forget, then, that these stories are not carved in granite; they can be re-storied, revised, amended and even sensed as accruing greater complexity. Each of our lives is like so many writers who continually negotiate their fictional creations to bring them more in line with the true authentic and poetic form they were originally seeded to be.

Each of us, even without knowing fully what we are doing, revise our narratives so to be more in line with our evolving authentic self. Doing it for any other reason betrays the myth we are destined to live out with as full an awareness as possible.

Continual reflection on our own story allows us to see anew our identity as it evolves through joy, suffering, failures, achievements and loving relationships. We cannot forget that our myth is always embodied--in our actions, rituals, celebrations, or even sitting silently and reading. A mythic life is a fully aware embodied life. Myths are not head trips alone. They are also embodied heart trips.

Meditating on our personal myth is an act of poetics, of shaping the myth to conform to our truest self. It is the work of a lifetime, so it demands enormous courage, fortitude and caring for ourselves and others. We are all in an interconnected series of mythologies, even when alone, sleeping and dreaming, which is another source for images of our personal myth to arise from our unconscious landscape, to be activated as guides for our waking voyage.

The journey inward is a mythic and poetic pilgrimage where self-discovery never ceases. How boring our lives would be if this were not true! And how devastating if we only minimally became conscious of its contours.

Works Cited

Jung, C. G. *The Archetypes and the Collective Unconscious.* Vol. 9,₁. Bollingen Series XX. *The Collected Works of C. G. Jung.* Translated by R.F. C. Hull, edited by Sir Herbert Read, Michael Fordham, et. al., Princeton UP, 1971.

Vaihinger, Hans. *The Philosophy of "As-If": A System of the Theoretical, Practical and Religious Fictions of Mankind.* Translated by C.K. Ogden. Routledge & Kegan Paul, 1968

18

TEMENOS OF IMAGINATION: CLASSROOM AS SACRED SURPRISE

Once, during a break in a course on Dante's *Commedia* at Pacifica Graduate Institute in Carpinteria, California, a student acknowledged with growing enthusiasm, the following insight: "I read Dante's poem and know that I understand little of it. But I understand so much of my own life having read and then discussed him in class."

Her perceptive remark launches the main interest of this essay on teaching and learning: the power of the text in the classroom to change perception, to shift orientation, to widen the orbit of what one grasps of self and world in some new conjunction. I think a text, be it fiction or non-fiction, if brought in as a guest in the classroom setting, has the capacity to unleash its energy into the collective psyche of the room, to be amplified, or like a light beam through a magnifying glass, have the power to start a fire, to kindle something deep in the woody pulp of the soul, to fire it up, to create a reservoir of *enthusiasmos,* the emotion of Dionysus, such that learning occurs on a deep level, one that can permanently alter a human life.

Rather than the more traditional academic format of the essay, I wish to offer some observations that while related, are not connected in the traditional paragraph structure. So, this essay is more experiential than scholarly, less interested in sources than in the experience of teaching and the phenomena that accrue from such an imaginal enterprise.

- I want to explore the experience of an engaged class, what I see takes place and what conditions often gather around such a pole of pedagogy; the result is nothing short of miraculous, where time and space alter to accommodate the transformation initiated by the text we enter as an imaginal field together.
- Who and what is in the room: students, teacher and text? How the three find their own original alchemical mix is the central drama of the entire process.
- Humor—its great asset is to relax and open both students and teacher so that engaging the text and being engaged by it originates the adventure of learning.
- Submission to the central, but not exclusive, authority in the room—the poem or the non-fictional work as it converses with the storied bodies of the students engaging it.
- The other authorities that rotate and intermingle their own authoritative voices are the teacher and individual students. At times one or the other assumes center stage in the dramatic action of learning. Student replaces teacher, teacher assumes the imagination of student. these designations are fluid in an organic way in learning.
- Each brings their own narrative structure and beliefs to those inhabiting the poem.

A few assumptions are active in this process as well:

- The text is not an object to be dissected like a cadaver but an organic subject that changes and accommodates changes in the reader. It too has a soul, an animated content and context wherever it finds itself.
- Submission to the work and to the voices in the room changes the barometric pressure gathering in the temenos of the classroom's shared space.
- The work has its own autonomy, but it is more than willing to oblige the particular congregation of engaged participants who gather around it in a manner similar to how a tribe gathers around

a communal fire, to be illuminated and even warmed by a series of tribal narratives.

- Stories have a sacred and numinous quality that cannot ever be fully rendered, but it can be experienced, felt viscerally and responded to with a spirit of largesse, probing questions and tentative assertions.

- One should be willing to be guided by the work, not master it, assault it or conquer it, to be then discarded as a dried husk, deprived of its knowledge.

- The reading of a text is not done exclusively for information but for some deeper level of human transformation. And in this process the text itself undergoes its own change. Perhaps it becomes more itself in this mutual conversation. Something of the text is completed in its being engaged, much as any of us moves towards a greater fullness when engaging with others.

- Relinquishing or yielding some key components of one's own authority, prejudices, narrowness or ideological huffing, encourages the text's voice to speak with greater amplitude and density.

- What one grasps from a literary text is tentative, its shelf life good for this reading only; subsequent readings will yield further and often different insights. Such is testimony to the organic nature of the work and the unfolding nature of its audience when in deep relationship with it.

- Deep in the core of a poem is a living mythos comprising the nugget of the work's existence and power. Each reading may take the reader closer to its hot center, to its nucleus of knowledge and perhaps simultaneously into the inmost center of the reader's being.

- A work read silently in private is quite different from the one that enters the classroom: the collective wisdom, energy and gathering of just this set of commingling mythic imaginations changes, often influencing the work's trajectory, orbit and ultimate meaning. Meaning often contains both individual as well as archetypal or universal possibilities.

- Rereading can be an imaginal action central to understanding on a deeper level.
- Spiraling back in repeated re-readings allows the imagination to bore further down to the more mysterious pockets of the work's own ontology. Such spiraling deeper may touch on the personal and collective unconscious of the text—that's how organic I sense the story is.
- Reading passages aloud changes the dynamics and the atmosphere of the classroom as a temenos; the air changes, the energy becomes more charged, and the participants are led, and often lead the rest of us, into the deeper recesses of the plot through sound rather than just sight.
- A field of energy is created in the room that is both fragile, ephemeral, yet miraculously durable in its own way—as a morphic field of resonance, reflection and reverie.
- At stake in the conversation where an energy flow begins to be created between the work and the individual who sits within a collective, is language itself as the fundamental but not exclusive mediator of meaningful experience. In reading together, we all become more sensitive to the language used, not for information alone, but for a style of consciousness that emerges through it. We all contact and participate in a collective myth that the text brings forward.
- Language itself is redeemed in the act of learning through and by means of the work's story.
- Less dogmatic assertions that push the text off center stage so that the student's own narrative becomes the central attraction, more than insights, while moving through the mythology of the student, bends like the rays of a rainbow,back to the pot of gold of the text, a form of the ancient grail of experience that echoes its meanings.
- Reading aloud by the teacher or student changes the meaning of the work in that it adds to the echoic power of words heard, makes oral and voiced what otherwise remains silent; thus, it operates on another level of consciousness.

- Joy should be a part of the entire experience. By this I mean a felt sense that one has deepened, grown and become more aware as a human being to the possibilities inherent in the imaginal life of self, story and world.

- A level of *poiesis* is activated in the interchange of text, student and teacher wherein something is made, shaped, formed, adapted, that transforms the body of people gathered around the text—the fire in the communal imagination that illuminates all.

- Meaning arises as a fourth presence in proportion to the relinquishing of personal concerns and agendas by all participants.

- Meaning, insight and recognition are liquid qualities that stem from some engagement with the archetypal realm of those verities that do not fade, die off, grow old and feeble, but rather are inflected anew in various ways in the moment of the event of just this reading at just this time with just these persons engaging the moment. It is a moment of eternal re-knew-al.

- One's powers of discernment are enhanced as a result of the meeting of text and participants. From here emerges the third thing: insight.

- All dimensions of one's existence are touched and tempered in this alchemical process of change: psychic, spiritual, incarnational, emotional, cultural and symbolic.

- Powers and actions of contemplation, meditation, annunciation and reflection are brought into play in a choreographed ensemble of mysterious interactions.

- The four functions of C. G. Jung—sensing, intuiting, thinking and feeling—are activated in the process.

- Pacing and rhythm are important realities to be aware of in the shared experience of deepening into the work's nuanced complexities.

- Knowledge, which may be the corridor to wisdom for its own sake, is one of the primary goals of the experience with the text and one another.

- For its part, the text loves conversation and its own participation in such an enterprise; it will, as a subject in its own right, respond to the conversation with its own style of speaking.
- The imaginal world that a text opens up is more, not less, real than the so-called "real world" outside the classroom as temenos.
- The imagination has its own way of knowing, perceiving, relating, grasping and understanding whatever text-as-feast is put before it.
- A work of literature or poetry offers guidance in the form of clues, codes, repetitions that lead one into how it should be read.
- A work is paradoxically at once finished and incomplete, needing readers and discussion to complete its circuit.
- At the same time, each of us who comes to the work is also incomplete and requires the text to complete us through conversation with it and others.
- The text is, like the psyche, autonomous, yet needs us at the same time. Paradox, then, is at the heart of learning, for it balances autonomy with relationship, independence with co-dependence, independent understanding with collective insights.
- No one meaning, conversation or reading is ever adequate to what a text has to offer and what it demands from us. Hence, the pleasure and challenges inherent in rereading.
- The text is self-conscious; part of the act of reading and conversing around and through it is to expose that self-consciousness and our own self-consciousness in the process.
- The classroom is another micro-version of the hero's journey as outlined by mythologist Joseph Campbell: a departure from the normative world of convention and habit in order to enter the woods of the text, initially alone, but not to dwell within that isolation; a wrestling with the forces of interpretation, mis-apprehensions, and then a voyage out of the woods of the work carrying what one has claimed as one's boon of insight, knowledge and a deeper grasping of the invisible reality that lurks just below the surface of the words on the page. The page with its markings is the terrain, the dark wood of understanding.

A=departure
B=Initiation
A=Return

in an unending cycle of engagement

- Apprehension of the forms that support the visible reality is part of the journey of reading towards understanding, accompanied by a joy in the voyage of learning.
- The text has the capacity to create *communitas* among its participants.
- After a class of many hours of engagement in which we experience an alteration of consciousness, all participants may require a period of decompression emerging from the imaginal space created by the collective psyche of the group.
- A neutral zone can serve as a space of transition before all who entered the space can gradually reclaim the lives they held in suspension for this adventure.
- The boons are often a terrain of riches; each gathers what they need from the experience and attends to what is lingering, echoing, to what excites, what illuminates. So, a period of reflection should occur in some form, as one ascends from the depths that learning encourages.
- In years of teaching the same works: Melville's *Moby-Dick*, Homer's *Odyssey*, Toni Morrison's *Beloved* and Dante's *Commedia*, never does the same work enter the classroom twice—the work's power to be mercurial, shape-shifting, protean, elastic and malleable continues to stretch to accommodate the new narratives in the room. Its power is constant.
- What one is called to underline in private reading is important to pay attention to in the classroom; there the personal mythos of the reader-student is seeking voice.
- The desire to write in the margins, to add a piece of one's own story to the stew of stories swirling around the text, is an essential moment to contemplate for what it may reveal of one's own life narrative and identity.

- Students often want to see their own lives shift from prose to poetry, to see that dimension of their being and to nurture it.
- Reading is mimetic and memorial as it includes assimilating parts of one's own plotline to discover where one integrates, resists, deepens and then expresses what is gleaned from their imaginal experience.
- A movement from analogy to ontology—to the mystery of being itself—is part of the journey not simply into the conscious plot of the work, but down and into *its unconscious*, both personal and collective, for each work contains these mythic dimensions of its being as well.
- Tapping the work's own unconscious creates a *poiesis* of soul-making—where some lasting insights are achieved. They are made by the interaction of reader, text and a sharing of insights.
- Reading is a ritual that reveals the myth inhabiting and directing the work to burst forth in a moment of surprising discovery.

In all that is above, one learns that truly to read is not a passive activity but more an organically active conjunction of one's own narrative within the journey afforded by the text. Then its deeper textures may reveal themselves in the voyage into a rich psychic reality, energized by the imagination and reflected on through remembrances.

19

CONVERSATION AND CIVILIZATION'S RENEWAL*

Recently on a flight from Salt Lake City to San Antonio, I found myself sitting next to a man for the two-and-a-half-hour journey. I learned very soon after we began a conversation even before the plane left the airport, that he was a lieutenant-colonel in the United States Army and had attended a military conference in San Antonio. He was a 25-year veteran who had led troops in both Iraq and Afghanistan as well as continuing to teach courses on military history. I quickly learned he knew his stuff.

Knowing little of the history of the various military branches, but having some knowledge through my own teaching of mythology and culture, I asked him, after offering a few characteristics of what a myth is, if each of the branches of the military grew out of and sustained their own unique mythologies. I suggested that far from being "lies," myths carry the deepest values an individual or an entire people hold and promote; it is what shapes us as the individuals we are and becoming. With that thumbnail idea in mind, we proceeded to have a *conversation* about the mythologies of the military that lasted until we landed some three hours later. We continued for a time to stay in touch.

I use this very rich experience to introduce a new book I have been reading: *Reclaiming Conversation: The Power of Talk in a Digital Age* by Sherry Turkle. Her research and discoveries are astonishing but, in many cases,

* Originally published as "Civilized Conversations in a Digital Age" in the "Opinion" page of New Braunfels' *Herald-Zeitung*, Sunday September 22, 2019. 4A.

not surprising. Working with young people in schools, she has measured how texting, emails and other technological means of communication have lowered the level of empathy one feels for another and others. The smart phone, she believes, has altered not only behavior with one another, but the prospect of intimacy itself. Smart phones sit at the dinner table and restaurants like an additional guest, face-up, ready to be pounced on when they ring or buzz. Fear of boredom is the major player among 18-24 years old, Turkle has discovered, so the computer or cell phone is the instant escape route from solitude, being alone or feeling bored, isolated and left out. It is also the default corridor to escape conversation.

Her research revealed that the technology we lionize is also the technology that can silence us, especially in muffling conversation, either on the phone or face-to-face. Her subjects tell her that they would rather text someone than talk to the person directly. Fear of not getting it right is the main reason presented for not wanting to have a conversation with another: one might say something and get it wrong. There is no time to edit and so control the communication. She uses the image that far from conversing more, we connect more; connecting overrides conversing; consequently, we can find ourselves in a "technological cockpit," isolated from any ideas, notions, feelings or beliefs that do not agree with our own. Conversation, real conversing, however, throws one into ambiguity, into a place where ideas take on their own life, and are far less controllable and sometimes not so agreeable. But the tradeoff can also lead to new insights and realizations not considered before. That is, if one is open and curious about other ways of experiencing reality.

She insists that there is hope in retrieving conversation, which is directly linked to civilization. Civilization brings up its original meaning: civility. Bullying, Turkle suggests, especially when performed on-line, may be experiencing such an acceleration because we do not see the other person's reactions, his/her feelings, or the trauma incited, when bullying's vehicle is technology. Empathy is erased or sharply restricted by technical instruments because the other person is not present in an embodied way as an individual. So, technology can numb us to the reality of the other.

Conversation moves in another direction: it promotes intimacy and uncertainty; in conversation one is not fighting to be right or to win, but to understand more fully the point of view of another and one's own. "Face-to-face conversation unfolds slowly. It teaches patience. We attend to tone and nuance. When we communicate on our digital devices, we learn different habits. . . . We dumb down our communications, even on the most important matters. And we become accustomed to a life of constant interruption" (35) that allows only the briefest of sound-bites. Conversation needs duration and durability. Real conversation, not passing information back and forth, can serve as "a crucible for discovery" (37). Ideas, she notes, come from speaking.

What matters most in conversation is risk. "The thrill of 'risky talk' comes from being in the presence of and in close connection to your listener" (35). One gives up control and allows ideas to have their own way, to see where they lead, what connections might be stirred in the crucible of time and duration, not in the pauses between exhausting interruptions.

Turkle's research reveals that the average adult checks his/her phone every 6.5 minutes; teenagers send an average of 100 texts per day. Eighty percent sleep with their phones and will check them when they roll over during the night; 44% never unplug from their devices" (42). The behavior is both compulsive and addictive. Instead of spurning interruptions, we tend to welcome them to keep the wolf of boredom at bay. Stillness is eliminated; solitude turns to loneliness and terrifies; we multi-task and concentrate on something for only a few minutes or even seconds. Our lives can easily become scattered and stuffed with busyness so at day's end we are left with little to reflect on; in fact, reflection seems a lost art, a first cousin to conversation. The end result is a shallow and incomplete sense of who we even are as persons. Perhaps more than a little of the brutality we see today in human interactions is a direct mirroring of how technology is insisting and training us to relate to one another. But is technology itself the problem? No. Abusing it is.

Nonetheless, Turkle remains hopeful; she believes we can reclaim conversation, and with it an earlier form of intimacy, community and basic human respect for one another's point of view without necessarily acquiescing to it. Truly and authentically listening is often enough because the other feels heard. Shrill attacks on what another thinks or believes reduces our humanness, and with it, civilization itself is dealt a wounding blow.

My knowledge of the origins of various branches of the military is so much richer from my plane partner's grasp of its history shared in conversation. His understanding of what comprises a myth—personal, national, and now global—was also enhanced, I like to think.

True conversation is one of those rare win-win human delights. Not winners and losers. Out of it we can reaffirm the joy of learning and teaching as among the highest of human achievements.

Work Cited

Turkle, Sherry. *Reclaiming Conversation: The Power of Talk in a Digital Age.* Penguin Books, 2016.

20

◆◆●◆◆

PORNOGRAPHY DOES NOT STOP
WITH SEXPLOITATION*

Sometimes a word gets stuck in a groove of familiarity and is then limited, even condemned, to just one definition or description. But we learn from the *Merriam-Webster* online dictionary that the word *pornography* can also refer to "a depiction of acts in a sensational manner so as to arouse a quick intense emotional reaction." It goes on to affirm that in the early 1950s the phrase "the pornography of violence" gained wide-spread usage.

This connection between pornography and violence leads me to the outrage felt across the United States and eighteen other nations over the brutal killing of George Floyd by a member of the Minneapolis Police Department.

One photograph showing a prone defenseless Mr. Floyd depicts an image of such power—what I am calling a pornographic image—that it has sparked a global outcry for changes in police brutality against citizens, followed by attempts to cover up the truth surrounding the assault. As many have commented, the knee of a white man on the neck of a black man has been repeated, with infinite variations, for 400 years.

Each of us is outraged in shared ways and in individual responses by the pornography of the events recorded by a seventeen-year-old

---

* Published on Pacifica Graduate Institute's Alumni Affairs website on July 14, 2020. See https://pgiaa.org/faculty-voices/pornography-does-not-stop-with-sexploitation/

bystander; its violence is palpable. The brutality of demeaning another human being through excessive force is deeply visceral; the image inflicts a deep moral wounding on any human being who has the capacity and will to feel compassion for the suffering of another. Unfortunately, and for a myriad of reasons, that compassion can be suffocated by anything from an ideology that stops human feeling to self-loathing, to self-alienation, to greed for power and control. But compassion and outrage were evident in the bravery of the young black woman who decided not simply to stand and watch passively but to take action with her cell phone and record the pornographic cruelty.

My other impulse, to recoil from its brutality, arose from the particular detail of the officer's hands in his pockets, his sunglasses above his forehead, his posture of casualness, his demeanor, his body language that bespoke "I've got this; no worries. All is under control." His hands in his pockets expressed the behavior of a monster out of control. He seemed to me to be at worst enjoying, or at best expressing indifference, in making another human being suffer, even unto death. His callous demeanor as well as his fellow officers' refusal to intervene also expresses the grim face of pornography. Pornography feeds on the fear of others who stand by as impotent observers.

The pornographic imagination seems to seek a number of common goals: turn the other into something less-than-human; dominate that other, be it an individual, a race, an ethnic group, or those who disagree with you—the pornographic need—and for some it is a need that expresses a distorted desire to love. Master the other in no uncertain terms. Call it what you will: restoring order, following orders, getting the job done. But at all costs, dominate.

Susan Griffin's brilliant study, *Pornography and Silence Culture's Revenge Against Nature*, reveals that when the pornographic imagination silences voices of dissent, something alarming happens: "Language ceases to describe reality. Words lose their direct relationship with actuality. Thus, language and culture begin to exist entirely independently of nature" (52). We can all be grateful that the outrage and generally peaceful demonstrations across our fifty states and in numerous countries were not silenced, not muzzled, not muted by the vigorous energy of pornography, which can assume the form of muffling others through domination. Justice demanded a peaceful recoil; compassion for others insisted on a fully human response. The verdict for the officer: guilty on all counts.

While in no way diminishing the sea-change in attitude and awareness that Mr. Floyd's death has catalyzed in the most decent and constructive terrain of our human nature, other forms of the pornography of violence include: trafficking in children; separating migrating parents from their children and placing the latter in cages; stifling increases in minimum wage as a means of keeping entire populations at a level of intolerable existence; voter suppression; governors denying federal assistance to bring millions of Americans into the health care system because the program was designed by an opposing political party; cutting welfare programs, including school meal vouchers; lying about the Covid-19 pandemic with the resulting deaths of tens of thousands of people who could have been saved; over-fishing the oceans and lakes of the world until the earth gasps, exhausted from continual abuse driven by the insatiable greed for *more*.

What is just below the skin of pornography is lust: a lust for power, for control and for accumulating wealth at the expense of others' well-being. That "wealth" may be monetary, social, political, spiritual or physical. The excessive lust wanders the world like an addict suffering in shame in a full-blown sickness who will, without intervention, destroy the host carrying the malady.

The "natural" response to Mr. Floyd's assassination was to sing/cry out in protest, to rebalance the natural order, to reclaim some shred of justice from a culture that has often become self-consumed, numbed by its own desires. Compassion and a clear path to equity through equality can restore a proper balance between nature and culture, placing compassion well in front of pornography as well as communal decency in front of willful appetites that, out of control, shred the social fabric holding us together in a common humanity.

Work Cited

Griffin, Susan. *Pornography and Silence: Culture's Revenge Against Nature.* Harper, 1981.

21

◆●◆

PEACE IS AN ATTITUDE:
SEEING INTO THE INVISIBLES*

I take seriously the plant's point of view.

~ Michael Pollan, *The Botany of Desire*, xvi.

Peace has a purpose. But it is an enormous topic as well as a complex feeling and attitude toward self and the world. Rather than treat it conceptually, I want to share an experience that I had years ago while pilgrimaging for three and a half months retreating into various monasteries and Zen centers in the Western United States. I gathered these experiences into a book, *A Pilgrimage Beyond Belief: Spiritual Journeys Through Christian and Buddhist Monasteries of the American West,* from which parts of this chapter were taken. See the experience which follows as a vignette that I hope carries some insight into the cultivation of inner peace, the only locale where it must, to my mind, take place and grow before any change in the world can be truly effective and lasting. In my pilgrimage I found peace most deeply and most frequently on my walks in Nature. It is also where I journaled each evening for the duration of my pilgrimage. Perhaps that is where many of us need to begin: in Nature—our own interior landscape and the elegant world surrounding us.

---

* Originally published as "The Attitude of Gratitude." *The Herald-Zeitung,* Thursday, April 16, 2020. "Opinion" page. A-4.

At one monastery in Oregon, I found in their tape library an arresting talk by the Benedictine monk Brother David Steindl-Rast, a writer whose work I know from reading him previously. Listening to him was a very different and far richer experience. So let me begin with that, then take you outdoors with me where something of peace's profound presence entered my interior space.

Brother David's voice was animated, vibrant, emotional and joyful; I relished his style as he outlined the qualities he believes constitute meditative prayer: wholeheartedness, leisureliness, faithfulness, authenticity and gratefulness. All of these qualities involved the heart rather than the head; the heart, he suggests, stands for the whole person, the deepest root where a person is of one piece, the realm where one exists with self, others and God. A God experienced in the heart constitutes for him the ultimate reality. All of us, he claims, are made for happiness; this condition grows directly from discovering and creating meaning in our everyday lives. Religion is the human quest for ultimate meaning, "so the term 'God' is not necessary" (*A Practical Guide* cassette tape). There are, for Brother David, many deeply religious atheists in the world also searching for meaning.

His idea of the difference between free time and leisure was helpful and encouraged me to continue the quest; on my pilgrimage I had an abundance of free time, but it was not a synonym for leisure. He states that leisure, rather, "is to allow time to work for its own sake wherein I allow myself to be open to what is happening right now." This leisurely attitude is a virtue because it allows one to *give* it time and to *take* time. The heart in its rhythmic beating continually pumps and rests, pumps and rests. It gives and takes, gives and takes, and so it is the best model for leisure's rhythm: a constant give-and-take in time.

Our lives and vocabulary, Brother David reveals, is full of "take" language with very few "give" responses. For example, I take a test, a seat, a nap, a vacation, time, a shower and a drink. Some despondent souls, reaching for a solution that eludes them, may even "take" their own lives because they cannot not "take it" anymore. Our learning, however, must include the word "give": to give ourselves, to give over to . . . to give in. Giving in, giving ourselves over to God, giving up old habits—"dead branches" he calls them—can help us incorporate the "give" back into the "give-and-take" of life to restore the heart's rhythm.

Brother David's simplicity in such a profound meditation stirred my own heart, giving it more time to make me aware of its rhythm. And then his punch line on for-*give*-ness (as opposed to always *taking*-offense, which was one of the most destructive forms taking can, well, *take*). For-giving, by contrast, is one of the most generous forms of giving. Christ, he suggests, took on the sins of humanity and for-gave them. Christ was the fullest model of the give-and-take of suffering and forgiveness, the great gift-giver. Grace was a given; it was freely given to us as a gift. We can take it or shun it. Somewhere I recalled here that it is better to give than to receive, to give rather than take. I take that to be true. I vowed to do better to give it more space in my life.

Grace may then be God's way of showing us a gift without measure; we can choose freely to take it in grateful acceptance, or we can reject it. Our choice would determine how we entered into this give-and-take relationship with God. I thought too of Meister Eckhart's writings on compassion: "For the person who has learned to let go and let be, nothing can ever get in the way again." Forgiveness is one of the highest expressions of compassion. Both are ways of letting go and letting be. In compassion we give—or for-give; in consuming we take. How to allow compassion to replace consuming was a titanic challenge for me, one which I wished to transform into action.

I "took" his thoughts with me next day when I drove north of Portland to Souvie Island where I "took" a hike along the Columbia River on a beautiful cool sunny day, a gift God had "given" me without conditions. I watched enormous cargo ships glide up the river in perfect silence as I hiked to a lighthouse through the forest and threaded my way between herds of cattle that made me skittish. These cud chewers looked at me suspiciously from above rheumy noses. I climbed a fence and walked humbly by two bulls that suspected me of having an eye on their hefty harem. I tried to appear deferential, to give them a clear sense that these beautiful cows were just not my style, lovely though they were.

I observed and moved within such a welcoming natural terrain with new eyes. It was a revelation to see throughout nature how the living and the dead existed side by side and how new life sprang from the decay of old matter. Some clotty soil suddenly let go along the bank of the river and slipped into the flowing stream to punctuate my musings. Motion and stillness, give and take, new life from old—the patterns continued to surface and I sensed that things invisible to me for so long were now revealing themselves. All is revelation, all is relation, all is realization. The leaves, covered with dirt, reentered the earth, having fallen from great heights. It was fall and all was falling, returning to the earth, heading down home and participating in the give and take of an ancient and enduring cycle. Many of them, already crispy brown, returned to replenish the soil for next year's growth. They gave themselves over to the enduring cycle of life and death.

As I walked, a leaf, acting very forward, spiraled down and landed on my cap. It wanted a last horizontal ride before finally falling on to the bank of the river. I obliged it. Water spiders jerked in joy along the slick calm liquid surface as the Columbia River, deep and silent as God's presence in the stream of my own life, flowed without a ripple. I reflected on how we are each given a certain amount of time on this earth; we can spend that time taking or giving or combining the two. To give of one's time or person to another is one of the great gifts a person can bestow. In such a generous act, one is repaid with the presence of peace. Perhaps I must take the time to give it.

Leaves that had fallen into the water floated along the top, while each shadow followed and mirrored in a darkened similitude its twin floating along the shallow water close to shore. Dead logs and branches lined the muddy bottom. Leaves quietly hosted the sun, palms gently facing out. A leaf bobbed and weaved its meandering descent into the river. Sounds began to increase under the thick bushes to my left. A spider's web caught the sunlight in its gentle sway, and for just an instant, out of the corner of my eye, I caught the filaments of perfect symmetry. This scene was too delicious to pass by, so I sat for a moment on an adjacent log to enjoy the patient and confident engineering of the web, still wet from last night's moisture. I wanted to pause to take it in more carefully.

This doubling of nature awoke in me the belief that I—each of us— was a double of God, a double of divinity; that what took place in the visible order was divinely duplicated in me, an idea I gave myself over to. I waited for these instants of insight in the natural order, where God spoke quietly but clearly, if only I had the eyes and the ears to take it in by giving myself over to God's conscious presence.

Then, as I gazed at the web, it suddenly disappeared. For a moment I thought I had hallucinated it. But the sun's light had shifted just a shudder to the right to make it disappear. I knew the web was right there, almost where I could reach out and touch it in its invisible presence between the two small shrubs to which it was anchored; an invisible presence now, yet I knew its existence was a matter of a few feet from my face. How many other webs were right in front of me, which I did not see because the attitude of the light, or because my angle of vision. blinded me to them. I recalled once again a physicist's belief that we have visible to us only about four percent of the created order. The rest is hidden in not such plain view.

Okay, but there are moments, like this one, as I shifted my position mere inches on the log, when again the spider web revealed itself to me as the sun once more caught it to make it magically visible to sight. So it must be that we can, depending on our disposition, see parts of the universe that may become visible when we are seated correctly or find the right angle or the appropriate attitude for their appearance. *It* needn't move, but *I* must be willing to. I thought that this phenomenon could also reveal God to us through moments of grace, if grace were understood as a gift by which we are given an angle of vision of God's presence, when His light pivoted so subtly. Grace may be thought of as a light which, when slanted in the right attitude, reveals what is invisibly before us, pulsing its own reality, daring to be seen by anyone with sufficient grace to see. I felt welling up in me a gratitude inspired by grace and the gift of the imagination to be aware of what is now invisible, now visible—a give (gift) and take of dimensions of reality going on all the time. This, I thought, is what poets and artists give expression to: those instants of vision when the light catches the invisible and allows the full measure to be seen for a moment in time. Then it retreats into memory to be retrieved in moments of solitude.

Sitting alone on a log next to the deep flow of the Columbia River contemplating a peek-a-boo spider web and delighting at how little prompting I needed to enjoy the mystery of the world, I felt the absence of any boundary existing between the physical and spiritual realms, between the natural order and supernatural presences, between the world's tangible body and its invisible gracefulness, between time and eternity. It was an instant of grace, freely given and gratefully taken; I found myself in the thick of the give-and-take of creation. All the low points, the loneliness, the feelings of depression, of sadness, of grief, of emptiness, of loss, of wanting to head home, evaporated in the face of this spider web, which had once more playfully disappeared in the forest but not in my imagination.

Its ability to remain on the margin between visibility and invisibility was its strength, like the eyes of the insects it wanted to ensnare were so multi-faceted and keen that only a web that could disappear would ever hope to snag them. This web's presence, when perceived, was akin to the effects true praying and insightful poetry had on the senses. Both of them made visible what was hidden in plain view, just in front or next to us or coming up from behind. Our failure was in lacking the right attitude by which to see it. I believe more strongly now that it requires an attitude of peace, of serenity and of acceptance—a thorough giving over of one's self—so to coax the invisibles into presence.

Both prayer and poetry make visible what is hidden in plain view, just in front of or next to us, in an object or a person. My weakness was not having the right attitude by which to see it. I shifted my position to defer to this reality. What I was given in return was a miracle of vision.

Zen Web

The spider's mandala
rests serenely anchored like a large enmeshed
wheel between two scrub bushes
linking forest and river.
The sun gives it shape and an angle of clear vision.
It vanishes when the sun blinks
 behind a swaying leaf.
The spider rests Zen-like at the center, in perfect
Zazen, waiting, praying, proud of its design
spun from a memory it did not recall.
Only when the web fades, becomes clear

force, does the spider move wavily in mid-air
above the ground towards a small moth
flapping against the sticky filaments of Zazen.
Two scrub bushes, keeping the tension of the moth
between them, bow slightly toward one another.
Buddhists of the forest embrace the flame of death.

Developing an attitude of peace in our daily lives places us finally in the intimate space of death. Knowing our mortality, our woundedness, our frailty and imperfections can enhance, not detract, from cultivating an attitude of peace and for-giveness towards oneself and others. Then the world can indeed change for the better through the invisible webbing of communal nurture.

Works Cited

Eckhart, Meister. https://www.azquotes.com/author/4339-Meister_Eckhart

Pollan, Michael. *The Botany of Desire: A Plant's-Eye View of the World*. Random House, 2002.

Slattery, Dennis Patrick. *A Pilgrimage Beyond Belief: Spiritual Journeys Through Christian and Buddhist Monasteries of the American West*. Angelico Press, 2017.

Steindl-Rast, Brother David. *A Practical Guide*. Cassette tape. n. d.

22

CALL ME ISHMAEL:
A QUEST FOR WHOLENESS*

It may seem out of keeping for some that I call this epic whale tale a religious narrative as well as a spiritual quest. But it cannot be otherwise. 'The Call to Adventure' advocated by Joseph Campbell in his classic exploration, *The Hero with a Thousand Faces*, offers another way of speaking about a mystical quest, a yearning for a sense of wholeness and a desire to tell one's story with such persuasive force that it may influence others by deepening their self-understanding and adding a chapter or a footnote to their own narrative.

Published in 1851 when Herman Melville was still a young man—he died in 1891—the epic is a powerful rendering of what the psychologist C. G. Jung would later call a "numinous experience." I will say more of that in a moment. *Moby-Dick* is also concerned with telling a good story, finding the right particulars to weave into a comprehensive whole. The psychiatrist Robert Coles writes in *The Call of Stories* that "the beauty of a good story is its openness—the way you or I or anyone reading it can take it in, and use it for ourselves" (47). Depth psychologist James Hollis considers how "the serious study of literature increases our capacity to see the archetypal nature of individual cases, unique stories, and particular dilemmas, as well as the formative work of the Collective Unconscious in shaping our behaviors and cultural patterns" (*Living Between Worlds* 33).

---

* Part of this essay was presented to The Unitarian Universalists of New Braunfels, Texas on Sunday, August 30, 2020.

I don't know about you but I sense the same beliefs: I have never met a person who does not enjoy a good story. We are, in fact, our narratives. How we tell them is a matter of craft, care and deep reflection. I am suggesting that Melville's whale narrative is as much concerned with exploring narrative itself as it is with hunting down a white whale that dismembered the captain of the Pequod, one Ahab, who, like Ishmael, is another character with a rich biblical name. Stories are meant to be used to disclose something shared in us and, through us, with the world, as Hollis' insight reveals. Such storied expressions can actually be a richer experience than an actual event it converts into a story.

We can see and deepen our understanding of our own stories by parsing them through another, especially a classic narrative. They reflect and mirror one another in very surprising ways. Just think for a moment of Ishmael's name. We may wonder: "Ss that your real name or your stage name? Is it your poetic name because you want us to understand you through the poetic prism of your prototype?"

To begin responding to these questions, let's make one quick visit to Genesis 21 where Abraham, now 100 years old, fathers a son, Ishmael by the Egyptian slave Hagar. In a moment of excessive pride at having been the mother of Abraham's son, Hagar mocks Abraham's wife, Sarah. In response, Abraham gives provisions to Hagar and "sent her away: and she departed, and wandered in the wilderness of Beer-sheba" (21:14). Dispirited, she sends the infant away from her so she will not hear him as he dies, but God hears the cries of Ishmael and speaks to Hagar: "'Arise, lift up the lad, and hold him in thine hand; for I will make him a great nation'" (21:18). Ishmael's name means in Hebrew "God shall hear."

So, let's think of these first three words when the narrator of *Moby-Dick* directs us to "Call me Ishmael." Now if you say this aloud, then you, the reader, are directing *us* to call *you* Ishmael. And God will hear your plea, your desire, your wish, your insistence. Will he answer? Stay tuned! Stay attuned! Stay attentive! Stay awake!

We might entertain a quick connection between this moment in Scripture, poetry and Joseph Campbell's thinking. He believes that before you can refuse or heed the call, you must first be able to hear it. But what allows some to hear the call and others to remain deaf or indifferent to it? The psychologist C. G. Jung writes in *Psychology and Religion: West and East* the following: "Religion appears to me to be a peculiar attitude of mind which could be formulated in accordance with the original use of the word *religio,* which means a careful consideration and observation of certain dynamic factors that are conceived as 'powers': spirits, daemons, gods, laws, ideas, ideals or whatever name man has given to such factors in his world as he has found powerful, dangerous or helpful enough to be taken into careful consideration, or grand, beautiful, and meaningful enough to be devoutly worshipped and loved" (*CW* 11, par. 8).

The hero, for Campbell, is "the man of self-achieved submission. A yielding, a giving of self over—of serving something outside the self" (*Hero* 17). A few pages later he adds: "The hero is one who has died to self, gone beyond, to tap another dimension of reality—then returned to share the boon" (20). I suggest the whale voyage is exactly the call that Ishmael submits to and then enters a double story: first is the event of the hunt; second is the conscious, self-reflective creation of the narrative that allows us to journey along with him. No wonder he invites us to call ourselves Ishmael, so we can experience the wonderful, mysterious and violent voyage sailing for revenge towards the *anima mundi,* the white whale, the godhead, which embodies both the creative powers of nurturing and the violent forces of annihilation, of splintering the soul into a thousand pieces. The challenge for Ishmael and us: can we accept both conditions and live within the tension of creation-destruction of this figure from the deep?

And are his first words to us in the narrative proper, following the sections called "Extracts" and "Etymology," a request or a requirement? And can each of us talk about the whale voyage of our own lives, including what is requested of us over against what is required of us? The ability to discern the difference looms large in how we might live our lives and with what wisdom we might have contacted and returned with from our adventure. The word *adventure* has an interesting biography. From etymonline.com, in 1200 it was "aventure, that which happens by chance, fortune, luck; from Old French, 'chance, accident, occurrence, event, happening'; from Latin: '(a thing) about to happen.'" An adventure is life-in-the-making and one of our richest sources for spinning the threads of stories into a coherent whole. We are more than what happens to us; we are also the stories that creatively arise from those happenings.

Ishmael, as he tells us on the first page, is an *isolato,* an outcast, living on the margins of the social order. He is angry, depressed, despondent: "Whenever my hypos get such an upper hand of me . . . then I account it high time to get to sea as soon as I can. This is my substitute for pistol and ball. With a philosophical flourish Cato throws himself upon his sword; I quietly take to the ship. There is nothing surprising in this. If they but knew it, almost all men in their degree, some time or other, cherish very nearly the same feelings towards the ocean with me" (*Moby-Dick* 3). I hope you see at this inception of the epic of over 600 pages, that Ishmael is seeking community, brotherhood, fraternity, others, relationships, connectivity between himself, humanity, the natural order and the divine presence in creation. Relating now to the fullness of life, he is all-in.

In the first chapter, appropriately named "Loomings," he reflects on the power of the call itself. "Why is almost every robust healthy boy with a robust healthy soul in him, at some time or other crazy to go to sea? Why upon your first voyage as a passenger, did you yourself feel such a mystical vibration, when first told that you and your ship were now out of sight of land?" (5). To which he then gives enticing musings a mythological twist: "And still deeper the meaning of that story of Narcissus, who because he could not grasp the tormenting, mild image he saw in the fountain, plunged into it and was drowned. But that image, we ourselves see in all rivers and oceans. It is the image of the ungraspable phantom of life; and this is the key to it all" (5).

That "ungraspable phantom of life" may be different for each of us, but I am certain that we all feel the dread and excitement of that part of our life, that double of ourselves, tack about through self-reflection, which is the heart-beat of the Narcissus myth. To see double is mythic; to see reflectively is mythic consciousness. C. G. Jung takes it one step further: "Experience is not even possible without reflection, because "experience" is a process of assimilation without which there can be no understanding" (*CW* 11, par 2).

So, we are called twice in life: one, to what we heed and yield to if we are awake enough to discern the call, the vocation that gives our life purpose and direction. We are, I know you recognize, "making a living" or "earning a good salary." But these alone will not sustain us; we need more soulful reasons for living; we also deserve more, as Campbell's mantra, "Follow Your Bliss" points us toward.

The second vocation is to give those events that brought us to accept a calling a voice in the second journey or pilgrimage: self-reflection. We remember our narrative to others and ourselves, we witness ourselves in the consequences of being called and of opening ourselves to some avenues of mystery. To do so we must remain flexible and open, not tight-fisted and clenched by ideologies or absolute pronouncements. We may even have had the experience of looking one day in the mirror—I mean really looking—and wondering who it is gazing back at us. At those moments, when we see, not a complete stranger, but a compelling other in the mirror, we may be rewarded with a temporary glimpse of the mysterious "other" that is us. What we are finally drawn to in the world is always, on some level of awareness, a reflection of something deep within our own psychic and spiritual geography, some correspondence between the inner and outer worlds that comprise the contents of mythology generally.

James Hillman takes this idea a step further. As he explores the Platonic idea of the *anima mundi,* that which animates the things of the world, he asks us to change our perspective that soul is in us as we experience the dead objects in the world: "Rather, let us imagine the *anima mundi* as that particular soul-spark, that seminal image, which offers itself through each thing as its visible form. . . . soul is given with each thing, God-given things of nature and man-made things of the street" ("Anima Mundi: Return of the Soul to the World" in *City and Soul* 33). Ishmael's desire to go to sea is also to "go to see" the world as animated by this ancient idea of the animating presence in all things of the world. His quest is first and foremost visionary, not exploitative.

What calls Ishmael, then, on the first pages that leads him, finally to sea (see!), "was the overwhelming idea of the whale himself. Such a portentous and mysterious monster roused all my curiosity" (*Moby-Dick* 7). His intimate narrative style with us, the readers that are his double, invites us to contemplate what our own white whale has been that we continue to pursue, or once did. Pursuing the white whale does not have to end in destruction, although Ishmael divulges how it can. This draw is to what Jung describes in citing the German philosopher, Rudolf Otto's book, *The Idea of the Holy*.

Otto describes the *numinosum,* that is, "a dynamic agency or effect not caused by an arbitrary act of will. On the contrary, it seizes and controls the human subject, who is always its victim and its creator" (qtd. in *CW* 11, par. 6). It is so important to note that it is both victim and creator. But Otto goes on to clarify, "the *numinosum*—whatever its cause may be—is an experience of the subject independent of his will. . . . The *numinosum* is either a quality belonging to a visible object or the influence of an invisible presence that causes a peculiar alteration of consciousness" (*CW* 11. par. 6). We notice how similar Ishmael's calling is to the description of the *numinosum* in our lives.

Chapter One ends, then, on a note of exuberant excitement as Ishmael contemplates the whaling voyage in a lyric outburst: "The great flood-gates of the wonder-world swung open, and in the wild conceits that swayed me to my purpose, two and two there floated into my inmost soul, endless processions of the whale, and, mid most of them all, one grand hooded phantom, like a snow hill in the air" (*Moby-Dick* 8). Notice how the whales appear in doubles, in twos, as if one continually reflects the other in a mirror. How can we not remember another biblical epic hero, Noah, who brings the animals into the ark two-by-two?

Ishmael has already assented to the whale voyage in his imagination. But the voyage, while in front of him in narrative time, is already taking shape as a historical event behind him in chronological time. Yet they too mirror one another as well, it seems to me; so, our past and futures mirror who we are in the present moment. Discerning how this is so is already to begin entering mythic time, the time of memory, metaphor and sustained coherence in the voyage of one's lifetime.

Works Cited

Campbell, Joseph. *The Hero with a Thousand Faces*. Bollingen Series XVII. Third Edition. New World Library, 2008.

Coles, Robert. *The Call of Stories: Teaching and the Moral Imagination.*
Houghton Mifflin, 1989.

Hillman, James. *City and Soul.* Vol. 2. *The Uniform Edition of the Writings of James Hillman,* edited by Robert J. Leaver. Spring Publications, 2006.

Hollis, James. *Living Between Worlds: Finding Personal Resilience in Changing Times.* Sounds True, 2020.

Jung, C. G. *Psychology and Religion: West and East.* Vol. 11. *The Collected Works of C. G. Jung.* Sir Herbert Read and Michael Fordham et. all, editors and translators. Princeton UP, 1977.

Melville, Herman. *Moby-Dick, or The Whale.* Introduction by Clifton Fadiman. Illustrated by Boardman Robinson. Collector's Edition. The Easton Press, 1971.

23

FACING OUR FEARS:
PAN, THE PANDEMIC AND POLITICS*

The god Pan in Greek mythology is a curious deity. As a loner in the mountains of Greece, he spent his time seducing the nymphs of the forest and generally alarming and terrifying folks eking out a simple life in surrounding farms, villages and cities. Because he was not often seen, his howlings and growlings distressed all those who heard him; he was the great disruptor of ordinary life in individuals, families and nations. Whenever we feel collectively an overwhelming sense of fear, of threat, of vulnerability, whether it be to our values, our beliefs or our way of life, our first instinct may well be to panic. Then our shields go up and clear thinking goes down. We have given ourselves over to a pandemic in the soul.

Fear, a cousin, or maybe brother, to panic, can also be a corrosive presence in our thoughts and responses to what threatens us. I have been thinking of how much the stories we hear today are frequently fear-based and stoked often by mis-, dis-, and flat-out wrong information. In-formation may easily coalesce into fear-formation, with responses to it being seemingly senseless acts of violence. Both panic and fear are forms of terrorism in themselves and often cultivate responses devoid of reason or even a scrap of common sense.

I returned to a book that a former professor of mine wrote years ago: Robert Sardello's *Freeing the Soul from Fear* (1999). It could have been

---

* Originally published as "Facing Our Fears: Panic, Pandemonium and Politics." "Opinion" page of *The Herald-Zeitung*, Thursday September 23, 2020. 4A.

published yesterday, for the conditions that incite fear are universal and timeless. We often don't think about being afraid as an opportunity for self-reflection and personal growth, but Robert does. Let me share a few of his insights about Fear, an emotion that haunts us intensely today:

- When Fear becomes one of the major stories in our lives, we may descend into a decentered place; we are pulled out of ourselves in fear.

- Retreating to prejudices is one common way that individuals deal with Fear. The word "prejudice" means to pre-judge, to judge without facts or correct information. It is a comforting place to retreat to in the face of being fearful. Fear exposes each of us to judgments that can, in times of calm, be seen as irrational and disconnected from the reality we feared; they can actually feed the furnace of Fear burning within us.

- Fear disturbs the flexible boundary between me and the world.

- From Robert's observation above, I would add that Fear makes us rigid, self-enclosed in an insulated system that feeds on its own toxic juices.

- If we approach Fear by hoping to stop it through external means alone, we are probably using the wrong tools. Some deeper response must come from within us.

- As Robert understands it, the soul needs time to take things in; it cannot be hurried. When bombarded with one sequence of events after another, and often with little depth or understanding accompanying it, then Fear enters us and becomes its own tyrant, stoking itself into greater control over our thinking and behavior.

- Fear creates a disposition towards obsessions, compulsions and other forms of non-reflective thoughts and actions. They in turn dull consciousness and the ability to reflect. We then risk knee-jerk reacting as a substitute for a more thoughtful, creative response.

What might be an antidote to a fear-based individual or culture? Robert suggests several. He believes that the human imagination itself is a moral force, one which can free us from a Fear-based pattern of reacting in order to respond with compassion and love, beginning with oneself. Developing an inner silence while observing the outer world can also cultivate a calmer understanding attitude that takes the wind out of Fear's sails.

Cultivating as well a spirit of patience, waiting and receptivity can begin to counteract the urges of our instincts and passions. Thought is an antidote to the impulses of the instincts and compassion is an antibody to our passions. In such a shifted attitude, we do not deny that certain situations threaten us; we can, however, delete Panic and Fear as our only options.

Work Cited

Sardello, Robert. *Freeing the Soul from Fear.* Riverhead Books, 1999.

24

BEING CERTAIN ABOUT UNCERTAINTY*

Uncertainty continues to grow, expand and deepen around us, creating perhaps, its own virus, a virus gnawing at the heart. We hear the words today, "Everything is so fluid and we don't know what's next." My own levels of anxiety continue to rise, so I returned to one of my favorite books by a beloved writer to calm myself: *When Things Fall Apart: Heart Advice for Difficult Times* by the Buddhist nun, Pema Chodron. In addition to her gift for bringing some fundamental ideas of Buddhism into the Western world, she was instrumental in founding and directing Gampo Abbey in Cape Breton, Nova Scotia. It is the first Tibetan monastery in North America specifically established for Westerners.

Rereading some select passages lately, I began to notice how her insights on impermanence seemed so applicable to many of our feelings of uncertainty and its first cousin, insecurity, as the spread of Covid-19 weaves its way into all parts of the planet. I am relearning from Chodron how a pandemic does not have to lead to pandemonium unless we allow it and even encourage it.

She asks us, for instance, to consider another tact on our feelings of impermanence, going so far as to suggest that "Impermanence is the goodness of reality. . . . Impermanence is the essence of everything." She

* Originally published as "Being Certain About Uncertainty." *The Herald-Zeitung,* Thursday, March 19, 2020. "Opinion" page. A-4.

observes that "people have no respect for impermanence; . . . in fact, we despair of it. We regard it as pain. We try to resist it by making things that will last—forever." In doing so, she claims, we can easily "lose our sense of the sacredness of life" (*Things* 118).

My understanding is that her remarks on impermanence strike close to the heartbeat of uncertainty. In fighting either one, I can feel that reference points in my daily life can be shaken, begin to fall apart and need to be reclaimed not by force but by yielding to and becoming curious about my relation with both impermanence and uncertainty. I feel certain about this reclamation!

I am curious at this stage how any of our reference points of our life can be seen as our reverence points, places in which the sacred— what we treasure and value—have their most dramatic and heart-felt expressions. What I reference on a daily basis is what I reverence. I believe that it is an important question to pose to ourselves periodically: what in my life do I truly revere? Then refer to these touchstones regularly.

Chodron describes at one point how these can become focal points of wisdom, even opportunities to examine life-long habits of responding to them when they appear, which, if not in our current condition of uncertainty of where the virus will take all of us, then when? But her approach goes deeper: she suggests that if we can see ourselves nested within our feelings of impermanence and uncertainty from a place that is not ego-driven, then things transform vividly. Here is what she understands: "Egolessness is available all the time as freshness, openness, delight in our sense perceptions . . . we also experience egolessness when we don't know what's happening. . . . We can notice our reactions to that" (*Things* 51).

I find her focus on what is worth exploring to be curiously comforting as I try to be more relaxed with the uncertainty that faces all of us each day around the planet: will there be enough money, food, health, healthcare, cooperation, unity in the face of increasing adversity? When the same old patterns "of grasping and fixating" continue to drive us towards greater insecurity, wherein the patterns are repeated with renewed gusto, we can, she notes at the end of her reflections, "relate to our circumstances with bitterness or with openness" (*Things* 146).

Our greatest freedom may indeed reside in how we relate to the mess we feel around and perhaps within us, rather than fleeing towards some comfort cocoon to avoid the dilemma altogether.

Work Cited

Chodron, Pema. *When Things Fall Apart: Heart Advice for Difficult Times.* Shambhala, 2000.

25

——— ◆●◆ ———

MORAL INJURY
AND ITS CHALLENGES*

As the ravaging pandemic continues to infect the globe with new out-breaks, we count over 110,00 lives lost at the time of this writing, as a growing number of infections continue to rise in pockets of our country with alarming intensity. But the other epidemic that has burst on the international scene is the May 25th. 2020 brutal murder of Mr. George Floyd by a Minneapolis police officer; it has exposed another epidemic that many assert is more than 400 years old: racism. His death has galvanized an entire movement seeking justice. More than ever, it has ignited the power and grand sweep of what comprises a moral injury. An individual or an entire people can be mortally injured, and we have the numbers to reveal that destruction. But we can also suffer moral injury that corrodes the heart and soul of a people with equal devastation. The uprising and demonstrations in all fifty states and eighteen nations against this horrific act of inhumanity offers us all hope. Since I originally wrote this short essay, George Floyd's killer has been found guilty on all three counts leveled against him.

Larry Kent Graham's insightful study, *Moral Injury: Restoring Wounded Souls,* reveals the crippling results that injuring one another morally can inflict; it too requires healing as much as any physical assault on our biology, economy and on our democracy. Moral injury feeds on creating

---

* Originally published as 'Moral Injury and Its Challenges." *The Herald-Zeitung.* Thursday, June 10, 2020. A-4.

dissonance between what is perceived as the facts of a situation and inserting an alternative reality that can pull us away from our own best virtues. These two pandemics, running concurrently, can diminish and demoralize a people, paralyze them into inaction, where they lose any resolve to stop the spread of the diseases. We feel the deep gratitude in witnessing and participating in a counter-movement: generally, a peaceful push-back, yes, but also an affirmation of our basic human, compassionate nature.

The pandemic is an infection of the body; moral injury is an affliction of the soul. Using the word "politics" to mask it misleads and deflects what are moral concerns that place the conversation on another level entirely. Graham believes the nature of moral afflictions can be "a failure to live in accord with our deepest moral aspirations." "Moral" designates "a sense of right, fairness in obligations that we see in everyday life. Moral includes our core values, our virtues by our communities about what constitutes the best way of life" (*Moral* 10). Yes, it cost the brutal murder of a submissive individual who was nonetheless monstrously killed, in order to highlight them. The photos of this incident sparked an outrage that sliced deep within our moral center of compassion.

When we lose the memory and the practice of this moral compass, we become confused as to what to believe, or we place our self-interests ahead of all "responsibility" for others. Then moral dissonance revs its engines and alienates us further from being a functioning community sharing fundamental values of moral equity. Sowing confusion, or shifting with the winds and the whims by national leaders, is a failed strategy to confuse the moral compass seeking true north. Moral dissonance is not just about interior conflicts; it can arise from a moral climate in which history and culture have embedded us. Distortions deify moral dissonance. Restoring a balance between justice and outrage recovers our collective humanity that tends toward the good; that must be the trajectory of our new path.

When we become ensnared in a moral dilemma, which is where I think we are gravitating towards, what arises, Graham asserts, is a situation in which "we are required to choose or act against our moral good at the expense of another value we hold. We cannot escape such a dilemma when it comes into play; we must respond" (*Moral* 77). Our responses can advance us morally, or they can lead further into moral acquiescence. Masking the truth, fabricating fictions to mislead others from failed leadership as a fragile defense against revealing a situation out of control, fuels the fires of moral dissonance. We are pushed into a terrain well beyond "political parties" and enter a no-man's land of conflict and unrest in order to feed self-interests. This is the state of moral paralysis, or sclerosis in the communal body, that further crises will challenge us not to succumb to if we can sustain a conscious moral conscience.

The situation becomes more complicated when bodies of leadership who have some control over such a slide into chaos abdicate their responsibilities or actually encourage such tyrannous chaos. Silence itself can be used as a weapon against assuming the mantle of what that body has been created to preserve. A question I have carried for some time is: which pandemic injury will ultimately inflict the greater injury on us as a people and a species: mortal or moral? The global demonstrations have raised the spirits of so many in the protests against Mr. Floyd's unnecessary and hideous suffering and death. The justice meted out in a verdict against his killer has assuaged some, but other similar examples are always being birthed on the social horizon.

Work Cited

Graham, Larry Kent. *Moral Injury: Restoring Wounded Souls*. Abingdon Press, 2017.

26

BELIEFS' POWER AND FRAGILITY*

What has surfaced and demanded attention in this period of our national history is the crisis of belief. I was impressed with Jim Sohan's letter in "Voices" (Dec. 12-13, 5-A) in the *Herald Zeitung*, "Time to Stop Being Silent." Referencing fledgling democracies in the world, he writes: "The foundation of those democratic institutions is the belief of the public that elections are free and fair. . . ." Belief as foundation, belief as baseline. We have a natural impulse or instinct to believe in something. *What? Which?* and *Why?* are crucial questions to answer not once, but frequently.

It seems, in the period we are slogging through today, that a belief rests less on its being true than on its level of emotional value and persuasion for an individual or a community. Whatever each of us accumulates in our storehouses of beliefs will in fact shape the story we live by and further contour our identity as an individual. In other words, our personal narrative, regardless of how much or little we reflect on it, is an amalgam of what we believe, sense, intuit, assume, accept and reject about what we loosely call "reality." The efficacy of a belief is highlighted most often by how much affect or emotional response it elicits from its adherents. In other words, is it believable?!

When any of our beliefs calcify into an ideology that "this is the truth," rather than "this is my perception of what is true," then out of that rigid and tight-fisted stance often arises resentments, denials and violent

---

* Originally published as "Beliefs' Power and Fragility." "Opinion page," 4A. *The Herald-Zeitung*, Saturday, January 2-3, 2021.

responses to what others have settled on *what is true for them*. Acceptance, or even tolerance of another's angle on "reality," transports us in a different direction and loosens the grip of a tyrannous sense of rightness.

Things become more complex when the phenomenon of *fact* is introduced into the argument over what is true. In his insightful book on revising education, *Unbinding Prometheus: Education for the Coming Age,* physicist and university president Donald Cowan writes of "the myth of fact," which he claims has been "the prevailing myth of the modern age" (*Prometheus* 4). Fair enough. But he then points out an historical move that may be responsible for the conspiracy theories enjoying such prominence today.

He suggests that the myth of fact shifted in the early Renaissance [14th. century Italy] in a substantial way: "In it the observable objects of the world came to exist in their own right. Rather than taking their meaning from a context. . . in order to participate in a larger reality, facts began to be considered the unchallengeable substance of life. . . . (4–5).

What evolved has come down to us as "facts speak for themselves." They can be measured and verified and trusted as entities to believe in. But we have entered a different mode in our relationship to facts. "Fact-checking" has become necessary to counter the dizzy world of "alternative facts." Facts are then weakened in their ability for many to believe in. Moreover, the contesting energies between facts and fantasies—lies—becomes more acute.

When facts lose their *contexts,* their veracity diminishes; facts in large measure help us to construct our narratives that shape our identities. But if facts are relativized, so also is the core of reality itself. If individuals and groups or nations are no longer certain what or who to believe in, their identity as a coherent and cohesive body with shared senses of purpose and ideals to pursue are orphaned. In addition, the shared mythos on which a people's sense of purpose and callings rests is eroded at its base.

May our collective journey forward allow us to find a tolerant, accepting level of accommodation for one another as we struggle through the pandemic and the pandemonium of our recent past in order to forge a future we can all believe in. Through communal generosity we can retrieve it. Only then can we each participate in a shared myth that bequeaths to us a formed set of facts, and the values that hibernate within them, to embrace as our image of the real—a mucilage that binds us as a community.

Work Cited

Cowan, Donald. *Unbinding Prometheus: Education for the Coming Age.* The Dallas Institute Publications, 1988.

27

THE DECENT SOCIETY: A WAY FORWARD*

In the wake of a moving and heart-stirring Inauguration were planted the seeds of a new level of integration of our disparate and at times desperate parts of our national soul. It stirred a memory in me of a book I had begun reading some time ago that I found inspirational and aspirational. I retrieved it from my bookshelf and picked up where I had left off: Rabbi Avishai Margalit's *The Decent Society*. The word "decent" has meant, in its origins, "tasteful," "proper," "becoming," or "to be fitting or suitable." Decency claims a rightful place in any society, especially deeply-afflicted ones or in those who are struggling between two realities, two myths, one fading and the other not yet birthed.

Margalit reveals that "a decent society is one that does not humiliate or wrest self-control from its weakest members." To humiliate or demean another, he claims, is "a painful evil." A decent society "does not injure the civic honor belonging to it" (*Society* 28). In such a society, there are no second-class citizens—those who have been shoveled to the margins, whose relative absence of power and position are used against them for personal or corporate gain. How leaders of a people decide to discriminate "in the distribution of goods and services is a form of

---

* Originally published as "The Decent Society: A Way Forward." "Opinion" page. *The Herald-Zeitung*, Saturday, January 23-24, 2021. 4A.

humiliation even if the people deprived of them do not define themselves as belonging to the depriving society" (153).

We can and have, as a people today, denied selected others "civic privileges," and by doing so, cement them in place according to a prescribed definition of their status as we have deployed it. What keeps or retards a society from becoming more decent—and perhaps the goal of democracy is less to "form a more perfect union" than to form a more decent union—is to encourage all others by offering equitable opportunities to rise to their most gratifying potentials.

My sense today is that we have at this critical crossroads, this threshold in the political sway of things, an opening to decide whether to stay secure in our silos of sour hearts and prejudiced persuasions, or to engage with all of our talents and innate decencies to enrich the lives and spirits of all of us for a change, in order to change. Dreams we hold can become nightmares that hold us back, from using the pandemic, economic and psychological crises we are entangled in, to create something new, not desecrate the human possibilities we are.

Allowing ourselves to be inspired by new attitudes towards our noble natures and to at least acknowledge the darkness that resides in each of us, known or not, can lead to leaving our guns at home, both the literal guns we own and the metaphorical guns we aim at others because they differ from and may challenge us with other ways of knowing. My poem below is an attempt to express this desire:

Leave Your Gun at Home

> "Anything will give up its secrets if you love it enough."
> ~ George Washington Carver

If you wish to see the other in
you striding beside your shadow
Leave your gun at home.
If you desire friendship with a stranger
in conversing on topics you share
Leave your gun at home.
If you seek in the folds of a friendship
the virtues of acceptance love and warmth

in the oven of meetings
Leave your gun at home.
If when driving, walking, talking
or teaching
you seek an open response to all
you profess
Leave your gun at home.
For in the pistol's presence and the
bullets that zing from your mouth
and the full chambers of your heart
and the hammer of a quick response
full of leaden love
and the trigger of a twisted phrase
The other dies in front of you because
in your scattered hail of reports
You brought your gun from home.

Work Cited

Margalit, Avishai. *The Decent Society*, translated by Naomi Goldblum. Harvard UP, 1986.

28

◆●◆

THE GULLIBLE GALLBLADDER?*

Beliefs' power to establish our individual realities, or at least influence their production with persuasive force, is being challenged every day in the news. Some of these pronouncements have completely uncoupled from the more shared perceptions of historical fact. Given the forest of fictions we are all enmeshed in today, I want to relate something closer to home: surgery to remove a very pesky and stone-packed gallbladder.

When my wife rushed me to the hospital last June to have hospital staff explore why I was feeling so ill, I surrendered into a system that I felt had my well-being at heart. This was my **belief.** When a surgeon visited me after two days of tests, he announced, "Your gallbladder is enflamed, full of stones and is creating distressful conditions on your liver. We need to operate."

I did not **doubt** him for an instant. His reputation in the New Braunfels community was widely-held and sterling. I **believed** him without conditions; he scheduled the surgery for the next afternoon. I accepted his **diagnosis** because I trusted him as a surgeon. In addition, I **believed** him because:

- He had the voice and expertise of **an authority** in his field.
- I had **faith** that his staff was well-trained.

---

* Originally published as "Reality and Our Beliefs Are Connected." "Opinion" page. *Herald-Zeitung,* February 13, 2021. A-4.

- I **assumed** the removal of this organ would set me on the road to recovery.
- I **believed** I was not going to be the first person from whom he removed a gallbladder.
- I had **credible reports** of his surgical skills.
- My **opinion** of his skills and his caring for me as a person was genuine.

All of these feelings and thoughts together congealed in me a composite and coherent story, a myth, in short, of **belief.** I sensed through this experience and others that the myth that lives in each of us is intimately related to the beliefs we hold. Both mythology and believability—one's credo—are firmly rooted in the reality of history—our own and the communal body we participate in.

I have also thought about how our preciously-held beliefs, which include what we have decided to place our faith in, can either open and bridge me to new beliefs or build a wall so no other possibilities can scale the bulwark of my entrenched beliefs in order to entertain options. Then it may well be worth our time to reflect on how our beliefs may have hardened and calcified, unbeknownst to us, into ideologies that will brook no outside pesky intrusions.

One reason this area of our lives is so important, but that for many may not be a concern for reflection, is that our perceptions of what comprises our Reality and our Beliefs are inseparable. We believe people, things, situations, conditions—some far beyond being able to be proven in any literal sense—because they bequeath to our lives a texture and a con-text, a narrative truth that unifies around a set of beliefs that give our lives purpose and value. All of these and other qualities are fundamental to living a coherent life.

I end this musing with a few questions for you to consider:

- Why is it necessary for you to believe in anything?
- Might some beliefs you hold continually wound you?
- Do the beliefs you hold incarcerate or free you to be more of who you are destined to be?

- Are the stories you tell about yourself to yourself and to others in fact your beliefs in narrative form?
- Do your beliefs allow you to be supple, flexible and pliable so as to entertain others' beliefs? Or have your beliefs frozen you in place?
- How important is it that others believe what you believe in order for you to accept them?

29

THE MYTH OF FACT AND THE FACT OF MYTH*

Some books read once reveal their secrets plainly enough; others invite continual rereading for one to understand and metabolize its treasures. Such is physicist Donald Cowan's rich book, *Unbinding Prometheus: Education for the Coming Age* (1988). From 1962-77 he served as President of The University of Dallas.

Recently I returned to his influential book on reimagining education and came across his exploration of "the myth of fact," which seems particularly relevant today. He prefaces how facts are myths by stating what a myth is: "We live always in a myth—a large overarching metaphor that gives philosophical meaning to the experience of everyday life" (*Prometheus* 4). We can't see the myth we are living in, he goes on, because "like the air, it is necessary but invisible" (4). He then hones in on the four-hundred-year history in the West up to the present where "the prevailing myth has been *fact*" (4). Such a belief came about when "the observable objects of the world came to exist in their own right" and ceased "taking their meaning from a context. . ." (5).

Facts assumed the place in culture by which reality was gauged and defined. A fact, he writes, "is a phenomenon taken as truth—a communal event, not a subjective awareness or an article of faith" (5). Facts are acquired through measurement, often by instruments created to get at the

* Originally published as "How Myth Became Confused with Fact" in *The San Antonio Express-News,* February 10, 2021. A16.

facts of the created order. Facts helped to standardize knowledge and with it, beliefs. He then offers detailed descriptions of the moments in history that undergirded the ascendency of facts as the gold standard for describing reality generally. We could say, then, that myths structure our patterns of thinking, including our patterns of beliefs.

But as science began to reveal that there also existed uncertainty and relativity concerning facts, as Cowan points out, then "the myth of fact" began to erode, for "Doubt is the worm that gnaws at the myth" (7). The myth that operated effectively for hundreds of years began to show cracks, wear-and-tear, and with it a lessening of its authority, enough decay to become questionable in the popular mind, "which is where myth has its abiding presence" (8). In a more contemporary moment, former president Obama has called what originated in the political sphere only to spread outward, "truth decay."

Cowan phrases it a bit differently: "Rather, the myth's decay characterizes the decline" (8). Myths, like individuals and societies, are organic, living entities; they move through birth, development, maintenance and decline and extinction. I wonder if that is where we are today—in a period of turmoil and confusion, leaderless and fantasy-prone, energetically willing to support and act on lies while ignoring the facts. Are we feeling such tension and stress, not just because of Covid-19, but even more so because the "myth of fact" and the realities that stem from it are being shredded by what I call "the myth of fantasy," a deadening climax to the "myth of individualism" and the loss of a shared communal myth that creates a general consensus of coherence rather than chaos, of community over acidic conflicts?

Whatever a person wishes to believe becomes, with enough participation, a world "of alternative facts" that are created from a conspiracy against the shared facts as we understand them. A corrosive form of tribal fundamentalism crowds out a shared reality of *Communitas*, of communal coherence.

Myths frame us by offering a shared context that coheres and congeals a people around a communal vision of our history and what we can aspire to achieve. Our founding documents contain all the lineaments of the national mythos we were born into. But convulsions in the "myth of fact" threaten the fabric of our shared reality on which we were founded as a people. That is our current context and perhaps our foreboding destiny.

Might this moment of crisis—a word which originally meant "decision" or "turning point in a disease," be an opportunity to revision and revamp our "myth of democracy" to rejuvenate and renew its core values? I believe so.

Works Cited

Cowan, Donald. *Unbinding Prometheus: Education for the Coming Age*. The Dallas Institute Publications, 1988.

30

THE POWER OF THE PERSONAL: *THE FLIGHT OF THE WILD GANDER**

Anytime I read, and especially reread, Joseph Campbell's books, I feel like I am in a personal conversation with a priest or a confessor, one who understands the need for the transcendent in our lives and is prepared to point us in the right direction. I think this feeling emerges because Campbell's storytelling gene is part of all of his utterances, but especially when he works a concept by morphing it into a narrative with provocative images energizing the through-line.

In this collection of essays, he states his purpose as shaman and guide: "to lift the veil, so to say, of the Goddess of the ancient temple of Sais," who confirmed for all time, "no one has lifted my veil" (xi). This metaphor is one of the constants of Campbell's entire heroic writer's journey: to enter that terrain where the veil thinly separates the phenomenal world from the treasures of the mythic structures that support it. Bird and Goddess, flight and veil, oscillate and communicate throughout these rich selections. The wild gander is a rich metaphor for "Hindu master yogis" who in their trance states go beyond all the pales of thought to become best known as "*hamsas* and *paramhamsas*: 'wild ganders' and 'supreme wild ganders'" (134). This and other comments brought me years ago to write an essay on "Joseph Campbell: Mystic" (*Bridge Work: Essays on Mythology, Literature and Psychology* 47-68).

---

* Originally published as a "Mythblast" on the Joseph Campbell Foundation Website, jcf.org. February, 2021.

Such an image serves as a still point in a rotating circle of themes, but the one I find most captivating is that of "*brahman-atman,* the ultimate transcendent yet immanent ground of all being," in order to make possible the yogi "passing from the sphere of waking consciousness . . . to the unconditioned, nondual state 'between two thoughts,' where the subject-object polarity is completely transcended . . ." (135).

The mythic motif Campbell spirals back to repeatedly is the quest for the crack, the gap, the thin membrane that allowed him to glimpse and discern the symbolic, transcendent nature of the world winking back at us with not a little seduction, through the mask of the sensate realm of the human and world body in their fragility and mystery. Such is one of the many masks of God that reveal the yearned-for archetypal compost of myth.

Follow Campbell's thought, like one starving for nutrients would track the thin line of bread crumbs that, if followed with humility and curiosity, will lead one to this realm of mystery, while feeding one's soul in the process. One of his constant nutritious repasts harbors the belief that myths allow us to move *as-if* in a transport vehicle from the sensate order to one where we become transparent to transcendence. The veil lifts ever-so-slightly in this moment of meaning, but not before, as he points out throughout his writings, having the rich human experience; the residue or after-burn, is meaning-making.

I have sensed, as have other lovers of Campbell's work, that his rich *mythodology* is syncretistic, gathering and clustering, then clarifying the connective tissue between disciplines to uncover the vast complexity of the human and world psyche in their arcing towards coherence. He is both hunter and gatherer, spanning centuries of development in human evolution.

Which persuades us to glance with double vision at both myth and history, one inside the other, one connecting and transforming the other. We might, in Campbellian fashion, play with our own metaphor at the end here. This is my image: the invisible lining of a jacket or coat is what I would call history's inner myth; it gives shape and contour to the outer sleeve, which is history itself, yet it remains hidden. Yes, the sleeve can be turned inside-out to reveal the hidden myth and that is part of Campbell's mode of excavation: he turns the sleeve inside-out in order to explore the mystery outlining history. Okay, not quite a veil, but certainly another form of fabric-ation.

Nor can myths be divorced from the inventions and discoveries of the time in which they surfaced. In Campbell's writings I sense that myths, on the contrary, survive by accommodating such discoveries, especially those of science. This discipline has knocked down the walls "from around all mythologies—every single one of them—by the findings and works of modern scientific discovery" (81).

And then the wild gander takes flight once again to accommodate the new mythic template. Let it not land too quickly. Allow it to soar. Enjoy looking up at its grandeur.

Work Cited

Campbell, Joseph. *The Flight of the Wild Gander: Explorations in the Mythological Dimension. Selected Essays, 1944-1968*. New World Library, 2002.

Slattery, Dennis Patrick. *Bridge Work: Essays on Mythology, Literature and Psychology*. Mandorla Books, 2015.

31

THE INNER REACHES OF OUTER SPACE IS WITHIN REACH[*]

Some people have confused a mythology as nothing more than an elegantly-packaged ideology. Not so. It is no truer to say that mythic figures are to be read as literal facts. The confusion often stems, as Campbell rehearsed often in his writings, from assuming that something or someone is literal, not metaphorical, of another reality that invites the imagination into a world of multiple possibilities. Such a move towards literalism belittles the universal appeal and power of the mythic images to no more than "prosaic reification" (*Inner Reaches* xxiv).

Making the imaginal shift from literal to figural alters one's entire perception of the phenomenal world, to say nothing of its opening one to the symbolic power of one's dreams. I can only speculate here as to why this confusion arises. I think one answer may be in Adolf Bastian's brilliant understanding of "elementary ideas" and "ethnic ideas." The former transports us into the rich arena of archetypal images and situations; the latter sends us into the particular historical and specific ways that such universal realities are embedded in and flourish in a people's or a nation's particular culture.

A brief example may suffice to unfold such a distinction. In their book, *Your Mythic Journey*, Sam Keen and Anne Valley-Fox offer that "A myth can make a cow sacred in one culture and hamburger meat in

---

[*] Originally published as a "Mythblast" in the Joseph Campbell Foundation website. jcf.org, April 2021.

another" (xi). Same animal. One cultural myth perceives it as sacred, the other reaches for it in its promise to assuage an appetite. Both are hungers of different orders. The animal's universality is bent to conform or to support a local ethnic belief. Beef as belief. Animal as anima. Billions of burgers served. Campbell was keen to see that myths provide a dual vision: the transcendent and universal, but both remain rooted firmly in history's particularity.

Such a belief allowed him to retrieve an ancient idea that the human body itself is "in miniature a duplicate of that macrocosmic form" (13) which conveyed a sense of unity through the great chain of being's diversity. Correspondence and correlation are the lenses by which to uncover and further this ancient wisdom of analogies linking all diverse parts of creation. Visible diversity anchored in invisible unity. Such connective tissue is heightened when we are invited to gaze at a photo of the earthrise taken from the moon's surface (19) to reveal that a new cosmological perspective insists on and incites a revisioned mythology. I believe such a miraculous image accelerated our concern for saving the planet by seeing it absent all the artificial boundaries between countries.

Such a dramatic photo struck Campbell as a visionary correlative of a new myth. It also revealed his own mythopoetic way of discovering analogies that reveal relationships we might miss or ignore absent his acute insights. Closer to planet earth, he explores patterns, for example, between native American people and those of India, sensing "equivalences" in their images and beliefs. His method is "to identify these universals . . . archetypes of the unconscious and as far as possible, to interpret them" (69). Let's pause to reflect here that the act of interpretation is a mythic move of imagination.

Hermes is the god-guide in this human activity; hermeneutics, therefore, is a divinely-inspired talent and impulse. Without this rich act of being human—and Campbell is one of the most cogent minds in such an uncovering—we would stack up event-after-event with no cohering sense growing from such a futile performance. Without a unifying narrative, we have chapters following on one another with no cohesive plot line threading the various yarns of the disparate events in our lives into a cohesive whole. Perhaps we do interpret ourselves into being.

Interpretation is a fundamental act of learning. As he creates a unique form of such meaning-making, Campbell uncovers "an implicit connotation through all its metaphorical imagery of a sense of identity of some kind, transcendent of appearances, which unites behind the scenes the opposed actors on the world stage" (81). Life itself is dramatic, but to miss the experience because of an obsession with what it means is to miss the action that is before us and within us.

Art in all of its guises becomes the delivery system by which myth, history and aesthetics congeal on the same stage. But as is his *habitus* of finding correlations between worlds, he suggests that "the mystic and the way of the proper artist are related" (111). It is not too much to proclaim that all art is metaphorical to a large degree; Campbell's own language is that the figural realities on the stage of artistic creation can succeed in opening us to "a transformation of perspective" (109). Change your seat in the theater of life's continual drama and you will inherit a different angle on the plotline.

Like that magnificent image of the earth rise, the power of *aesthesis,* a showing forth or an unveiling, is the artist's sacred inspiration for expression. The artist's construction provides us with a mimetic reality, a way to activate our sense of analogy to recover our own mythic imagining, to see "with two eyes, and alone to him is the center revealed: that still point . . ." (117).

Draw a circle around the still point. Suddenly you exist at the center of it all. Why would one fuss any further?

Works Cited

Campbell, Joseph. *The Inner Reaches of Outer Space: Metaphor as Myth and as Religion.* New World Library, 2002.

Keen, Sam and Anne Valley-Fox. *Your Mythic Journey: Finding Meaning in Your Life Through Writing and Storytelling.* Jeremy Tarcher/Putnam, 1989.

32

---◆●◆---

THE MASKS OF GOD:
CREATIVE MYTHOLOGY
A PANDEMIC REFLECTION*

In the final volume of his massive four-part *The Masks of God* series, Joseph Campbell reflects on a wide assortment of historical, cultural, spiritual and mythical events in history that are extraordinary in their useful-
ness to us today as we move into the second year of a global pandemic.
Leaving aside the rich figure of the god Pan in mythology who could
easily overpower this entire essay, I return to one of the great inspirations
in Campbell's life, *The Decline of the West* by Oswald Spengler, published
in two volumes in 1926 and 1928 respectively.

Perhaps it is not too much to think of Campbell's four volumes as a
patterned set of publications that express his own critique of the West,
among other large concerns of culture. I hear resonances of Spengler's
authority throughout *Creative Mythology*. For instance, Spengler writes
early in Volume One; "Is there a logic of history? Is there, beyond all the
casual and incalculable elements of the separate events, something that
we may call a metaphysical structure of historic humanity, something that
is independent of the outward forms—social, spiritual and political—
which we see so clearly?" (*Decline of the West* 3).

* Published as a "Myth Blast" on the Joseph Campbell Foundation's website. jcf.org
June 2021.

To be honest, I want to return to Spengler's work and see it more deeply through the formed imagination of Campbell's passion and work within and through historical frames. As prisms, these two writers refract one another's perceptions about the universal order of the world through its marvelous range of particulars. What both epic writers share in their respective visions of the past as epic, mythic and formative, is an awareness of psychic patterns that undergird the phenomenal world. Discover the pattern and you sense a thread of the plot that holds the entire fabric of the cosmos together.

Each one of our on-going personal mythologies are chock-full of bundles of motifs that together form our mythic-historical worldview, which is a core value in *Creative Mythology*. Another that guided Campbell here and, in his explorations, generally is that the phenomenal world has its analogical corollaries in the interior life of the individual. Accessing these connections occurs so often through art, for example in James Joyce's *Finnegan's Wake,* which he calls a boiling vessel that contains "that same rich continuum of themes from our deepest, darkest past" (40). Return to the dark, often invisible past, Campbell intones, and there you will find the fine lineaments of the present and future. It seems that the structure of mythic time is evident in such an observation.

What Campbell is sensitive to is that moment when the heart suddenly opens under the influence of aesthetic arrest to encourage a more porous attitude to adventure; following this shift one becomes aware, like a bodhisattva, of the precious place of transcendence above and beyond all dualities and dichotomies, "the yonder shore" of Buddhism that accompanies one's bliss (157). He works this rich metaphor more thoroughly in *Oriental Mythology*. The metaphors he develops and deploys throughout comprise his heuristic. Metaphor as methodology, metaphor as *mythodology*, a way of being in the world and describing it, much as an artist does in working out apprehending something of their subject matter, then struggling to craft that apprehension into a coherent form for others.

One major goal of artistic creation in the making is that it "opens out in back, as it were, to eternity, and this requires of the artist . . . that he should . . . touch anew that still point in this turning world of which the immemorial mythic forms are the symbols and guarantee" (94). To achieve this creative goal, one works obliquely, by indirection, nuance, spirically, leaving the linear path behind. I fantasize Spengler standing beside Campbell as he wrote this idea, nodding his approval.

Synthetic seeing, pattern-plotting, gnostic-knowing—I sense these *mythodologies* as seminal to Campbell's mytho-historical consciousness that hosts both myth and history to be separate, yet share some understanding of being that shapes a unity-within-diversity. By means of the analogical, Campbell yearns for and strives to achieve some glimpse of the anagogical: "We term such speech 'anagogical' (from the Greek verb [meaning] 'to lead upward') because it points beyond itself, beyond speech" (189). Here he carries the energy and realization of the medieval poet, Dante, as the latter admits so often in writing his *Commedia:* I cannot find the words to describe to you, reader, what I am seeing; I leave it to your imagination to fill it in, for words fail me (my paraphrase).

So for Dante as for Campbell, the anagogical is yearned for and perhaps glimpsed through the analogical—the figural language that the artist is so gifted to offer us as fresh ways of seeing in order to promote a new way of believing. Myths, in addition to so many other characteristics that comprise them, are also belief systems, organic if they are alive, ideologies if they have stiffened into corpses.

To keep the life blood of mythic consciousness oxygenated and robust, we must exercise our right and obligation to renew the symbols, metaphors and figures *in* our own time *for* our own time. It is a matter of refreshing "the mythogenetic zone" which designates the geographical area "in which such a language of mythic symbols and related rites can be shown to have sprung into being" (90). Campbell's one perduring example among many, is the advent of science's rise, which dissolved boundaries and made obsolete so many beliefs that collapsed under science's overpowering presence. Another is the invention and rise of the individual in the Middle Ages, which shifted the energies of the macrocosm to the particular values of the microcosm as Manuele Gragnolati so eloquently explores in *Experiencing the Afterlife*.

This period of pandemonium in politics, biology and global illness is giving rise to new and renewed mythic orientations, including social justice, equality, a shared yearning for a moral order, for the preservation of Mother Earth, as well as a challenged respect for the facts over fantasies of wishful-thinking. I see where we are, on this eve of a New

Inauguration as a hopeful moment in the history of myth. Shaken, we continue to stand together for mutual support.

Works Cited

Campbell, Joseph. *The Masks of God: Creative Mythology.* Viking Press, 1968.

Gragnolati, Manuele. *Experiencing the Afterlife: Soul and Body in Dante and Medieval Culture.* U Notre Dame P, 2005.

Spengler, Oswald. *The Decline of the West, Volume 1: Form and Actuality.* Alfred Knopf Publisher, 1926.

33

---◆●◆---

MYTH AS FICTIONAL FABRICATION JOSEPH CAMPBELL'S *MYTHIC IMAGINATION: COLLECTED SHORT FICTION*[*]

Published by New World Library for the Joseph Campbell Foundation in 2012, this collection of short narratives witnesses so many of Campbell's favorite mythopoetic themes. Included are seven stories, ranging from 1931 to 1943. Reading the volume, I jotted down a handful of these constants in Campbell's later writings, including the monumental, *The Hero with a Thousand Faces* (1949): seeing anew; being transported from the familiar to the unfamiliar; an ordinary life slowly becoming most strange and mysterious; the inspiration to begin a quest; a life transformed and remythologized; self-discovery; the presence of the grotesque, the monstrous; entering sacred space and returning to narrate the adventure.

I can only make the briefest comments about so many stories in this limited space. Doing so will attune the reader to the kinds of stories the young fiction writer gravitated towards to give narrative form to insights that he developed subsequently into more thorough explorations.

---

[*] Originally published as "Myth as Fictional Fabrication: Joseph Campbell's *Mythic Imagination: Collected Short Stories. Myth Blast* on The Joseph Campbell Foundation's website April 2021. www.jcf.org.

"Moonlight in Vermont" reveals Freddy Bliss from Brooklyn who accepts new employment on a farm. At one point he is led by one of the farmer's cows across the fields. Animal wisdom guides him to Jennifer, the farmer George Waterford's daughter, who loves to pick corn by moonlight. Through her guidance Freddy is directed to his own interior life and finds his purpose; from there he is transported back to the ordinary reality of farming. What began as temporary employment becomes a permanent home for him.

In "Moth and Rust: A Story Cycle" (1942-46), Campbell pens four narratives under this umbrella. "The Forgotten Man" has a surreal plot, closer to dream than waking life. A white United States president wakes one morning to discover that overnight he has been transformed into a black man. His death is feigned as he travels to the South and connects with its black population; they in turn see him as a savior and label him "the Marvelous Wanderer." His contact with so many feminine figures contributes to his transformation from the president to a voice for the black community: "Something epochal had happened. He had found himself, come into himself again" (48).

In "The Belly of the Shark" (1942), George Ambrose Fitzray is journeying by steamer to New Guinea when the ship sinks. In the water with other men, George spies a shark approaching him: "The harsh gullet had yawned; he was gone" (63). His return is as miraculous as was his disappearance. One of the characters he meets on his watery survival through the shark's body instructs him: "Food is life and life is food" (67), echoing one of Campbell's mythic motifs that life feeds on life. That is a law of life itself mirrored in numerous world mythologies.

"The Lord of Love" (1945), set in a different narrative voice, is the only story with a female hero, Lilian Copeland, twenty-seven, whose sexuality is fiercely attractive to most men. At a moment that presages a transformation, she is attacked by her boss in his office but escapes before he is able to rape her. Lilian begins her own quest, launched at a Buddhist Temple; she admits to her mother: "I have to look for some . . . something I lost" (118). On an island in Polynesia, she descends into the Palolo Valley; in this serene, solitary landscape she discovers a peace and "a simple, direct contact with the untroubled quietude of the elemental dark" (121).

"Voracious" (1945-46) is the most extravagant of all the stories. It depicts the death of Arnold Hopper, who is severely wounded in combat. Of his death his mother tells a friend: "This loss is honest, the only honest thing in our lives" (141). Arnold then appears sometime later in his bed at home, where he undergoes a radical physical transformation. In this new, monstrous iteration, his appetite is as powerful as the Cyclops Polyphemus in Homer's *Odyssey*. He becomes a victim of all human appetites and exhibits intensely sexually aggressive behavior towards a host of women. The story widens to a conflict between two mythologies: that of the Native Americans living in the town of Indian Hat and members of the white population.

"Last Paradise" and a story in the Appendix, "Strictly Platonic," end the collection. The former is one of the most sustained quest narratives in the collection. Tom Waller, a librarian, discovers an island that no one knows about; he is called to it in his unique summons to venture. On his journey he is stripped of all vestiges of his previous life, including his glasses that bring his world into sharp view. There, he discovers through Hima, a young native girl, the existence of a "lava tube" (228) that runs through a mountain. Tom seizes on this discovery as a chance to become wealthy in growing sugar cane by siphoning stolen water through his constructed mountain tube. His self-absorbed quest rises to the petty heights of a rapacious pursuit for greater wealth.

The last story in the collection is the most tightly written. Campbell's own life is most overtly threaded throughout it. Jim Weston is a new college teacher who flunks the most popular and talented football player on the team at Welton College, Larry Cobb. He refuses to budge from his assessment of the student when pressured by a wealthy board member to inflate the grade. In his classroom, Jim and Larry physically fight and Larry is injured, making it impossible for him to play his last game at the college. Jim's moral center remains intact under repeated bombardments to abandon his moral principles.

An admittedly quick overview; nonetheless, many of the themes that occupied Campbell in his subsequent writings are given initial form in these ventures. He tells us that "the hero journey is a night sea journey . . . where the individual is going to bring forth in his life something that was never beheld before" (*The Hero's Journey* 76). Each of these narratives by a young, developing writer reveals the power of the quest to transform a life into one of deeper meaning through discovering one's authentic bliss. Many of the plots that drive these narratives will become permanent reference centers of Campbell's myth-making edifice that continues to influence and guide countless souls who use his work as beacons for their own life trajectory.

Works Cited

Campbell, Joseph. *Mythic Imagination: Collected Short Fiction.* New World Library, 2012.

Campbell, Joseph. *The Hero's Journey: Joseph Campbell on His Life and Work.* Edited and with an Introduction by Phil Cousineau. New World Library, 2003.

34

◆◀●▶◆

DEEP CREATIVITY: SEVEN WAYS TO SPARK YOUR CREATIVE SPIRIT

AN INTERVIEW WITH DENNIS PATRICK SLATTERY, PH.D. WITH ANGELA BORDA*

Dennis Patrick Slattery is a beloved Distinguished Professor Emeritus of mythology at Pacifica, with over fifty years of teaching experience and 30+ books published, including seven books of poetry. He is the co-author of *Deep Creativity: Seven Ways to Spark Your Creative Spirit* and will be co-presenting the Pacifica workshop of the same name with Pacifica scholars Deborah Anne Quibell, Ph.D., and Jennifer Leigh Selig, Ph.D., on March 5–7, 2021. I felt very privileged to discuss Dennis's work with him, as he is deeply thoughtful about the liminal realm of imagination and creativity within the context of mythology and depth psychology.

Angela: How does mythology intersect with creativity?

Dennis: Intersect is the right verb to use. The last volume of Joseph Campbell's four-volume *Masks of God* is entitled *Creative Mythology*. Myths themselves are creative expressions of the individual/communal soul.

---

* Interview with Angela Borda prior to a three-day conference on *Deep Creativity: Seven Ways to Spark Your Creative Spirit* with Deborah Ann Quibell, Jennifer Leigh Selig and Dennis Patrick Slattery. Interview posted on Pacifica Graduate Institute's website, February, 2021.

The call to create is a call to uncover the myth that is our own, that part of us which communes with other souls. Both require a belief in the invisible forces at work in the world. I think that the unconscious is a creative terrain from which many of our inspirations spring. Creating is a form of mythologizing ourselves further and becoming more conscious of what that feels like. Creative inspiration comes, in part, from the myth within that we are each living out. Creative expressions fuel, augment and cultivate that growing awareness. I would add that the soul in things of the world also inspire and cultivate their own intentions that creatives respond to.

Angela: How does creativity speak to answering the question of who we are and why we are? Is that at the heart of *Deep Creativity*, some deeper understanding of why we need to express ourselves? How does the importance or meaning of creative expression shift when it becomes a communal project?

Dennis: Creativity addresses and promotes our identities, shows their gaps and allows us to continue to story ourselves into being. But our stories will always contain this gappy quality. So creativity has an ontological element in that it is interested in our being as well as our becoming. The stories that we tell ourselves and those that we hear or read are often moments of awakening to our deep creative impulses. When my co-authors, Jennifer and Deborah and I gathered in a shared communal effort with a shared willingness to learn from one another, we energized one another, saw the same WAY that we wrote on from others' standpoints, and witnessed the creative genius of each of us. Said another way, we all shared a similar mythos of creativity. Deborah led the construction of the book with her breathing in/breathing out meditations at the beginning and end of each of the "Seven Ways." That fine initiating, body-oriented meditation alone helped Jennifer and me to align our creative energies with this ritual practice. I for one, would not have thought to construct such framing. Concentrating on our breathing the world in and exhaling it is a fine way as well as ancient practice to cultivate an awareness of our creative impulses as embodied temporal expressions.

Angela: You are a poet, a painter, a potter, really quite prolific in all that you've published. How have you continually renewed your artistic flame and is that represented in the principles present in the book *Deep Creativity*?

Dennis: I have continued to renew and periodically relight my artistic flame by remaining curious, interested and listening to what comes along that make me wonder, to want to know more. It is also self-trust—that I am guided by a desire to know who and what I am on this planet and to share with others what I learn through what I create—a lecture, an interview, a painting, a poem and the like. As with this interview. I was so excited to be asked to be part of the trilogy to create *Deep Creativity*; it came at the right time, a moment of *Kairos*, or auspicious time, for I had become interested in what creativity does to inform and form the soul in each of us and to contemplate the soul in things of the world as well. I thought I could understand much more by working with two creative geniuses that would open up pathways of knowing I could not achieve by myself. *Deep Creativity* is participatory, responsive, archetypal and alchemical, so yes, my own principles of creative renewal are present in the book.

Angela: Quarantine affected creative people differently. Some dug in and wrote that book they'd been meaning to write. Others found themselves unable to write or paint or create music during this time, have found it to be a time of paralysis or inability to express themselves. What is your perspective on this from the angle of depth psychology and will the workshop address periods of the apparently fallow, as well as to suggest how to emerge from that and evolve from it into a place of deep creativity?

Dennis: The virus and quarantine have required enormous creative adjustments: to routine, to familiarity, to being present with others, to life in an embodied way. But it has suffocated some, especially those whose supported life has been curtailed. Of course, it can lead to periods of inactivity, of a lack of creative energy.

The psyche has its own reality, its own impulses, its own desires. Can I be attentive to that reality in a new, even creative way? Is not being creative also part of the aesthetic hero's journey, where pauses, gaps, end-stops are part of the pilgrimage? Can I pay more attention to my dream life during this period, to follow the narratives/images that emerge from this lower depth that informs my conscious life? This will be part of the workshop we present. I may pay more attention as well in these periods of lesser creative urges, although they may be taking new forms that we have not yet noticed. We can learn much from moments of blockage and resistances, as I have written in one of my essays. Deborah and Jennifer also address these moments of resistance—a good place to ask if the resistance is trying to lead me onto another path, finally more fruitful? Is the resistance itself an attempt at a renewal of something—perhaps a way of creating we have not registered before? Trust, again, is the key to being willing to yield to these pauses in our creative life.

Angela: You teach a section of the workshop centered on viewing our lives as our canvases, as something that can be created and co-created. How do you hope participants will learn from this and be transformed by it? Does a participant need to be an artist to benefit from this or can anyone, even those who have never picked up a paint brush, find significance and growth and gratification in thinking of their life as a creative process?

Dennis: Life as a canvas is a rich metaphor, not to be taken too literally. Every early morning when I write in my journal, for example, I am adding to the painting in prose of my life's contours, aspirations, disappointments and projects. Some days feel like quick brush strokes; others feel like it is taking forever to sketch out in rough outline where I am supposed to put my energies now. And each of us might watch especially for presences from outside that come in the form of an invitation, an idea that stems from something seen, read, heard, overheard—all these have the capacity to add to and modify the canvas of life from unlived to lived. These are potentials, perhaps new insights to add to the canvas of coherence, of comprehension and finally to what we are called to accept as well as cautioned to avoid.

I like that you use the word "co-created." I think anything we create is in some format a co-creation, from sources within us and influences outside of us. Co-creation is a form of co-hearing, a "hearing with." A "seeing with." I picked up a paint brush after over 58 years of not drawing, coloring or painting anything; it came in the form of an invitation from a former student who had established herself as a fine acrylic painter of Texas wildflowers and other wonders in nature. Linda's invitation came when one summer I took our granddaughter to a painting class for young folks. I heard and decided to yield to the calling and have been picking up a paint brush now for nine years. But I have been picking up a pen for decades; that has been my print brush, my writing brush. We each paint ourselves daily through the stories we tell and those we hear or read. Sometimes, without knowing it right away, we can paint ourselves into a corner; we can paint ourselves into a new creative space; we can paint ourselves into a new way of seeing how ordinary moments in each day are grounds for the creative spirit to work with.

If one has never tried actual literal painting, now might be the time to let that part of one's mysterious myth have expression; or making pottery. But it can be waking up each morning to see the possibilities of what the day might allow one to begin or to continue painting.

Angela: Thank you so much for speaking with me, Dennis. I'm looking forward to your March workshop with Deborah and Jennifer on *Deep Creativity* and all your future endeavors.

Angela Borda is a writer for Pacifica Graduate Institute, as well as the editor of the *Santa Barbara Literary Journal.* Her work has been published in *Food & Home, Peregrine, Hurricanes & Swan Songs, Delirium Corridor, Still Arts Quarterly, Danse Macabre,* and is forthcoming in *The Tertiary Lodger* and *Running Wild Anthology of Stories, Vol. 5.*

35

◆◆●◆◆

A GROWING INTEREST IN COMPASSION*

The word "compassion," which entered the fringes of social discourse years ago, has now moved closer to the center of discussion for many. A Google search for its etymology shows its history reaches back to ancient times and cultures. In Greek "compassion" had its origin in the noun "patient," or "one who suffers. It is also connected to "patiens," from the Greek "paskhein," "to suffer." In the biblical sense, compassion means "someone else's heartbreak becomes your heartbreak." In Latin as well it carries the same sense of getting out of one's own preoccupations and placing the other as most important.

I recall hearing the word gathering steam when the biblical scholar Karen Armstrong gave a national TED talk on compassion, which won her first prize. From her winnings she convened a group of global religious and lay individuals to begin a "Charter for Compassion" in 2009. Her request in the 2008 talk included the following: "I wish that you would help with the creation, launch and propagation of a Charter for Compassion, crafted by a group of leading inspirational thinkers from the three Abrahamic traditions of Judaism, Christianity and Islam, and based on the fundamental principles of universal justice and respect."

From that initial establishment of a global initiative, she wrote and published what is becoming a classic text on compassion: *Twelve Steps to*

---

* Published in the *San Antonio Express-News* on September 6, 2020. A22.

a Compassionate Life. Resonating, of course, earlier 12-step recovery programs that have helped millions to heal from addictions, resentments, prejudices and other afflictions that narrow our world view and often keep compassion at bay, they range from "The First Step: Learn About Compassion" to "The Twelfth Step: Love Your Enemies." I found "The Third Step: Compassion for Yourself," particularly enlightening. She quotes Rabbi Albert Friedlander, who grew up in Nazi Germany and as a child was confused "by the vicious anti-Semitic propaganda" that pervaded the atmosphere of that moment in history. What his experiences taught Armstrong is "if you cannot love yourself, you cannot love other people either" (*Compassion* 75).

Recently, the 30th Anniversary Edition of Maureen Murdock's *The Heroine's Journey* was revised and republished. It has to date been translated into 14 languages, including Farsi, Korean and Polish. I was pleased with how often the word "compassion" was a part of her discussion of women who had never allowed themselves to step out from the shadows of a controlling mother or a "father's daughter" role. When she relates what a powerful experience she had participating in a five-day retreat for high school seniors, she concludes, "The compassion we experienced together will enable each one of us to move closer to understanding diversity, rather than being threatened by it" (*Journey* 190). It was a breakthrough moment for all participants because compassion spearheaded the penetration into new emotional awareness.

More recently, one of the leaders of a current men's movement called "In Search of the Compassionate Male," writer and retreat leader Clay Boykin, a former Marine Corps artillery officer and Park Ave. executive, suffered a heart attack. That crisis pushed him to reevaluate his life and make a decision about his new vocation for the next two decades: to explore "The Compassionate Male." His book, *Circles of Men: A Counter-Intuitive Approach to Creating Men's Groups*, offers a template for the development of a Men's Fellowship Network based on a particular model that has had the most success of the many he researched. He bases his book's structure on what he calls "The Twelve Secrets."

The first secret: "Language Matters—Be mindful of how you speak about your circle and within it" (*Circle* 25). The twelfth secret: "Transformation—It is what seekers are seeking" (35). Throughout his insightful ideas about forming men's groups, he urges compassion be shown by each man to every other man in the retreat circle. Vulnerability is, Boykin claims, "the greatest obstacle to man's spiritual growth," so compassion is always in the center of the circle when men gather.

The interest and effectiveness of practicing compassion continues to grow personally, communally and politically at a time when our nation and the world hunger for healing from forces and programs that do not revere or practice this humane behavior.

Works Cited

Armstrong, Karen. *Twelve Steps to a Compassionate Life*. Anchor Books, 2010.

Boykin, Clayton. *Circles of Men: A Counter-Intuitive Approach to Creating Men's Groups*. Men's Fellowship Network, 2018.

https://www.etymonline.com/word/compassion#ety-monline_v_17258

https://www.ted.com/talks/karen_armstrong_my_wish_the_charter_for_compassion?language=en

Murdock, Maureen. *The Heroine's Journey: Woman's Quest for Wholeness. 30th Anniversary Edition*. Shambhala, 2020.

36

THE LYRIC IMPULSE TO CREATE: CREATIVITY'S HUNGERS WITHIN A CREATIVE LIFE*

I do not believe that our soul's deep need for expression in the world through some form of creative outlet is either compensation or sublimation, like paying a debt through some form of service. I think it is closer to filling out parts of our identity that have yet to be lived, whether literally or symbolically. It may be closer to Jennifer's idea outlined in our book, *Deep Creativity,* of "creative immortality" in her essay in "The Way of Love." She relates how one of the girls she loved died suddenly when a truck hit her car and killed her (31). She writes soon after, "that love became the fuel that fed my creative fire" (32). She wrote poems furiously, so that "my writing becomes a form of worship, my pages both propitiation and supplication before the god of love" (32).

Her essay goes on to explore the rich mythology of Eros and Psyche; that avenue in is itself a creative aperture into her creativity. It is as if the hunger to create required finding or being given a form for her longing to express the two incidents her essay focuses on: the sudden death of her friend and the shock of having a loaded gun pointed at her forehead and discharged. Thank God it was loaded with blanks, still . . . I understand her examples and her reflections as nodal points that cultivate how

---

* Part of this essay was published in The *San Antonio Express-News* on September 26, 2020. A22.

the hunger to create is a form of a love to create; it reveals how we all need this form of loving in order to activate/incarnate desire.

In my own essay, "Creating Love Through the Love of Creating," I recollect and muse on when my love to create was suddenly snuffed out of me in the third grade by a well-meaning (?) Ursuline Sister who compared my crayoning of fall trees surrounding our school in Euclid, Ohio, to my friend Joan's sitting across from me, who was already an artist at age ten. I experienced such a demeaning critique slam into an already ashamed boy, a debilitating emotion forged in the home of our alcoholic father, whose timid personality was shed on the weekends through heavy drinking and raging at us all in his own shaming illness. But a ten-year-old me could not make the connection. I stopped painting for 58 years but wrote for much of that time, perhaps replacing the brush for the pen as a surrogate way of painting the canvas. Then fate stepped in to offer an opportunity.

One summer many decades later, I took our young granddaughter, Kris, to sign up for a painting class each day for a week in New Braunfels, Texas. It was offered by a former student of mine who had become an accomplished acrylic painter of Texas wildflowers and other natural beauties. She invited me to begin a new adult painting class for beginners; with a knee-jerk response I said yes. Here is what I wrote in *Deep Creativity:* "The story I related above, now shaped in memory to reveal to me decades later what it meant, illustrates how learning to trust and love one's own originality affords an enormous influence on how we shape our own history as well as create ourselves into the world" (41). Further down the page I finish this thought: "Suffocating the creative impulse is thus one of the most devastating tyrannies an individual can self-inflict or have inflicted on them by another" (41), well-meaning or otherwise just plain being mean.

Joseph Campbell, the famed mythologist of the last century, developed one of his favorite themes, "The Hero's Journey," that transformed the way myths were addressed. It contained one of his motifs "The Call to Adventure," which is an invitation and a call to venture, to venture out, to venture forth. Adventure comes from the Latin "adventurus" = a thing about to happen. In 1300 "risk or danger," Late 14th. century, "dangerous undertaking"; 1560, "remarkable occurrence." The word has 1,280,000 hits.

I invite all of you reading this to pose a question to yourself: when in your own life was the desire, the eros to create, met with resistance, suffocation or downright hostility? It could be a desire to study a certain subject, a desire to travel to a dreamed of destination, to live somewhere that has called to you for many years, or even to be a particular kind of person?

On the other side, when were you encouraged to create something, were supported by someone cheerleading you on to a destiny you would have missed, and consequently not become the person you are? Give yourself 15 minutes to write on each of these.

My mentor, Louise Cowan, taught us all in graduate school at the University of Dallas to pay attention to poetry and literature as offering their own mode of knowledge—a knowledge of form gotten at through the poem's particulars. She used to quiz us on Dostoevsky's *The Brothers Karamazov*, Gogol's *Dead Souls,* and Tolstoy's *Anna Karenina* in her Russian novel class. It was her way of coaxing us to follow the bread crumbs of the novel's specifics as guides to the Grail cup of insight. And finally, to an oasis of meaning.

One of her richest literary genres of the four—Lyric, Tragedy, Comedy and Epic—was Lyric poetry. If you love Mary Oliver's or Rilke's or Robert Frost's or Jane Hirschfield's poetry, you are attracted to the lyric imagination, which is part of the hunger to create that I am developing here. It has three territories of the heart as Louise defines them: anticipation, consummation and lamentation. First, we yearn or hunger for something or someone in our lives; that hunger might then be consummated in a relationship with another, but for our purposes, in a hunger to create that is carried to some form of completion; the last moment of the heart is a lament, a nostalgia, a still-lit desire for those original moments of a rich freedom and insights about our own beingness. It may fan out to include what we have lost in life that cannot be retrieved except through remembrance.

From a mythological point of view, perhaps what is longed for, then lamented in the pain of loss, is the original Garden, that archetypal realm before all dualisms, dichotomies and paradoxes have yet entered—a lament for Paradise Lost, a deep nostalgia in the soul that art, authentic creativity, yearns to retrieve in one's life. I believe it is the retrieval of a deep love for all of creation, even a yearning to converse with the soul of things and others.

She went on in her essay I am citing here to suggest that "Love is Lyric's natural dwelling ground." When we step into this landscape, we are surrounded by the force of Love itself as it guided Jennifer and Deborah's essays earlier. The power of Lyric that I identify with the creative impulse might be the same Love in a lower register that led God in Genesis to create the world, and then us, as an expression of His love. I say this because of what Louise observes next: "Beauty in Lyric is the splendor of form, the radiant ontological breakthrough in which flesh encounters spirit" (*Prospect* 13) A magnificent insight—the organic form of art, her Lyric poetry, is to adventure into what is splendid, spectacular and wondrous; it has the strength to excite an emotion that I know you have felt: a sense of awe—something awful, full of awe-inspired wonder.

Now in today's usage, something "awesome" is something cool, desirable, neat. But it originally meant "to inspire with fright, terror," but also "admiration, veneration." What we create and/or what moves us to a sense of reverence may depend on what Rollo May in *The Courage to Create* refers to as "*encounter*" (39), which may be "an encounter with an idea, an inner vision; . . . the material by which one brings this encounter to fruition are the media we use to achieve the experience of that encounter." The second quality he senses can inspire a creative encounter is the "degree of absorption, the degree of intensity. . .; there must be a specific quality of *engagement*" (40). I believe these latter qualities of an experience stem from a sense of awe that cries to be realized, to be achieved. I believe it is also a hunger for coherence in our story. To remember Louise's insight earlier, it is a moment when one senses and anticipates the possibility of an adventure down and in to a realm where "flesh encounters spirit."

All of the above leads me to a series of hungers. Louise adds at this juncture that "Lyric seeks the place where human nature encounters immortality, the obscure realm where the *imago dei* still resides" (5) and is intimately concerned with incarnation, namely, to make something of our anticipated moments of life itself and to consummate it, as Christ said on the cross, "Consumatum est," it is done, achieved, completed. To be able for any one of us to say that at the end of our lives—it is done, achieved, completed—might be our most prominent "awesome" moment of achievement. My poem below tries to express what I wrote above:

Narrative Longing

A storied life is not a sorry life.
"Can I?" he wondered,
"back out of a story
into the ground of experience
that rises to a quivering narrative
full of its own desire to be told?"
The woods in back of our house
darken when the sun is highest.
It cannot penetrate the shades of things
or the shadows of beings.
Only a vignette is sharp enough
to pierce obscurity's tender reeds.
Only the tight line of a plot transfers the energy
on which a natural glow rests quietly.
Can she separate the story
from the storied?
Is it any wonder streams find
other grooves to shine in?
Other truths to rise from?
Not real—only true.
Let the dark woods form the words
that lead you from bewildered shadows
to the other side of the story's shore—
The side not told,
the side still longing,
the story from this
special day forward
you all are destined to live.

(Leaves from the World Tree: Selected Poems 101)

Creativity, the call to create, resides therefore in a deep hunger that permeates and provokes every cell of our bodies. To create comprises one of the deepest callings in us to make ourselves matter in the world and to know on a deep level the form that such matter assumes and why it is always in process of trans-formation. As we journey through all or some of these hungers, please note which ones speak to you that you might make personal in a short writing meditation.

- A hunger to engage life more deeply than our busy everyday realities encourage or allow room for. Here possibly is an inspiration to deepen, to be called to a new depth, to a more present and response-able inclination toward our lives with a fuller consciousness. Here is the place of the pause, of deceleration and a certain deliberateness. Here stillness speaks.

- A hunger to relate more deeply with ourselves, others and life itself; such a hunger can and has healed a divorce or a lengthy separation we have imposed on ourselves or had it done for us and to us. We wake one morning and question where the last 6 months or 6 years have gone. Perhaps this hunger is a call to reconcile with disparate and occasionally desperate parts of ourselves, or to mend breaks with those from whom we feel alienated, including the other that lives within. It may be a call to remember with a more robust plenitude.

- A hunger for adventure: to enter the woods where there is no path to follow, as mythologist Joseph Campbell believed, or its outlines are shady and opaque; then one knows she is on her path, not someone else's. Fear may suddenly sprout right here, but so may courage find its foothold to continue the quest. Perhaps this search provides the venue to pose the question one has ignored or not been willing to face before. As creatives we might use our art to pose and risk answering the fundamental questions of our life's purpose.

- A hunger to leave a trace, some markers that affirm we were present on this earth, that we participated in life, and that we changed it for the better in some way. It is not boastful or bragging to paint a success portrait which honors what marks we have made in the lives of others, what tracks we have left already and plan to continue to "make impressions" of ourselves in the world's matter. That matter is there to be impressed by you.

- But—this hunger can also uncover creativity's shadow through constructions that destroy, that annihilate, that damage people, things, ideas, institutions and all those afflicted by it. So creative work includes shadow work, struggling not just in but through the dark. Connie Zweig's magnificent study, *Romancing the Shadow* (1997) opens with an epigram from the poet Rilke: "Perhaps all the dragons of our lives are princesses who are only waiting to see us once beautiful and brave. Perhaps everything terrible is in its deepest being something helpless that wants help from us" (qtd. in *Shadow* 3). I love the paradox of this insight that Connie uses to open her study. It sets the compass on how we might look twice or three times at what the shadow side of our creativity is asking/pleading for/instructing us to see with another visionary lens.

- A hunger to transcend our understanding of who we are with our limitations, abbreviations, emendations, narrowness, self-incarcerations and to connect with a realm of invisible presences that are eternally available to prod us into a fuller awareness. Such a transport, by means of imagination, allows us to go beyond our mortal limits in the act of creation, to both ascend and deepen beyond our normal range of possibilities, to step beyond it in the divinely-inspirited act of creation. We might, to test this idea, look back and remember something we had created, accomplished or achieved and to question: who did that? What allowed me to create in this way that so transcended my daily life and placed me in a zone of creativity that, once achieved, I returned to my quotidian life?

- A hunger for communion and for community; to incarnate our imagination to connect with a larger collective myth that carries us beyond our personal set of mythic structures to allow more in. The deep desire in each of us for what Victor Turner labelled *communitas*: "I prefer the Latin term '*communitas*' to 'community,' to distinguish this modality of social relationship from an area of common living'" (*The Ritual Process* 96).

- A hunger to risk something, to step out of our current cultural obsessions with safety and security, which can incarcerate us from life more than encourage participation in it; to risk feeling the essential groundlessness of our lives when it passes more swiftly as we grow into our full identity. In short, to live within and celebrate our vulnerabilities. Victor Turner might call it a condition of "liminality" in this way. A sacredness is allowed into communal experience: "Liminality implies that the high could not be high unless the low existed, and he who is high must experience what it is like to be low" (*The Ritual Process* 97). To be in-between, to recognize a certain groundlessness, where creativity may have its most fruitful genesis and development.

- A hunger to feel in our bones a deeper courage—life lived from within the heart—and to feel the hearth fire of ourselves burning in the heated glow of the coals of our unlived potentials.

- A hunger to awaken, to become more conscious, more aware, of what our place in the cosmos is for, and what our purpose in life fully involves.

- A hunger to give a coherent shape and order to what may feel at times like a series of disconnected days and endless strings of unrelated events without linkage or purpose.

- A hunger to break free from the shackles of our own often self-imposed conventional limitations, definitions and descriptions of what, who and where we are.

- A hunger to feel at times what it is like to live closer to our full capacity, to push against all those "I can't" s that envelope us in a stamped, self-admonishing envelope mailed to ourselves far too frequently.

- A hunger to live outside of or out of the totalitarian control of our ego, with all its busy constricting labels, and into a more functional relationship with our Self, the place and purpose of our higher and deeper calling.

- A hunger to kick up the dust or to kick through the wall of our conventional storylines, those endless narratives that more often than not constrict, restrict and choke the flow of our vital life spirit that often repeats the following messages: "Don't you dare"// "Don't risk it"// "It's not safe"// "You might fail."

- A hunger, paradoxically, to accept our incapacities, our limitations and our former failures. Such acceptance can happen most effectively in liminal space, where the boundaries are, for a moment, suspended.

- A hunger for ritual, for incarnating our thoughts, insights, revelations or understandings into a coherent form, for giving it integrity and for proposing it tangibly to the world.

- A hunger for sacrifice, for giving up something that has outlived its shelf life, to make room for what has been birthed into being or wants to be, for relinquishing, for absenting from our life something that no longer serves us.

- A hunger for the bliss that lies in the deepest recesses of us that we perhaps rarely tap into, much less ever connect and befriend. Here the act of creation is a moment of transformation; we long for these moments of conversion but often seek them in the world rather than within the terrain of our own mystery, our own miracle of becoming. Within the lyric heart-scape, we may yearn for what has been rather than using that energy to motion towards what could be.

- To follow one's bliss, as Joseph Campbell made it public knowledge, is to accept the pain and the challenge of its difficulty. Bliss may not be a joy ride but it is an authentic deployment of who we are and what our purpose is. It is also to invite the liminality in life, a rich wellspring of creativity. This call to a path of bliss may be only a whisper, so we have to be attentive and still to hear it. This same whisper may occasion on the road a series of blisters, for bliss does not mean a path without challenges and obstacles, as any creative pursuit requires and any creative will acknowledge.

- A hunger for the journey into opposites, into contradictions, where the act of creation may occasion a reconciliation of them through a joining, a unifying of what was split and gnawing away at one's sense of wholeness and unity. Here again, it is to make room for both the high and the low, the horizontal road map of our daily pursuits and the vertical descent into the terrains of the heart longing to be expressed.

Works Cited

Cowan, Bainard, editor. *The Prospect of Lyric.* Introduction by Louise Cowan. The Dallas Institute Publications, 2012.

Deininger, Craig and Dennis Patrick Slattery. *Leaves From the World Tree: Selected Poems.* Mandorla Books, 2018.

May, Rollo. *The Courage to Create.* Norton, 1994.

Quibell, Deborah Anne, Jennifer Leigh Selig and Dennis Patrick Slattery. *Deep Creativity: Seven Ways to Spark Your Creative Spirit.* Shambhala, 2019.

Turner, Victor. *The Ritual Process: Structure and Anti-Structure.* Aldine de Bruyter, 1995.

Zweig, Connie, Steve Wolf. *Romancing the Shadow: Illuminating the Dark Side of the Soul.* Ballantine Books, 1997.

ABOUT THE AUTHOR

━━━━━━━━━━━━━◆●◆━━━━━━━━━━━━

Dennis Patrick Slattery, Ph.D., has been teaching for fifty-three years, the last twenty-seven in the Mythological Studies Program at Pacifica Graduate Institute in Carpinteria, California. He is the author, co-author, editor, or co-editor of thirty-two volumes, including seven volumes of poetry: *Casting the Shadows: Selected Poems; Just Below the Water Line: Selected Poems; Twisted Sky: Selected Poems; The Beauty Between Words: Selected Poems of Dennis Patrick Slattery and Chris Paris; Feathered Ladder: Selected Poems* with Brian Landis; *Road, Frame Window: A Poetics of Seeing. Selected Poetry of Timothy J. Donohue, Donald Carlson and Dennis Patrick Slattery;* and *Leaves from the World Tree: Selected Poems of Craig Deininger and Dennis Patrick Slattery.* He has co-authored one novel, *Simon's Crossing,* with Charles Asher. Other titles include *The Idiot: Dostoevsky's Fantastic Prince. A Phenomenological Approach; The Wounded Body: Remembering the Markings of Flesh; Creases in Culture: Essays Toward a Poetics of Depth;* and *Bridge Work: Essays on Mythology, Literature and Psychology.* With Lionel Corbett he has co-edited and contributed to *Psychology at the Threshold* and *Depth Psychology: Meditations in the Field;* with Glen Slater he has co-edited and contributed to *Varieties of Mythic Experience: Essays on Religion, Psyche and Culture;* and *A Limbo of Shards: Essays on Memory, Myth and Metaphor.* His more recent books include *Our Daily Breach: Exploring Your Personal Myth through Herman Melville's Moby-Dick; Day-to-Day Dante: Exploring Personal Myth Through the Divine Comedy;* and *Riting Myth, Mythic Writing: Plotting Your Personal Story.* With Jennifer Leigh Selig, he has coedited and contributed to *Re-Ensouling Education: Essays on the Importance of the Humanities in Schooling the Soul,* and *Reimagining Education: Essays on Reviving the Soul of Learning.* With Deborah

Anne Quibell and Jennifer Leigh Selig he has co-authored a book awarded a Nautilus Book First Place Prize for best book on Inspiration and Creativity in 2020: *Deep Creativity: Seven Ways to Spark Your Creative Spirit*; with Evans Lansing Smith he has co-edited *Correspondence: 1927-1987* on the letters of Joseph Campbell. He has also authored over 200 essays and reviews in books, magazines, newspapers, and on-line journals. His most current publications include *From War to Wonder: Recovering Your Personal Myth Through Homer's Odyssey* and *An Obscure Order: Reflections on Cultural Mythologies.*

He offers riting retreats both in-person and on Zoom in the United States and Europe on exploring one's personal myth through the works of Joseph Campbell and C. G. Jung's *Red Book* as well as on topics of creativity, the mythology of belief and the nature of stories and personal identity.

For recreation he takes classes painting mythic themes in both watercolor and acrylic. He also enjoys riding his Harley-Davidson motorcycle with his two sons, Matt and Steve, through the Hill Country roads of Texas. He enjoys being a grandfather to three sweet young women: Kris, Eleanor and Siena.

For more about Dennis, visit www.dennispatrickslattery.com.

Made in the USA
Middletown, DE
29 September 2023

39766444R00210